D0909412

Education and
Social Change
in China

EDUCATION AND SOCIETY
Series editor: Paul R. Hanna

Publications in the *Education and Society* series, a research project of the Hoover Institution on War, Revolution and Peace, address issues of education's role in social, economic, and political affairs. It is hoped that insight into the relationship between inculcated values and behavior and a society's approach to revolution and development will contribute to more effective education for the establishment and preservation of justice and peace.

UNCONDITIONAL DEMOCRACY: Education and Politics in Occupied Japan, 1945–1953   *Toshio Nishi*

EDUCATION AND SOCIAL CHANGE IN CHINA: The Beginnings of the Modern Era   *Sally Borthwick*

Education and Social Change in China

The Beginnings of the Modern Era

Sally Borthwick

HOOVER INSTITUTION PRESS
Stanford University, Stanford, California

Hoover Press Publication 268
Copyright 1983 by the Board of Trustees of the Leland Stanford
    Junior University

Library of Congress Cataloging in Publication Data
Borthwick, Sally, 1945–
Education and social change in China.

Bibliography: p.
Includes index.
1. Education and state—China—History. 2. Social change.
I. Title.
LC94.C5B67   1983   379.51   81-83853
ISBN 0-8179-7681-7

Manufactured in the United States of America

Design by P. Kelley Baker

For Alan

Contents

Illustrations

Editor's Foreword

In *Education and Social Change in China*, the second publication in the Hoover Institution's *Education and Society* series, Sally Borthwick describes the educational reforms introduced in China during the late Qing (Ch'ing) dynasty (ca. 1890 to 1911) and analyzes why these reforms produced the results they did. The story is a fascinating one, with profound implications for China's modernization efforts today and for those leaders in contemporary developing nations trying to establish Western-type educational institutions and educate a new generation of leaders and professionals.

Sally Borthwick's interpretation of China's first modern education reforms and their failures offers the following lesson: a society that embraces sweeping reforms beyond its powers of execution and ignores its traditional educational institutions places itself in a vulnerable position.

Building modern educational organizations is an expensive business that can threaten to undermine social stability and the political order. Once the initial structure has been constructed, the educational process becomes increasingly expensive for the state. Poor countries are unlikely to be able to afford these long-run rising costs. Even if they can afford the costs, unintended intellectual and political processes set in motion by these educational reforms can prove to be politically destabilizing. Worse yet, the nation that fails to make maximum use of its traditional educational organizations, does not upgrade them, and cannot integrate them with the new institutions being created wastes precious resources, alienates many professionals and students, and aggravates existing strains between modernizing and traditional segments of the society.

Borthwick's account of the traditional school system in China shows that the late Qing rulers already possessed the foundations upon which to graft a new educational order, if this step could be done properly. But instead, reformist zeal, official misperceptions, and planning errors combined to create a new urban school system, terribly expensive and never coordinated effectively with the older system.

To compound the problem, the new system failed to contain the two necessary educational tracks: one to train and supply society with middle-level and high-level skills; the other to supply a small pool of highly trained professionals to serve as leaders in government and the public sector. The lopsided educational systems of urban high schools and higher-level institutions produced only an overabundant supply of graduates without special skills or developed professional capabilities. As a result, school graduates quickly became alienated from the society they were supposed to serve. Many even became politically radicalized and joined revolutionary societies bent on realizing the goals of national strength and wealth set, but not attained, by the new education.

The result was an educational disaster and a tragedy for early modern China, one that China never fully overcame during the interregnum period of 1911 to 1949.

Sally Borthwick's publication is the first in a projected series of studies that will deal with education and its problems in twentieth-century China. The Hoover Institution is proud to present this scholarly and persuasive treatment of modern China's first educational reforms.

PAUL R. HANNA

Hoover Institution

Acknowledgments

The basis of this work is the doctoral dissertation I presented at the Australian National University in 1978. I wish to thank those who supervised that dissertation at different times: Dr. Stephen Fitzgerald, for his guidance in its later stages; Dr. Wang Ling, for his encouragement and support throughout my scholastic career; and Professor Wang Gungwu, for many illuminating suggestions. I also benefited from the assistance of colleagues in the Department of Far Eastern History: Dr. John Fincher, Dr. Lo Hui-min, Dr. David Pong, Dr. Louis Sigel, and Mrs. May Wong—and from the hours that William Liu of Sydney spent with me, conjuring up the vanished world of his childhood in Guangdong. I am grateful to my examiners—Dr. John Chinnery, Professor Kwang-Ching Liu, Professor Liu Ts'un-yan, and Dr. Yen-ching Huang—for many valuable comments. Finally, I thank the Australian National University for providing me with a scholarship and fieldwork assistance.

The revision of the dissertation was much advanced by the stimulating suggestions given by Dr. Ramon Myers of the Hoover Institution. I am indebted to him and to Dr. Paul Hanna for their interest in and support of the project, to John Ziemer for his meticulous editing of the manuscript, and to the Hoover Institution for making possible the use of its resources during a two-month stay at Stanford in 1979.

Last, I wish to thank my husband, Alan Thomas, for his patient toleration of five years of working nights and weekends.

Introduction

Since the Cultural Revolution, there has been a sharp rise in Western interest in the Chinese approach to education, an interest fueled by the Chinese assessment of educational policy as basic to national development. Among the issues raised in the debate over reaction, destruction, and reform have been the suitability of Western institutions and methods for China, the relative utility of technical and moral knowledge, the fate of unemployed youth, and the worth and feasibility of centralization versus dispersal and discipline versus independence. The issues are not new ones in the history of Chinese education, but the student will have great difficulty in tracing their earlier course. Writings on education in pre-1949 China have hitherto had a strong bent towards the political, understood as a record of government decisions, and the intellectual, understood as the mental development of a few outstanding men or as shifts in educational philosophy. This is particularly marked in the many histories written from the point of view of professional educationalists such as those by Yu Shulin, Chen Qingzhi, and Chen Qitian. With the exception of Chen Dongyuan, writers on the history of education in China have tended to limit their material to edicts, memorials, and regulations on the one hand and to the writings of educational theorists on the other. Evelyn Rawski's *Education and Popular Literacy in Ch'ing China*, a comprehensive and well-documented study of the hitherto elusive subject of traditional Chinese schooling, provides a useful corrective to an overly theoretical picture of premodern education, long thought of solely in terms of the examination system; the twentieth century, however, is still to a large extent a field of conflicting generalizations.

The present work attempts to survey early modern education in action, looking at the gap between the ideal and the real and examining the social determinants and implications of the new schooling. The time span chosen, the last years of the Qing—roughly 1890 to 1911—enables a study of the interpenetration of old and new values and relationships as China prepared to make the transition from an agrarian, family-based society to a modern, industrialized nation—a transition the new schools were supposed to expedite since they were themselves symbols of hoped-for order, discipline, and control—the "civilization" of the future. The study ends in 1911, for as Marianne Bastid observes in her picture of local educational reform, "the Republic brought in its train new problems."[1]

My work began with very concrete questions about both the new schooling and its competitor, the traditional school: How many hours were spent in the classroom? Where were schools located? How much were school fees? What were teachers' wages? How many pupils attended a school, and how far was the school from their homes? These led to questions on the motivations of the state in patronizing and the people in pursuing school education, which in turn opened up wider issues of the nature of state control and social organization in preindustrial and industrialized societies. It has naturally been impossible, in the space of a single work, to make an exhaustive analysis of themes of such magnitude, even for a single society over a limited period, but I believe that these lines of inquiry are fruitful ones.

The words "modern" and "traditional" are well known as shorthand references to points in a series of historical events. By "modern" I refer not necessarily to institutions of the present day, but to what was "modern" to China in the 1900s: the forms of society evolved in industrializing Europe and transmitted to the East.

Secondary works on Chinese education for this period are relatively scarce. One of the main topics that has drawn the attention of general historians has been the connection of students with revolutionary movements preceding the fall of the Qing. Others have singled out outstanding figures connected with the introduction of the new schooling. Articles by David Buck and Richard Orb discuss educational reform in a single province, but neither has produced a study covering the whole nation. Nor have Abe Hiroshi and Wang Shuhuai, although their articles give valuable insight into many commonly neglected aspects of the new schooling, such as peasant riots against schools.

I have used official documents with caution, preferring to check and supplement them with material from contemporary periodicals, autobiographies, and even fiction. The most useful periodicals for my purposes were *Dongfang zazhi* and Shanghai's *Jiaoyu zazhi*. *Xue Bu guanbao* and *Zhili jiaoyu zazhi* were also valuable sources.

Autobiography provides the researcher with much information, both subjective and objective, on schooling and pupils' reactions to it. For the traditional private schools, or *sishu*, data as basic as hours of schooling, texts, fees, the size of classes, and the school year have to be derived from informal autobiographical material, as no systematic treatment of these subjects exists. In the case of Western-type schools, regulations and decrees issued by the Beijing government provide copious but misleading information; here autobiography can be a valuable corrective to the versions of educational authorities. A case in point is Guo Moruo's account of his experience with "modern" schooling in Sichuan between 1906 and 1909: where educators envisaged professionally trained teachers inducting eager twelve-year-olds into Western science, Guo's class of adults, diverted unexpectedly from their preparations for the imperial examinations, faced ill-prepared graduates of the same examinations who lectured on pseudoscientific topics such as the five elements and the eight hexagrams.[2]

Such are the advantages of autobiography as a source. At the same time, it has its limitations. Autobiographies and memoirs are scarce, random, subjective, and usually written long after the event. They are not representative of the experiences of the mass of people, or even of the middle ranks of society. For the most part, autobiographies are written by a tiny fraction of a minority group, the highly educated who become prominent in later life. In the present instance, most of this group came from gentry families; reminiscences by those of peasant stock are as rare as they are valuable.

The use of fiction as a source is not common in historical writing, but it has obvious value for studying not only historical events but the reactions and responses of participants and observers. In addition, fiction, like memoirs, has the advantage of offering unexpected perspectives on events treated in standard fashion in more orthodox chronicles.

This work falls into four sections. The first two chapters deal with the indigenous educational institutions still operating at the end of the Qing, with special emphasis on the sishu and its social integration. Chapter three treats the attempts of reformers and missionaries to publicize alternative models of education as a means of saving China and the first schools to experiment with modern subject matter and methods. In chapters four and five, I look at the adoption of a nationwide school system modeled on the West's from the perspectives of the central government and of provincial and local officials and gentry members charged with implementing the scheme, as well as the part played by the new schools in fueling gentry demands for autonomy. Chapter six looks at the new schools' effects on social mobility and career prospects, and chapter seven examines the internal dynamics of the schools and their political repercussions. The conclusion evaluates the successes and failures of the wholesale educational modernization undertaken in China at the beginning of the century.

1
Indigenous Educational Institutions

The rulers of nineteenth-century China were deeply concerned with ideological control at all levels. The punitive or prohibitory aspect of this control was centralized: the central government could order a book burning or the suppression of a heretical sect or require that the death sentence be approved by the emperor. For prescriptive control it relied largely on the internalization of a body of precepts almost immanent in their diffusion, the Confucian norms and constants instilled in every chanting schoolboy.

The court was less concerned with administrative control, which was negligible in terms of China's size and population. Organs of government went down only as far as the county, an administrative unit comprising tens of thousands of households. The county magistrate's chief tasks were to dispense justice and collect taxes, some of which he retained for expenses, the rest of which he remitted to the center. The central government consumed revenue; it did not allocate or distribute it.

A masterstroke of earlier emperors had maximized the limited administrative functions of the center by combining the selection of officials who performed them with examinations in the classics, a touchstone for the rectitude of the scholar-gentry. The possibility of a prestigious and remunerative position in the bureaucracy ensured the voluntary compliance in an imperially approved course of study of millions over whom the government could exercise no direct control.

Only a fraction of the hundreds of thousands who took the lowest-level examinations passed at any one session. The few who passed obtained the title of *shengyuan*, becoming nominal students in a network of government school-temples that no longer had any educative function.[1] Approximately one in thirty of those successful in the lowest examination gained the degree of *juren* at the triennial provincial examinations that qualified scholars for selection for government office; one in two hundred would become a *jinshi* at the metropolitan examination that ensured it. Even among jinshi, fewer than a third achieved the cherished membership in the Hanlin Academy—a reservoir of talent from which the highest officials were appointed.[2] Thus each locality had a large group of men to whom the government had given status but not employment, as well as numerous outright failures. For such men, no other career had as much prestige as that of an official. Many wasted their lives waiting in vain for an opening. "Most owe their rent and board and have pawned all their clothes," wrote a contemporary observer of office seekers congregated in Hubei's provincial capital toward the end of the century. "They can't think of going home. It is hard to find words for the awkwardness of their position and their loss of shame."[3] Mean occupations were below the dignity of a scholar; regulations forbade shengyuan to undertake employment as store bookkeepers, yamen runners, and other lowly positions. Respectable but undistinguished positions as personal secretaries or shopkeepers required connections in commerce or government; the work of a teacher or a doctor was often ill-paid and arduous. Many scholars resented their failure to advance.

The Qing government was highly sensitive to the capacity of dissatisfied scholars for stirring up trouble. At the beginning of the dynasty, it had tried to outlaw involvement of shengyuan in political activity. The eight regulations designed to keep shengyuan apolitical repeated some prohibitions from the preceding Ming dynasty (1368–1644): "Shengyuan are not allowed to make submissions on civil or military affairs. A single proposal will be considered a breach of the regulations, and the offender will be stripped of his degree and punished." It also added new ones, among them one designed to prevent the repetition of the scholar cliques formed in the last decades of the Ming: "Shengyuan are not allowed to form parties, sworn alliances, or societies and dictate to officials or make themselves arbiters in the countryside. They may not publish at will what they write. Offenders will be punished by the proctors."[4]

Tablets bearing the injunctions were placed in the government school-temples among other symbolic representations of an ideal world.

Pious exhortation, however, was insufficient to prevent the gentry from manipulating their privileged status to their own advantage. Many scholars continued unruly, litigious, and combative, pressing their demands on officials and lording it over the common people.[5] The existence of the regulations meant, however, that any approach to government had to be indirect and informal, dependent on personal connections. The prohibition of associations and open political debate explains the note of daring with which private groups studying matters of national import were introduced in the 1890s. A conservative critic of one such group objected not to its undue Westernization but to its resemblance to the outlawed secret societies.[6]

Imperial concern with law-abiding behavior did not stop at scholars, but extended to all sectors of the population. The Sacred Edict of the Kangxi emperor (r. 1661–1722) enjoined on all the observance of Confucian teachings on harmony, frugality, and respect for learning, adding to them such civic duties as full payment of taxes and refusal to harbor fugitives from justice. Government schools were to be promoted "to bring into line the behavior of scholars"; at home, the young should be instructed to eschew wrongdoing.[7] Education was valued as a means of transforming conduct. In the words of the Qianlong emperor (r. 1736–1796), "studying the classics and debating philosophical principles is no education at all" unless based on the practice of Confucian virtues.[8]

The Rural Compact

The *xiangyue*, or rural compact, originated in the Song dynasty (960–1279).[9] It was revived at the beginning of the Qing in the mid-seventeenth century for the edification of a wider audience than could be reached by ill-attended and irregular lectures at the school-temples. Local officials were to appoint scholars to expound at public lectures the maxims of emperors, most frequently the Sacred Edict of the Kangxi emperor and the Amplified Instructions of the Yongzheng emperor (r. 1723–1736). The imperial house had great confidence in the powers of this instruction. If faithfully carried out, it would "open the minds of its hearers. Not only will the careful and compliant delight in it; even the wild and unruly will feel some constraint."[10] Local officials, who had more pressing tasks than the supervision of moral uplift, rarely shared the imperial enthusiasm. Moreover, the center provided no funds; they had to be raised locally from reluctant taxpayers. A conscientious official might deliver the readings himself. Elsewhere, the task fell to unwilling commoners or unsuccessful scholars or was completely abandoned.

Where the rural compact persisted, it lost its moral purpose, becoming assimilated to local defense or police organizations or even to tax collection. It could serve as the venue for the transaction of business between the magistrate and members of the lower gentry, who thus circumvented the rules forbidding them to frequent the yamen.

The Qing emperors encountered two obstacles in their effort to elevate their subjects through acquaintance with the imperial views on the conduct of life: they could not rely on their subordinates to propagate these teachings, and they could not rely on the people to follow them. A surface harmony might have been created if every villager or townsman had been familiar with these precepts, a goal constantly urged by the emperors. Japanese leaders of the Meiji period showed that the content of the Amplified Instructions could be used effectively to foster consensus when they manipulated imperial rescripts modeled on the Instructions to build national unity. China, however, had no governmental framework to support the implementation of propaganda programs at the level of the village or market town, although lineages and families did carry out this function informally.

The Examination System

From the point of view of the state, education (*jiaoyu*) performed two functions: the transformation of the masses (*jiaohua*) and the cultivation of talent for office (*yucai*). Only at the end of the century were they conceptually united in the idea of a universal schooling that would at the same time nurture talent and transform the customs and morals of the masses. Throughout the greater part of the dynasty, the two were carried out by separate institutions: the rural compact, aimed at the common people, and the *keju*, or examination system, aimed at prospective officials.

Unlike the rural compact, the examinations were highly centralized. The chain of command was headed by the emperor himself. At the lowest level, the examination for shengyuan status, the final sessions were conducted at the prefectural seat by the provincial director of studies, an official appointed by the emperor who acted independently of the governor or governor-general and reported back to the court on the completion of his three-year term of duty. Specially appointed officials sent out from Beijing gave the provincial examinations, and the final metropolitan and palace examinations gathered scholars from all over the empire at the capital. The government set quotas by county for the lower examinations and by province for the higher in an attempt to give fair representation to each area and to ensure that no one region dominated the system.

No separate board of education existed. The examinations were under the jurisdiction of the Board of Rites—appropriately, since they were probably the most widely observed of the dynasty's rituals. The ritual was a secular one, linking man and man—scholar and examiner or fellow-students—rather than man and the divine, although spirits were called in to supervise the proceedings.[11] The successive examinations were in a sense stages in an initiation process whose trials welded together those who underwent them. A lasting relationship subsisted among those who had passed at the same examination and between them and their examiner, whose "disciples" they were henceforth. Partly for this reason, the emperor gave the final examination himself in an attempt to ensure that successful candidates owed their first loyalty to the throne. Common survival of a grueling ordeal and common achievement of scarce honors gave graduates a tendency to close ranks against those who had purchased official ranks or obtained educational qualifications outside the regular system. This cohesion contributed to scholars' reluctance to change the examination system.

The regulations and conventions governing examination procedures were a mixture of genuine testing (of stamina, tractability, and meticulous care as much as of intelligence), bureaucratic precaution against abuse (candidates were searched on entering the examination hall), and social reinforcement. The last was a major component. The public posting of the results at the site of the examinations, official banquets for successful candidates, mounted messengers bearing homeward the news of their triumph—the panoply of success not only encouraged the victors but spurred on laggards to another try. A shengyuan high on the list would be famous throughout his district; the scholar who came first in the palace examinations brought glory to his whole province. The element of chance in examination success was rationalized in popular Taoism—in beliefs held by the gentry as well as the common people—as the working out of a candidate's accumulated karma. Another superstition held that success derived from the geomancy of the candidate's native place. Such beliefs strengthened the legitimacy of scholarly prestige and of the court as its patron, as well as reinforced native place or lineage solidarity and cohesion.

At first sight, the examination system of Qing China seems to have possessed the characteristics of a "modern" institution: it was centralized, operated on a national scale, and fulfilled (in the selection of officials) a rational bureaucratic function implemented through a series of impersonal, universalistic regulations. On analysis, the similarity appears superficial. To say that the proclaimed universal and rational values of the examination system were shot through with irrational beliefs and operated for the maintenance of particularistic interests is not to differentiate it from the institutions of Western society, in which the same is the case. The difference is rather that in Qing China the examinations were almost the only point at which the central government cut deeply but briefly into lives normally little affected by events outside their locality.

The functions of the central government were limited by its funds. Its writ extended through the examination hall and the yamen of the centrally appointed county magistrate, but not necessarily far beyond. Local society had its own dynamics and suffered under or resolved its own problems in defense, agriculture, education, and social relations with little direct assistance or interference from the center. A large proportion of local worthies had no degrees; many whose talents the government had formally acknowledged with the award of the title of shengyuan led lives of straitened obscurity. The wide mesh of the examination system represented perhaps the maximum extension of direct control of which the central government was capable; more was not financially, technically, administratively, or politically possible.

The state created the examination system for its own purposes. Those who were scholars from avocation rather than ambition often felt uneasy within its rigid constraints. The pull of divided loyalties is evident in the words of a Ming scholar: "The examinations are the system of our sacred dynasty; for scholars not to practice for them respectfully is to estrange the present and oppose the past and is thus not in accord with the principle of Heaven. If Confucius and Mencius were reborn, they would sit the examinations." Nonetheless, he continues, a mechanical approach to classical studies undertaken simply as a stepping-stone to degrees fetters the scholar.[12] Qing scholars faced the same dilemma in attempting to reconcile pure learning with preparation for the examinations.[13]

The Academy

The *shuyuan*, or academy, originated in the Song as an alternative for the scholar who did not wish to pursue an official career. It was at that time a center of free discussion and research, largely independent of the system that selected men for office. Succeeding dynasties saw frequent attempts by the government to bring academies under official auspices, while, to the detriment of independent research, local gentry and aspirant gentry tended to use them as a convenient means of practicing for the examinations.

The Qing dynasty overcame an initial suspicion of academies and made them objects of official patronage and regulation. The Yongzheng emperor made grants from the treasury of 1,000 taels to each of 21 leading provincial academies in the hope that they would become centers at which "virtuous and accomplished provincial scholars expound and recite the classics morning and evening, strictly ordering themselves and their behavior, their attainments inspiring scholars from near and far to emulation."[14] The intent was to bring scholars and scholarship under control. The Qianlong emperor continued his predecessor's policies. In a revealing edict, he ordered that the "highly inappropriate" title of *shanzhang* ("mountain leader"—a term suggesting independence, used since the Song for the heads of academies) be replaced by the bureaucratically neutral *yuanzhang* ("academy leader").[15] These gentlemen were to serve no longer than six years. Provincial officials could recommend those with meritorious records for official rank.[16] Both rulings were widely ignored. As with the rural compact, the center had no means of enforcing compliance.

Direct grants by the central government to academies were unusual. Yongzheng's signaled imperial favor rather than economic support; operating costs would have swiftly exhausted 1,000 taels. By the Jiaqing period (1796–1820), some academies in Guangdong had annual expenses of nearly 5,000 taels.[17] Academies were normally funded locally, through endowments of land or money from which rental income or interest could be drawn to meet current expenses such as the head's salary or student allowances. Deprived to a large extent of the opportunity to propagate independent views, they became organs for the advancement of the material interests of local individuals or groups.

The Qing dynasty saw an increase both in the number of academies and in the proportion of those founded through official sponsorship, although an influx of commercial capital tended to reverse this trend in certain areas during the late Qing.[18] The quality of an academy tended to depend on its proximity to sources of income. By the late Qing, the majority were urban foundations, with those in provincial capitals enjoying the highest reputation.[19] They thus contributed to the attraction of urban life for gentry members.

The establishment of academies involved the cooperation of different sections of the elite.

> It is seldom easy to disentangle the precise roles of gentry and officials in the foundation of particular academies. From the very beginning of

the process, official approval and recognition were required . . . But since the local social unit invariably stood to gain by a new *shu-yüan*, through enhanced reputation and improved chances in the competition for the coveted degrees, its leading gentry were consistently and strongly motivated to found and sustain one . . . Thus one can seldom be certain in the case of a founding recorded as "official" whether it was the magistrate (using his bureaucratic power as necessary to extract contributions) or the local gentry (manipulating the magistrate as a convenient figurehead) who took the initiative and played the leading role.[20]

The position of academy head was often held by former magistrates or (an unauthorized practice) by local educational officials. Of 515 recorded appointments of academy heads in Guangdong, 52 were former county magistrates and 104 educational officials. Educational officials were supposed to relinquish their official posts before assuming a headship but did not always do so.[21] Academic cooperation with officialdom was institutionalized through the practice of holding two essay competitions a month. The head of the academy set the theme and marked the papers for one, the magistrate for the other. Outside scholars were permitted to compete for the small cash prizes offered and often used the occasion to polish their examination technique.

Often intended and actual advantages of having an academy in one's district merged. Their use as an adjunct to the examinations was not in itself forbidden; indeed, the Qianlong emperor had ordered that the monthly tests continue to use the eight-legged essay form set for the official examinations, although within the academy its study was to be confined to the duller students.[22] Elsewhere, he stated that preparation for the examinations should be the Confucian scholar's last concern.[23] Imperial exhortation was in no position to compete with local self-interest, however, and the reputations of many of the best academies derived from the examination successes of their graduates.

At its extreme, the domination of the examination system led to a distortion of the original role of academies. Frequent edicts censured the appointment of unqualified heads and the use of personal connections in the appointment of staff and the admission of students. It became common for heads to draw their salaries without giving lectures or even putting in an appearance in the academies in which they were supposed to reside. Similarly, students attended solely for the small stipends they received; some even drew the money and stayed away. The compiler of one imperial encyclopedia prefaced the section on academies with some comments on their decline: "The post of head was filled by tired, decrepit persons; scholars vied with one another in frivolities. Day and night the latter read nothing more taxing than eight-legged essays. But the general run of them [stayed] merely for the tiny allowances; some of them even refused to leave when their hair had turned white."[24]

It would be easy to join the chorus of condemnation that arose at the end of the nineteenth century from those who wished to see the academies replaced by modern schools. Such condemnation, however, is anachronistic; the majority of scholars in the Qing saw nothing wrong with an academy's producing examination graduates. On the contrary, this testified to its success. For those who wished to pursue pure learning, several famous academies, founded or revived by farsighted officials in the nineteenth century, sponsored critical and broadly based investigation into ancient and modern learning along the lines of Han learning, the dominant trend of philological and literary scholasticism during the Qing. Dedication to the pursuit of truth and to its practical application enabled these academies to make, through their students and teachers, an indirect but important contribution to China's progress in this century.

The rules of various academies reflect the tension between their lofty goals and the petty preoccupations of daily life. Even those students who had the benefit of daily contact with the Song philosopher Zhu Xi must have found his rules for the White Deer Cave Academy a counsel of perfection. They enjoined on students the observation of Confucian virtues in social relations and personal ethics and "wide learning, deep inquiry, careful thought, clear discernment, and sincere practice" in study. Students were to put fame and profit last and seek understanding for its own sake.[25]

Heterodox in his own day, Zhu Xi had become a paragon of orthodoxy by the Qing, and the Qianlong emperor held up his rules as a model for all academies. For a course of study, the emperor recommended that drawn up by one of Zhu Xi's followers and based on the master's work.[26] This course should not be understood as the equivalent of a modern school curriculum any more than Zhu Xi's rules can be taken as the equivalent of modern school rules. Both were predicated on individual self-cultivation under the guidance of a master; neither set a fixed term to learning, nor did they assume that all students would be doing the same thing at the same time. Some academies did attempt to introduce a certain group discipline into academic life, though not into the actual sequence of studies—these continued to be tailored to the individual student's rate of progress. One early set of rules called on all students to rise, wash, and dress at the first stroke of the bell at dawn. By the second stroke, they were to be at their desks reciting or in the lecture hall making obeisance to past sages, depending on the time of the month.[27] At their most strict, however, rules for academic conduct were in the nature of outward and visible signs of an inward and spiritual grace, intended to instill in scholars a dedication to learning, respect for teachers, and a fraternal regard for fellow-students by making habitual the behavior associated with these qualities. They were not rules of convenience externally imposed to facilitate the management of large numbers of people (academies rarely had more than a few score students) but the outward manifestations of the scholarly self-cultivation developed by the neo-Confucians.

Many sets of rules drawn up for academies in the Qing follow the hortatory model set by Zhu Xi. Others, slightly more realistic, show by their limited goals the extent to which academies diverged from the ideal. One academy in Guangdong had "the establishment of a course of study" among its aims, an indirect comment on the frequent absence of any defined course; another provided penalties of ten days' loss of stipend for plagiarism of a whole essay, but only five days if half the essay were copied.[28]

Publicly Funded Schooling

Academies can be thought of as part of the "cultivating of talent" (yucai). The idea of using classical training as a means of improving customs and reforming manners among the masses (jiaohua) existed in the Qing but was not carried out through government agencies. For the most part, it was left to the people of each locality—the family, lineage, village, or guild—to arrange for themselves. The state was nominally concerned with the provision of free elementary education through community (shexue) or charity schools (yixue), and the Kangxi, Yongzheng, and Qianlong emperors all issued edicts ordering the establishment of such schools. As with the rural compact (with which the operation of the charity school might be combined), the center allocated no funds for this purpose; the promotion of free education was left to the discretion of the magistrate and the goodwill of the local populace.[29] Charity schools in no sense formed a national education network.[30] Only 5,846 are recorded for the late Qing, accommodating, according to Evelyn Rawski's study, a possible total of 134,000 out of 40.3 million school-age boys. She concludes that "the available schools . . . provided negligible opportunities for education" at the national level even if considerable underrecording is assumed.[31]

Although the government would gladly have extended indoctrination in the Confucian precepts on which its rule was founded to the lower orders, the Qing economy lacked sufficient surplus resources for the achievement of universal literacy. In its absence, the masses were supposed to acquire the teachings of Confucianism from the example of their betters. Many Confucian tenets did filter downwards. One writer describes the distress of a tenant farmer who lost his pigtail (required of Han Chinese by the Manchu Qing dynasty) after the 1911 revolution at having damaged part of the body he had inherited from his parents: "Hsun-hsin was quite illiterate, but as the sayings of Confucius and his disciples were perpetually quoted in our daily conversation, he knew them and strove to obey them." [32] Apologists for Chinese illiteracy attempted to rationalize its prevalence: "To us, at least to the village folks, education does not necessarily include the mechanical appliance of reading and writing. It rather consists in the apprehension of lofty ideas and the understanding of the philosophy of life." [33] It was education of this nature that was purveyed by readings of the Sacred Edict. "Lofty ideas" usually meant such teachings as were conducive to order and stability.

The idyllic view of education as possession of the right ideas tended to originate with the gentry for peasant consumption. No gentleman would leave his son ignorant of reading and writing, a fact reflected in the popular term for an educated man: *dushu ren*, or "a man who reads books." Schooling was conceived as a means not of raising the status of a whole group but rather of admitting selected members of lower groups to elite status. [34] To maintain the perception of justice in the system's operation, it was essential that the poor but talented should have an opportunity to compete. The elite-determined criteria were exclusively literary; since such talent appeared only after the child had already embarked on a course of study, the majority of the population were not even entrants in the race. In practice, the deserving poor were often scions of educated families who had fallen on hard times—a common occurrence since the nineteenth-century rates of mortality and morbidity left many families without a breadwinner.

Charity schools were one means of equalizing educational opportunity. They functioned rather like academies, in that they, too, derived funds from an endowment of land or money. As with academies, their foundation was often the result of a joint effort by officials and local people, although gentry members or groups of villagers acting independently also founded them. Their only irreducible cost was the teacher's salary; since this was low, an endowment of less than fifty *mou* of land (approximately three hectares) sufficed. Rural as well as urban areas could afford to establish such schools. [35] Standards varied: higher-level schools offered an education equivalent to that obtainable in the less ambitious academies, others took students at all levels, but the majority provided only elementary schooling for the poor. As indicated above, they were by no means capable of providing schooling even for that fraction of the population that qualified by inclination and ability. In Yunnan, which had the highest rate of attendance, recorded schools could have accommodated only 3.3 percent of the potential students.[36] Another means of defraying the expenses of a boy's education was attendance at a lineage school, which offered free places to poor members of the lineage. Unfortunately, lack of data makes it impossible to quantify either the number of schools or the number of such positions available.[37]

The case of Wu Xun (1838–1896), a beggar who devoted his life to collecting money to set up charity schools, is an instructive one. Despite later attempts to make him an apostle of universal education, his life was predicated on the right of a small literate elite to dominate the uneducated masses; he did not wish to change this, but merely to ensure that lack of money did not prevent those with an aptitude for study from entering the ruling classes. The school he founded produced several students who passed the lowest examinations.[38] Unable to read or write, he himself took his place humbly at the bottom of the social ladder. On the opening day of the school his money had set up, he "made his obeisances to the teacher and then to the pupils. When food was brought out to feast the teacher, Seven [Wu Xun] stood outside the door. When the feast was over, he ate up what was left, saying 'I am a beggar and would not presume to contest the teacher's place of honor!'"[39] It is hardly surprising that Mao threw him out of the pantheon of model worthies.[40]

Private Schooling

Both academies and charity schools played a marginal part in Chinese education. Its true parameters were the examination system, crowning the educational edifice, initiated by and corresponding to the needs of the apex of Chinese society, the central government; and the lowly sishu, or private, one-teacher tutorial school (discussed in detail in chapter two), which arose in response to the demands of the family units that formed society's base.

Sishu, unlike academies, community schools, or charity schools, were purely private, as their name indicates. Not only did they receive no support from officials, they received no recognition in any form. Gazetteers and official compilations did not include them under the heading of "schools" (xuexiao); no public funds were diverted toward them; no registration or supervision was provided. This absence of sishu from the bureaucratic dictionary had serious consequences for later Chinese educational policy; namely, the government never considered using them as a base for the new school system.

Academies provided allowances for all their scholars, and charity schools were free. The sishu, however, invariably charged fees. Since sishu provided, to all intents and purposes, almost all elementary education, this meant that at the base of a system meant to operate on merit rather than wealth was a built-in inequality. Nonetheless, the need for literacy in daily life and the respect accorded learning ensured a widespread demand for schooling, a demand filled by a constant supply of educated men seeking to make a living out of years of classical studies otherwise irredeemable in cash terms. The classical education in which the sishu specialized exclusively was available to most families with any disposable income. Thus schooling was not confined to an elite, although it derived a large part of its prestige from association with elite culture and a large part of its utility from association with elite power.

The examination system mixed rigorous external regulation with abandonment of the candidate to a solitary wrestle with his fate. The academy attempted to realize the ideal scholarly community through rules designed to inculcate self-discipline—but found the ideal dissolved through indifference and neglect until "the name remained but the reality disappeared." The sishu differed from both, running through its hourly, daily, yearly routine with a total absence of systematic regulation. Custom and individual need, not externally imposed rules, dictated practice. The sishu teacher was integrated with the surrounding community but independent of the hierarchies above him. The sishu thus combined autonomy and integration in a manner totally different from its modern counterpart.

2
The Sishu and
Its Place in Society

Modern Schooling

China's indigenous schools had molded themselves to fit the contours of a society very different from that of the industrialized West or industrializing Japan. The school systems of the latter were not isolated developments, but grew up in conjunction with modern hospital and penal systems, disciplined armies, and, subsequently, police forces, and with increased regularization of the tasks and control in the organization of the labor force in the manufacturing sector.[1] New technology and new institutions interacted in a spiral of increasing political and economic integration, which provided channels for the diffusion of ideological and the strengthening of administrative control (in contrast to the static nature of China's sishu).[2]

In modern Western society schooling has normally involved attendance of all male and female children between certain ages regardless of the will or wealth of their parents. Although entry to school is at a fixed age, there is relatively little concept of that age as a turning point, as marking a new period of one's life; indeed, the content of a child's activities during the first year of school overlaps to a large extent with that offered to children in a middle-class home—games, stories, constructive play. It is the structure of activity within school rather than its content that differs from home life. The child becomes a member of a class—one of twenty or thirty, or, in the old days, of forty, fifty, or sixty. For the first time, he or she is a unit in a large group and embarks on a process of habituation to coordinated, regulated action that will later suit manners to tasks in the factory, the army, public service, or the business world. The discipline required for the management of large groups is inculcated along with the ABCs, as the child learns to arrive punctually, respond to bells and words of command, stand at attention or march in line, begin and end activities in unison with classmates (even if these are of no more gravity than an afternoon nap). Performing these actions imprints their virtue on the infant mind, and "rules" and "obedience" take their place among the earliest abstract concepts learned.

Integration of Curriculum

The curriculum soon evolves from its original formlessness to differentiation—nature study, arithmetic, reading, writing—and further differentiation—history, geography, calculus, French, physics, chemistry. Especially in primary school, subjects are supposed to reflect the child's natural interests and immediate surroundings. In high school, knowledge is still understood in "practical" terms; that is, it gives the pupil information about the operation of the natural and social world. Thus the learning imparted in school is seen as a distillation of observations made outside it. Texts are written by authors whose standpoint in time and space is not far distant from that of the pupils who use them (with the exception of those used in literature classes, school textbooks are rarely more than twenty years behind their readers).

Segregation of Organization

The apparent relevance of the message of these classes is contradicted by their medium. Lessons take place in a classroom built for the purpose and never used for any other, equipped with items of furniture, such as blackboards, rarely found elsewhere. Teachers are trained and employed to deliver lessons and are seldom encountered by pupils in any other capacity. Similarly, textbooks written for use in schools are never read outside them. School subjects are thus drawn into a world of their own, set in a frame that implicitly denies the connections that pedagogical theory explicitly claims.

The class is a unit of the school, itself a discrete, articulated organism. Except in the countryside, a school will usually have hundreds of pupils and a dozen or more staff members. Within the school, progress is sequential by age and work covered; a year is normally spent at each level. The school, again, is a unit in the whole educational system. Horizontally, a school is set up in each area with sufficient children of the required age to support one; vertically, it is a stage in a tripartite, graded system whose divisions, like those of hospitals and penal institutions, fall along broad age groupings. The school differs from these institutions in that the longer the stay, the greater the advantages enjoyed in later life.

The educational system is, as a rule, government run and government funded. Even institutions not directly under state control, such as universities and private schools, are subject to government regulation and must conform to standards the state sets down. Bureaucrats and professional educators cooperate to regulate the operation of schools by determining texts, staff qualifications, the school calendar, and the level needed for graduation; thus the school system is characteristically highly centralized. Differences of opinion may occur between professionals and bureaucrats over questions of priority or principle, but no one questions the right of each to play a role in the formation of the system. The same does not hold true for parents, who participate only at the base level and then in a token, marginal role.

Although the pattern of schooling is uniform, differences in the quality of teaching, facilities, and equipment mean that not every child gets an identical education. Differences of provision compound with differences of background, as pupils enter school with a varying array of vocabulary, concepts, attitudes, and habits, depending on their parents' occupation and education. Quantity of education received, in terms of number of years spent in educational institutions, correlates closely with family background and in turn determines the student's future occupation and status. Despite the apparent egalitarianism of universal education, it is one of the main mechanisms for formalizing the streaming and selection of the occupants of different social strata.

In broad strokes, these are the common characteristics of the modern school system that developed in Europe and the United States in the nineteenth century in response to particular economic, political, and technological conditions. This system was not necessarily the only or the ideal form for an industrialized society and is now in some respects being superseded in its place of origin. By virtue of the prestige that military and commercial might conferred on its original possessors, however, it became the model for the school system developed in Japan from 1872 on and thence transferred to China in the early twentieth century. To a large extent, it remains the system in use in China today.

The Sishu

The sishu differed fundamentally from the type of school outlined above both in its place in society and in its internal organization. It
had existed in the same form in China for several centuries[3] and typ-
ically consisted of one class, of boys only, taught by one teacher.[4] At its
smallest, in a family school, the class might dwindle to one pupil, the son
of the house; at its largest, one might find sishu with "thirty or forty or
even fifty or sixty students."[5] Numbers varied from school to school and
fluctuated at different times. Surveys of those schools taking children
from a number of families show average class sizes ranging between 8
and 24.[6] Unfortunately, statistics are insufficient to assess the difference
in class size between rural and urban schools and in different parts of
China. Apart from these variables, class size also depended on the reputation of the teacher. One schoolmaster recalled starting with very few
pupils—their combined fees equivalent to only four yuan a year. Subsequently he earned two hundred yuan over ten years, signifying, if his
fees remained constant, more than a fivefold rise in the number of
students.[7]

Although a general distinction may be drawn between *mengguan*, or
schools taking elementary pupils, and *daguan*, or schools for advanced
students, many sishu took pupils at all levels. Within each sishu, pupils
were not subdivided into groups on the basis of age, ability, or achievement. Rather, each pupil was a single teaching unit, proceeding through
the curriculum at his own pace. His work was appraised individually, not
automatically graded in relation to his fellows. From this point of view,
the teaching scheme could be said to be individualism run rife, but it derived not from a respect for individual development but from limits imposed by custom and convenience.

Although the master's teaching might be delivered to a group by way
of a single lecture or text, its apprehension had always been a matter for
the individual student; tradition dating back to Confucius and strengthened by Zhu Xi militated against togetherness in learning. There were
practical obstacles, too, to the modern institution of graded group learning. Before the development of good roads and public transport, a
school had to be within walking distance of its pupils unless they boarded
away from home. Since its catchment area was limited in size, so was the
number of pupils. Even supposing the amalgamation of two or three sishu in a large village or small market town, the thirty or forty pupils thus
brought together would be insufficient for the economic operation of

groupings similar to those of the modern school system; nor was the schoolmaster, usually wholly dependent on his pupils' fees, likely to welcome their partial diversion to an assistant or colleague.

Sishu attendance was not universal, compulsory, or free. No school of thought advocated universal attendance regardless of sex or ability, although the ideal held that poor but talented boys should have the opportunity to study. The government's attitude to popular schooling was one of benign neglect; not only did it not subsidize the general run of elementary schools, it neither certified nor inspected them. The government bureaucracy impinged on the schoolmaster only as the possible destination of an exceptionally fortunate pupil. The master was employed not by the state but by his pupils' parents. Their control may have contributed to the longevity and conservatism of the sishu, which continued to propagate values acceptable to parents even when such values diverged from those espoused by modernizing governments of the Republican period.

Modern schooling "grades" its pupils not only in the classroom but in their adult life, usually through school-associated examinations. The results of this sorting appear to correlate closely with family origin, but family origin alone is generally powerless without appropriate certification. In China, however, the formalization and legitimization of officially recognized social stratification were carried out through examinations that were independent of schools. Schooling itself offered no formal qualifications, but merged with family background as one of the intangibles affecting success or failure in the examinations.

Types of Sishu

Family background strongly influenced the type of schooling received. Sishu conveniently divide into three general classes: the family school, or *jiashu*; the communally established lineage or village school (*zuxue* or *cunxue*); and the privately established school, founded and run by a single teacher accepting applicants solely on a cash basis. The different types overlapped: a family school that advertised on street corners was difficult to distinguish from an open-entry school; the lineage school lay somewhere between an extended family school and a restricted village school (especially in the south, where single-surname villages were common); and a school independently set up by the teacher sometimes enjoyed the "moral and material assistance" of sponsors in the same way as a village school.[8] Although educationalists' definitions vary, usage sanctions "sishu" as a generic term for all types of indigenous private tutorial schools, as distinct from all forms of "foreign" or "modern" schools.

The Family School. In the simplest form of private schooling, a family (in the Chinese context, this meant all relatives living under one roof) hired a tutor for the education of its own children. The class might be swollen by the children of neighbors or relatives, but basically the arrangement was an exclusive and thus relatively costly one, especially if the teacher lived on the premises. Education at home was the prerogative of a privileged group, purchased in the expectation that it would contribute to the maintenance of privilege. Teacher and employer often came from the same social stratum and had a prior relationship based on kinship or acquaintance. Memoirists recall receiving their early lessons from a relative or friend.[9] Even where the link was not a direct one, a teacher might well have been recommended by a friend.[10] Both the existence of prior ties and the family head's right to determine his son's tutor distinguish this arrangement from the typical modern school, in which parents are unacquainted with their children's teacher before and often during the course of their education.

The greater intimacy of the relationship did not guarantee the teacher's status. If he was a young man temporarily pressed into service by friends or relatives while studying for the examinations or pursuing other avocations or an old one doing a favor for a friend, teaching might be regarded as a mutual convenience.[11] It was almost axiomatic, however, that those who pursued a career of elementary teaching lacked sufficient property to live off and all hope of advancement through the examinations. Theirs was a dependent and precarious position.

Some teachers were old retainers, or even enjoyed an almost hereditary position, but this appears to have been the exception.[12] A teacher's office was called into being by the needs of a specific child or children, and his appointment was at best tied to their years of schooling. Apart from this, a teacher might leave his job because of age or illness or have his services terminated because of strains on the family budget. Sometimes a teacher would follow his patron away from his native place. It was not impossible for a wife to follow her husband on his travels if he lived separately from his pupils.[13]

A rather cavalier attitude toward the appointment and retention of teachers at the elementary level reflects their lack of special qualifications either in subject matter or teaching method. Although such works as Wang Yun's *Jiao tongzi fa* (Teaching the Young) gave guidance on teaching, they were not required reading. The science of education, with concomitant prestige for its practitioners, was not elaborated in nineteenth-century China. A further problem appears to have been an oversupply of would-be teachers, seduced into a literary career by hopes of examination success that did not materialize.[14]

The teacher's dependence could be abject where personal connections did not mediate a cash relationship. A comic play from Shandong records the desperation of an unemployed teacher grasping at a contract to teach a miller's two dull sons for six thousand odd cash a year and his keep (two meals a day, for the sake of economy, straw bedding, and a dogskin coverlet); for this he had to provide not only mental but manual labor.[15]

Unless obtained at a discount, as in the case above, a teacher's board was costly. An urban clientele with a modest income, if desirous of the benefits of home education, would often hire a teacher to come in daily. This practice, involving the teacher's coming to the pupil rather than vice versa, was regarded as somewhat degrading to the teacher: the *Book of Rites* was quoted as evidence that in ancient times the opposite had been the case. A parsimonious employer might add insult to injury by "not providing meals but making the teacher walk home to eat them, in bitter cold and burning sun . . . and there are poor fellows, penniless scholars, whose pay is in arrears . . . though they beg for it, their pleas are ignored."[16] The education received under these conditions was probably no better than the conditions of employment, but this may have been a matter of indifference to a father who simply wanted a business assistant.

Miyazaki's conclusion that "'teachers from whom we receive instruction' [as opposed to examiners] were not given much credit. In what was a hard, clear-cut business transaction, the students considered their obligations to teachers fulfilled when they paid the exact tuition fee" may be an overstatement in the case of higher education.[17] Even at the elementary stage, the teacher's lowly position was often softened by personal ties. Nonetheless, Miyazaki's words are a useful corrective to the view that the teacher-pupil relationship was sacrosanct in traditional China.[18] Writers recalling the teachers of their childhood may do so with dislike, affection, indifference, or pious respect (though the latter is less mandatory for teachers than for mothers), but they rarely indicate that the relationship persisted in any form in later life. Only children owed their teachers unqualified respect, but this they outgrew with their childhood. The teacher's relationship with his pupils was often based on past ties, but was rarely the foundation for future ones.[19]

Although women were not allowed to sit the examinations, they were, in gentry families, more commonly given an education than is sometimes believed. Daughters frequently attended classes with their brothers until they reached their teens, when they were taken off to learn women's work. Families with a pampered only daughter might even call in a tutor specially for her. In highly cultivated families, female accomplishments could rival those of the men; missionary-educator Robert Morrison noted in 1834 that "Governor Yuen of Canton (now member of the cabinet at Peking) had a learned daughter who died recently; after her death, his excellency published a hundred of her verses." Lower down the social scale, daughters and wives of small shopkeepers and craftsmen must often have learned, from family members, to keep accounts; and lower yet, singing girls and "those despised little girls who act in theaters" could read the texts from which they worked. The Confucian classics were normally beyond a woman's reach, but Buddhism was less discriminatory. Nuns who could read the sutras formed another small group of literate women. There was little objection to women's education in itself. Later conservative opposition to girls' schools was directed largely against the impropriety of young ladies' being seen in public, outside the home, and not against their being taught to read and write. Even the most thoroughgoing revisionist must conclude, however, that education for women was the exception rather than the rule. A Confucian tag had it that "lack of talent is virtue in a woman," an attitude reinforced by the lack of economic advantage in educating a daughter. Even the most brilliant would be unable to take the examinations; even the most capable would be lost to her family of origin on marriage. Evelyn Rawski estimates that "only 2 to 10 percent of females [possessed] some ability to read and write,"[20] compared with a literacy rate of about 30 percent for males.

Communal Schools. Although the village or communally run school offered little opportunity for female education, in other respects its intake was more catholic than that of the family school since it catered to a lower range of incomes. Such schools were set up through the joint efforts of a number of families. The most detailed account of this process dates from the 1930s, when Liao T'ai-ch'u, a sociologist from Yenching University, surveyed sishu in the Shandong county of Wenshang.[21] Supplementary evidence from late Qing sources and the recollections of participants attest the diffusion and durability of the methods he witnessed.

According to Liao, family heads would form a board dominated by "the village elders, or at least prominent members of the community possessing land, prestige, or ready cash." One or several of their number would be responsible for hiring the teacher, either locally or from outside,[22] while others would drum up enrollments by canvasing all families with school-age children. Since the canvasser knew each family's circumstances, his propaganda was exactly targeted. The admissions officers were . . . known for their knowledge of the locality, of the people, and also for their eloquence. They would talk to [the father of every potential pupil], persuade him, tell him the usefulness of Confucius' teachings . . . After talks of this kind no father could find courage enough to resist such a temptation unless he was absolutely bare and had not a cent to spare for his child's future or not a minute his child could stay away from his work in the farm. Even if this was really the case, his child might also be admitted free of charge and could be allowed to come any time he wanted through the recommendation of the admissions officer.[23]

Liao takes a rosy view of the ease with which sishu could be entered; elsewhere, however, he indicates that sishu schooling was confined mainly to families owning more than 1.2 hectares (18 *mou*) of land, a small percentage of peasant families.[24] Remission of fees appears to have been an occasional indulgence rather than a regular means of enabling the children of the poor to attend.

It is interesting to compare the canvasser, as a one-man propaganda team, with later communist attempts to enlist the support of peasants for worthy but not necessarily popular causes—with house-to-house visits to encourage contraception, for example. The school system introduced from the West in the late Qing and continued under the Nationalists conspicuously lacked mechanisms of enlisting popular support at the grass-roots level.[25]

It was to the interest of most of the participants to have as many children attending the school as the teacher could control since this spread the burden of his hire. This contributed to a flexible attitude toward school fees. Relative ability to pay was normally taken into account in assessing charges. Generally they were low, probably because of the surplus of would-be teachers. According to a satirical Shandong proverb, "The number of those who wish to teach school is in excess of the number who can read."[26]

Arrangements for schooling were social as well as educational. Their dual character is exemplified in the process known as *yi xue* ("discussion of schooling") by which school fees were fixed each year. Educationalist Shu Xincheng gave an account of its operation in his own schooldays:

At the Qingming festival, family heads would gather at the school, bringing plentiful supplies of wine and food. The teacher was kept busy receiving them, and though we were at school, we had no lessons that day. After a little chat they would all move out of his way and go to discuss in a room opposite how much each should undertake to pay in the way of school fees. Once this had been decided, each would write his share on a piece of red paper, and one of the older men present would be selected to hand the paper from his sleeve to the teacher with a few congratulatory words. Then the wine and food each had brought were put on a table with dishes prepared by the teacher, and they would sit down at table and drink together while the pupils ate at the side. This was called "discussing schooling"; that is, family heads would weigh up each family's financial situation as the basis for apportioning school fees. Once the amount was settled, it would be written in a book and given to the teacher. Further installments would be paid at the Duanwu and Mid-autumn festivals. This sum was to support the schoolmaster's family. As far as his personal life at the school was concerned, each sponsoring family would take turns in providing him with oil, salt, firewood, rice, and meat and vegetables each month.[27]

A foreign observer refers to the compilation of "a red card, called a school list" with the names of pupils on it, prepared by mid-autumn, the winter solstice, or the end of the lunar year.[28] Procedure naturally differed somewhat in charity schools, where the teacher's salary was not paid by parents, but the contract of one such school makes similar provision for a feast at the teacher's arrival and for seasonal payment of his salary.[29]

Installment payments, payments in kind, and the fitting of fees to circumstances meant that it was not difficult for families with some surplus income to send at least one son to school. If the canvasser did his work well, supply and demand would be a close fit. Given this subtle and sociable arrangement, it is small wonder that the flat rate charged by later schools on the Western model condemned them in the eyes of the old-fashioned as "roping in students to soak them for the fees."[30]

The system was not as egalitarian as it appears on the surface. As indicated above, farm laborers and many tenant farmers and small landholders living at or below the subsistence level could not have afforded even the most modest fees. Within the sishu itself, treatment often varied with the amount of the fee. Low fees simply entitled one to a place in the classroom; generosity meant a large share of the teacher's attention. Thus Shu Xincheng was permitted to start school for the small sum of 1,200 wen per year in cash (approximately three British shillings at the prevailing rate of exchange), two fat hens, and a few dozen eggs simply because, being less than four years old, it was assumed that he would not require much attention.[31] Conversely, Hu Shi's mother paid record-breaking fees of twelve yuan a year, six times the normal, to ensure her son special treatment.[32] A hostile short story makes the point through caricature: of a poverty-stricken schoolmaster who took his meals at each student's house in turn and surreptitiously stuffed his sleeves with food for his wife, "everybody said that he taught his students not according to their level but to the quantity of food and drink provided."[33] From the schoolmaster's point of view, deficiencies in fees could be made up in number of pupils; owing to the teaching methods used, an increase in numbers did not necessarily mean a commensurate increase in effort.

Schools Run by the Teacher. The third form of sishu, the school set up by the teacher, is of interest not so much because it differs greatly from the arrangements already discussed, but because such differences as exist take it in the direction of a modern school in the sense that no personal relationship, direct or through intermediaries, necessarily existed between schoolmaster and parent. In such a school, no formalities of appointment were required. The schoolmaster simply hung up a signboard and waited for pupils. This act assumes a certain number of pupils in the vicinity (few would attend a school not within walking distance of their home), and thus an urban location, or at least a large village and popular teacher. This ad hoc organization could lead to even greater flexibility in attendance and payment of fees; it was possible to pay by the month, or even, for very poor families who could not afford a large single outlay, by the day.[34] Like the hiring of teachers on the open market, this transaction could shed its social elements, becoming purely the sale and purchase of services. The process does not seem to have been carried to its conclusion; even in Beijing in the 1930s, sishu pupils still tended to come "from relatives in the neighborhood."[35]

A variation on this type was the daguan, or school for advanced students, at which a well-known scholar would prepare pupils for the examinations. Such schools might be residential (since scholars of such standing were not to be met with in every village, their instruction formed an exception to the rule that schooling was usually obtained in the pupil's home locality) and took in pupils from their teens into their thirties. In Wenshang, they were known as *cuanju* ("stove house") since those who attended did their own cooking. Shu Xincheng's autobiography contrasts the self-reliance nurtured in this type of school and the hand-and-foot service offered in the modern school that he later attended.[36]

The division of schooling was not formalized as it is in the Western or modern system. One master, if sufficiently capable, could teach all levels from beginning to advanced in the same class. A school's level depended on the teacher's reputation; only the best could confine themselves to higher-level students.

Few pupils received all their education from one teacher. A typical case is that of Chen Heqin, who in six years of sishu education studied under four masters at three schools.[37] If a family head did not change his child's teacher because of dissatisfaction with the teacher's performance, he did so because of a change of abode or fortunes. (Many students changed from family to outside schools or switched to self-study for economic reasons; others had their education broken off altogether.)

Availability of Schooling

Chinese scholastic lore has always exalted the role of individual application in studious achievement. A modern study takes a more cynical view, concluding that in the examination system, "the advantages were heavily in favor of those who had wealth and influence."[38] Schooling, standing at the juncture between family means and individual effort, showed the influence of both. At the elementary level, texts and teaching methods were similar in all schools, but even here individual attention—of the type automatically obtained in a small family school and purchased at extra cost in others—helped ensure that the child memorized and reproduced his lessons accurately, a desideratum in an examination system that penalized the minutest inaccuracy. The acquisition of more abstruse skills depended on the possession of wealth that permitted a prolongation of studenthood, sometimes into old age. Examination success depended to some extent on the utilization of one's forerunners' experience. Although books of model eight-legged essays could be bought, the training given by a successful candidate was preferred. Those with the right connections and income might even obtain the aid of a juren.

Even deeper than the division between those who enjoyed different levels of schooling was that between those who obtained some schooling and those who had never crossed the schoolroom threshold. There has been some debate in recent years about the literacy rate in Qing China. Given the dubious quality and limited quantity of statistics for the period, exactitude is unlikely. My own estimate would be that up to 40 percent of males attended a sishu at some time in their childhood. Many of them did not learn to read while they were there, and others would subsequently have lost their rarely used skills.[39]

The ubiquity of sishu can be deduced from the common derogatory term for a village schoolmaster, "Mr. Winterhearth of Three Family Village."[40] ("Winterhearth" refers to the practice of teaching children from farming families in winter, the slack season in agriculture; "Three Family Village" to a village so small that it had only three families.) In Wenshang in the 1930s, Liao T'ai-ch'u found "at least 1 szu shu in every village—big and small. In big villages and townships one expected more than one."[41] Shu Xincheng's home, a Hunan village of twenty or thirty households, supported two elementary sishu at the turn of the century. At that time, he reflects, the sound of chanted lessons was to be heard in every hamlet of ten houses. (The amount of noise from such chanting served as an index of an area's cultural standing: the more noise, the more culture.)[42] Writing of Shandong in the 1890s, a missionary observed that "it is far from being the fact that every Chinese village has its school, but it is doubtless true that every village would like to have one."[43]

Given the high level of demand for education and the number of underemployed educated men, it would appear that the state could, with a relatively small infusion of capital, have increased school attendance considerably. Active officials could and did found charity schools by the hundreds without lacking for teachers or students.[44] Most twentieth-century educators, however, opted for ambitious educational modernization rather than the upgrading of traditional schools.

Motives for Schooling

In the absence of state subsidies, who went to school? Well-to-do families would hire a tutor as a matter of course. Below them was a wide band of households whose small surplus income could be used for schooling if other expenditures were curtailed. Given that a schoolmaster would eat up—sometimes literally—this surplus, what determined whether the possibility of schooling was realized?

In looking at the factors that made schooling a desideratum, one must remember that it did not affect the individual alone. Education was a family investment, made with hopes of benefiting past, present, and future generations of the family.

Two of the main motives behind the pursuit of schooling were family honor and material advantage. Family honor was served by members who were successful in the examinations. Such success, to a far greater extent than achievement in the modern school, reflected on the family as a whole, "bringing glory to one's ancestors." Ma Xulun's mother urged him to his studies with the twin goads of his grandfather's high degree, which had to be emulated, and his father's failure, which had to be redeemed.[45] Honor was a potent motivation not only among the gentry but also in families only a generation away from manual labor. Shu Xincheng wrote that his mother's hopes were especially earnest: "She wished me on no account to follow in my ancestors' footsteps and become a horny-handed farmer, but prayed reverently before all the gods and Buddhas in the locality that when grown to manhood I might be an educated man and get some sort of office to make notable the forebears of the Shu and Xu families" (Xu was the maternal line).[46]

Shu's mother was not an isolated example. Women appear to have been particularly sensitive to the demands of family honor as defined by the examination system. In some cases widows championed their son's claims to education single-handedly against indifferent relatives—Hu

Shi and Luo Dunwei were the highly successful products of such maternal enterprise.[47]

Maternal influence has played its part in Chinese education since the fourth century B.C. when Mencius' mother moved three times to give him suitable surroundings for study. It is hard to tell how much the role of virtuous wife and mother was projected on to women by men, how much it represented women's response to a male-dominated society. Memoirs written by men serve both to record and reinforce desirable feminine behavior. One writer remembers that "in the evening, mother would be spinning cotton by the tiny flame of the oil lamp, or sometimes twisting threads, while we brothers would sit round the table chanting our lessons in loud voices. That picture of 'teaching one's sons in the lamplight' still springs of itself from my pen."[48] The literary flavor of this passage reflects the interplay between reality and stereotype in descriptions of the maternal role. Although most of the incidents recorded in memoirs probably took place, they are strained through the mesh of conventional piety; it is rare that a woman emerges from her son's autobiography as a living human being.

Failing the memoirs of Qing matriarchs, one can only conjecture why women valued the education of their sons so highly. There was a certain basis of realism to their hopes: if she outlived her husband, a woman would be financially dependent on her son. It was naturally in her interest that he should have the status and income potentially available through education. Then there were the social rewards, such as the esteem of neighbors, and the emotional satisfaction of having carried out the duties proper to one's sex in an exemplary manner, and finally, perhaps, an unconscious gratification at having fulfilled through one's son goals that one was not permitted to entertain for oneself.

Schooling was also expected to offer material advantages, or at least to prevent loss. The common people valued literacy as a form of self-defense against the extortions of the lettered. Shu Xincheng's great-grandfather, a tenant farmer, had his grandson attend a few years' school "because he had once been cheated."[49] A Zhejiang author recalls his father's stories of family humiliation; he received an education because his grandfather "believed that once in the charmed circle of scholar-officials, all humiliations would be left behind."[50] A degree was a powerful armor—its holders were immune from the grosser forms of physical punishment—but failing this, the ability to read official documents, receipts, or bills was obviously of use in dealing with yamen underlings or rapacious neighbors.

More particularly, literacy was necessary for the conduct of litigation. As late as the 1930s certain areas of Shandong were known for their beautifully written complaints and accusations, a product of the high standards of the local sishu.[51] Among boys sent to school with this accomplishment in mind was the future chairman of the Communist Party of China, Mao Zedong: "My father . . . wanted me to master the Classics, especially after he was defeated in a lawsuit because of an apt Classical quotation used by his adversary in the Chinese court."[52]

It has been suggested that schooling was also seen as having a moral function, as inculcating values that would preserve the family and its code of beliefs—ancestor worship, proper socialization by age and kin— and as "developing and inspiring a penchant for moral regeneration and improvement."[53] This was certainly what schooling was *supposed* to do. In Confucian theory, moral and intellectual development were indivisible: to understand the meaning of classical texts was to understand moral principles. Nonetheless, it is questionable whether the school was a prime agent in childhood socialization and whether morality loomed large in the calculations of parents hiring a teacher. Knowledge of Confucian tags had a social, even monetary, value, as the anecdote in the preceding paragraph indicates, and hence it is hard to assess the intrinsic worth ascribed to them. Textual content aside, the school was probably most effective in inculcating through practice a school-based morality of study: diligence, perseverance, respect for learning, unwearying submission to monotony in the hope of a tangible rather than a spiritual future reward. Even this discipline appears to have rested in many cases on rather tenuous day-to-day control by the teacher. Chapter nine of the famous Qing novel *Honglou meng* (Dream of the Red Chamber) describes name-calling degenerating into a brawl in the hero's lineage school while the regular teacher was on temporary leave.[54] Chen Tianxi remembers that his younger brothers took advantage of their teacher's absence to empty their chamberpots over each other, then wiped up the resulting mess with the pages of their textbook—acts a far cry from the decorum preached in its pages.[55]

The foremost agent of socialization into kin and sex roles was the family, where children could participate in customs and rites affirming family solidarity and continuity—the New Year reunion dinner, the ancestral altar, sweeping family graves at the Qingming festival—and learn the daily minutiae of respectful behavior—correct terms of address, when to be silent and when to speak, how and to whom to bow and to kneel.[56] The school could teach *about* family values, abstractly and through anecdote, and was thus, unlike the later "foreign" or modern school, seen as reinforcing them, but Confucian familism was not dependent on the school for its transmission. Women were after all effectively socialized without benefit of formal education into a system in which they were at some disadvantage. One finds, for example, the "virtuous woman" who ministered to an ailing mother-in-law or husband with a medicine brewed from her own flesh.[57] Her piety and that of chaste widows and rape-resisting suicides would be retailed in local gossip and maternal homily as well as being commemorated in official histories and memorial arches, reminding even the illiterate of what was expected of them.[58] Sishu teaching—unlike that later given in the new schools—was seen as reinforcing Confucian values rather than downgrading or displacing them, but its role in their preservation was limited. Similarly, sishu education was conducive to but was not the primary locus of Confucian intellectual endeavor, which tended rather to find a home in the great academies.

Schooling as Induction

So far I have been speaking of schooling in the context of reflected advantages for the family unit. In a sense, however, schooling performed this function only by first drawing the pupil out of his family and into the community of scholars. This is evident in the ceremony surrounding the child's first lesson, known as *po meng* or *qi meng* (the "breaking" or "enlightening of ignorance").[59] This marked his departure not only from his individual childish ignorance, but from the ignorance that enshrouded all who were unfamiliar with Confucian teachings. The lesson was prefaced by obeisance toward an altar to Confucius and by the pupil's formal acknowledgment of the teacher to whose care he was entrusted. The choice of a first teacher was held to be of great importance, not necessarily for the sake of his pupil's school career (the teacher might disappear after the first lesson) but for what it presaged about the future. Ma Xulun's father invited the first-place juren in the previous year's provincial examination to give young Ma his first lesson, hoping that the boy would follow in his temporary mentor's footsteps. (The juren was on his way to Beijing for the metropolitan examinations and did not reappear in Ma's narrative.) The young student, outfitted with a varying assortment of the tools of his new trade—schoolbag embroidered with auspicious symbols, the "four treasures of the study" (paper, brush, ink stick, and inkstone), and the Four Books or another suitable text—would then recite after his teacher a line from the classics or a later Confucian text until he had memorized the characters of which it was composed. Around this Confucian core grew up accretions of custom and superstition designed to ensure the harmony of the pupil-teacher relationship and the pupil's future success. The ceremony could be preceded by an offering to the "bodhisattvas"—Taoist gods who had insinuated themselves into the Confucian canon, where they presided over the examination fortunes of scholars.[60] At its conclusion, offerings might be made to the ancestors, or friends and neighbors—if the family was a rich one—invited to a feast for the teacher. Such festivities would not be repeated again in the student's scholastic career unless he passed the examinations. Within the classroom, the cakes brought by the new pupil signified, by a play on words, a high position in the examinations. Suzhou shops made specially shaped cakes for the occasion. Bao Tianxiao recalls that his schoolbag, embroidered with a first-place jinshi on a white horse, was turned inside out by the teacher; this stood for a scholar called to high office. This goal was reinforced by inspirational verse:

> The emperor values heroes bold, and writing would have you learn.
> Other occupations are lowly in rank; study alone is high.
> As a little child you must study hard; writing can make your career.
> The court's full of nobles in purple and gems; scholars, every one.
> In the morning, a farmer he was; at eve, he ascends to the palace.
> Generals and ministers are made not born; a boy should make his own way . . .[61]

These rituals were all designed for men, who alone could sit the examinations. Women had their part to play, however, in the provision of delicacies or embroideries and thus enjoyed a vicarious involvement. In Suzhou, the wife's brother took the child to his first lesson rather than father, and her family outfitted the pupil.

Such academic ritual illuminates popular attitudes to schooling during the late Qing. School attendance was a single aspect of deep-rooted beliefs about the purpose of study and the relationships involved. On the one hand its present participants—teacher, pupil, family—were linked through the preparation and conduct of these rites; on the other, ancestors, gods, and the First Teacher, Confucius, were called to witness. The ceremony bespeaks the integration of schooling with intellectual, religious, and social life.

Comparison of the Sishu and the Modern School

In all these particulars traditional Chinese schooling differed from the modern system. Although the content and purpose of the latter have socially recognized significance, no sanctity attaches to its forms. No ancient rite demands that a child who reaches a certain age in the course of a year be taken to a place within a fixed distance of his home and left there for six hours. These are bureaucratic dictates, designed for the smooth functioning of the system they regulate, but possessing little intrinsic meaning for the households they affect.

China's traditional schooling differed from that of the modern West not only in the nature of its ties with the family and the government but in its internal organization, which, in many respects, could be said to be the mirror image of that of modern schooling. The modern school integrates its curriculum with the outside world, but as an institution cuts off all links with it. The sishu closed off its curriculum from everyday life, but (in rural areas especially) was organizationally integrated into the surrounding community.

Segregation of Curriculum

In the modern school, teaching methods and curriculum purport to be practical, related to daily life, or at least to the principles governing the operation of the natural and social worlds. Children's readers reflect the life of the average middle-class child. Later specializations—modern languages, the social and physical sciences, mathematics, domestic and industrial crafts—are supposed to be relevant to the interests and careers of older pupils.[62] Such instruction is not necessarily devoid of moral content. Especially at the junior levels, primers are often the vehicle for the diffusion of national myths and the encouragement of civic virtue. This was especially true of the Japanese system, which from the 1880s onward introduced an emphasis on ethics not found in its Western models. Even here, the beliefs inculcated were state-selected rather than a reflection of values already held by the community. At advanced levels, subject matter tends to be insulated by its specialization from ethical and religious beliefs.

In China, the traditional curriculum was more remote from everyday life but less compartmentalized. Its subject matter was unitary. Compared with the modern curriculum, it did not show clear lines of demarcation. The *Three Character Classic*, the child's first reader, was also a primer of history, bibliography, ethics, and general knowledge. The Four Books could be regarded primarily as works of moral philosophy, but also served as sources of political history; the Five Classics included works of history, poetry, and divination, overlaid with neo-Confucian interpretations. An educated man was expected to be familiar with his country's history, but neither his teacher nor the examination system demanded that he study history as a separate discipline. He could get by without reading historical sources for the post-Qin millennia. For the Confucian educationalist, the classics were not merely *primus inter pares* as sources of knowledge about humanity; they were the records of the sages, imprinted with the perfections of their creators. Traditionalists looking at the new curriculum and its texts were baffled by the sight of modern men taking other moderns as their authority: "Are textbook writers the new sages, then?" asked the late Qing reformer Kang Youwei.[63] A mastery of the classics could be followed but never equaled by studies in other fields. In sishu, practicality yielded to doctrine to such an extent that even arithmetic was seldom taught, a knowledge of the abacus being left to parent or employer to provide.[64] The advanced accounting skills needed for financial administration could be acquired from teachers who specialized in training young men as private secretaries to officials.[65]

The Confucian classics and the preceding primers were remote from their young readers in other ways. They were written in classical Chinese. The earliest dated from nearly three thousand years ago, the most recent was a few centuries old.[66] Without explanation, they were unintelligible. Although the *Three Character Classic* emphasized the importance of explanation, it was customary for a student to memorize the primers, the Four Books, and the Five Classics before he was taught their meaning. The reform propagandist Zheng Guanying evokes the amazement of one who, after ten years of intermittent schooling, finds almost accidentally that the gibberish on the page in front of him has an intelligible meaning.[67] Harassed and often ignorant schoolmasters concentrated on producing value for money in terms of level of noise—from the recitation of texts—rather than level of understanding. It was taken for granted that children did not understand the books they read: the teacher of Gu Jiegang, one of the leading classicists of the Republican period, expressed disbelief when the precocious Gu claimed to grasp the meaning of the ancient *Zuo zhuan*.[68] Even though autobiographies are the records of a relatively privileged class, it is remarkable how many of their authors left the sishu understanding no more of the works they had memorized "than a monk reciting the scriptures." Ma Xulun, later to become a noted philologist, had to pass the usual hurdles in his youth. He recalls classes with "ten-odd students in a small room, all squawking nonstop . . . I got away with just opening my mouth and making noises with the best of them. All Mr. Zhang required of his students was recitation . . . I was on the third book of Mencius, but didn't know what it was about."[69] The Five Classics were even worse: Ma found the *Book of Odes* and the *Book of History* "a lot of nonsense syllables."[70] Even Gu Jiegang found the court poetry of the *Odes* an intolerable burden.[71]

If much of the continued use of these materials for young children was due to inertia and the vested interest of teachers in familiar methods, they nonetheless had both pedagogic and social utility. A student who had completed the "Three Hundred Thousand"—the three basic readers: the *Three Character Classic*, the *Hundred Family Names*, and the

Thousand Character Classic—would have committed to memory about two thousand characters, a sufficient base for further reading. These two thousand he would have acquired in a comparatively short time—the time taken to memorize about seven hundred three- or four-word lines of verse. He might not understand them perfectly, but their content was of sufficient gravity to convince the young student and his relatives that he had begun the study of man's affairs. In contrast, primers written in China during the first half of the twentieth century tended to the repetitive vacuity of their Japanese or American models. These did no great injury to the Japanese or American child, who acquired through them a knowledge of the alphabet and its correspondence with phonemic and thence semantic units, but they retarded the progress of the Chinese learner. Since Chinese has a morphemic script, sound forms no bridge between the words in a child's vocabulary and the characters on the page, each of which has to be learned as it appears. The concentrated recognition of characters is a necessary preliminary to a student's reading career, a task economically performed by the "Three Hundred Thousand."[72]

Knowledge of classical Chinese was a marker of elite status. For those outside the scholar-gentry, mastery of the language of the classics meant the possibility of understanding and thence evading or manipulating the demands of those higher in the social scale. Its omission would have signaled a second-class education. In addition, centuries of diffusion of Confucian precepts interacted with the strong family orientation of Chinese society to reinforce confidence in the Four Books as the fount of correct action in the home as well as abroad. So great was the influence of these works that in Sichuan in the 1920s, some country folk "still insisted that their children must read the Four Books and the Five Classics, and didn't like [modern] textbooks."[73] The content of modern works was suspect. According to Liao T'ai-ch'u, in Wenshang "some people even doubted whether the characters they taught in new schools were the ones 'invented' by Confucius, or whether they created a different set."[74]

The sishu not only gave the child adult texts but demanded of him adult standards of behavior fitting the stereotype of the "educated man." This union of the adult's and the child's worlds differed markedly from the child-centered teaching methods evolved in the West in the nineteenth century by disciples of Froebbels and Pestalozzi, which placed a high value on engaging the child's interest and allowing him freedom to play and run around. In China, most people sent their sons to school to get the childishness whipped out of them, not encouraged. A Hunanese proverb ran, "A boy is tamed by school, a girl by marriage."[75] In the same

1. Harsh Discipline in a Sishu (*Xingqi huabao*, no. 36 [1907])

vein are "He won't grow into a man without a beating; beat him into an official" and, from the *Three Character Classic*, "To rear without teaching is a fault in the father; to teach without severity is a fault in the teacher."

Teachers who took such injunctions literally could make their pupils' lives a misery. Common punishments were blows with a ruler or bamboo rod, or kneeling in front of Confucius' picture for as long as it took an incense stick to burn. The supposed educative functions of these punishments was easily lost in casual brutality. Guo Moruo recalls that when he first attended school he was beaten round the head so often that his scalp was a mass of sores. His mother, in lieu of protest, made him a hard, padded cap, but was powerless after the teacher discovered it.[76]

With their classical texts, emphasis on rote learning, and severe discipline, the traditional Chinese curriculum and teaching methods could be said to be remote and formal, their only kinship with the surrounding world that which was insinuated into it by generations of repetition and imposed on it by the imperial examinations. In these respects it was the opposite of the Western school.

Integration of Organization

In areas where the new schools imposed uniformity, compulsion, and rigidity, however, the sishu was arbitrary, fluid, informal, responsive. Those boundaries that define the modern school as being other, different from the outside world, were absent in the sishu. A sishu never had its own premises in the sense of having a building designed for its occupancy; this would have needed an administrative structure and income beyond the resources of the small community it served. Classes might be conducted in the study or spare room of a well-to-do household, in a room in the teacher's own house, or in public premises such as a temple or ancestral hall.[77] School furnishings were often brought from home,[78] or, in the north where heated brick beds were common, dispensed with. This simplicity meant that schooling could occur whenever teacher and pupil, books and writing implements, were brought together.

The role of the teacher was no more fixed than that of the room he occupied. The teacher played a dual role in society: whether from economic need or goodwill, he would lend a hand in a variety of tasks to his illiterate and semiliterate neighbors. In a literary vein, he would write their letters, choose their children's names, compose couplets for the New Year or a wedding or funeral notice. He wrote their pleas and complaints for lawsuits and acted as their intermediary in other dealings with the outside world—the hiring of an opera troupe, for example, for a village festival. Many teachers doubled as doctors, another trade for which literacy was the main qualification; other dabbled in less reputable sidelines, such as fortune-telling or peddling.[79]

The sishu's adaptability was equally evident in its calendar, which was a movable one. Apart from those that offered winter classes, it was usual for sishu to open after the lunar New Year and close before it. In this they conformed to Chinese custom and the agricultural year, unlike the new schools, which copied the Japanese system and opened in autumn. Traditional festivals such as Qingming and Mid-autumn were celebrated with a holiday. Within this broad framework, every sishu "ran a different calendar . . . [and] every student had his own calendar."[80] In a rural sishu, the school year was broken whenever pupils' help was needed in harvesting or other agricultural tasks, or when local festivals were held and opera troupes invited. A teacher with private business or public duties might close the school or entrust it to an older pupil during his absence. To such permitted holidays, students added time taken off for visits to friends or relatives or simple truancy.[81]

Attendance was easily broken off but just as easily resumed. Nor was there a fixed starting age: a beginning reader of ten might be chanting the same lessons as a precocious four-year-old. A pupil who missed days or months of schooling because of health or money problems or a shift of residence would not find that his class had been promoted above him or that he was so many lessons behind his fellows in a set text. The sishu's simple curriculum could be taken up at any point. Tuition was individual rather than group, and each pupil proceeded at his own pace with only the tapping of the teacher's ruler to hurry him along.

This pattern of schooling does not appear to have been peculiarly Chinese, but rather to have been the common mode of preindustrial but commercialized societies in which education had left the home but had not yet taken up its abode in the elaborated structure of a school system. Contrasting persistent support for the old style of private school with parental reluctance to send children to the new, free public schools in nineteenth-century Britain (a period of transition in schooling comparable to the early twentieth century in China), Thomas Laqueur writes:

> . . . the private school was more attuned to the rhythms of working-class life than was its public competitor. The miners' leader, John Wilson, may have been an exception in attending a different school every few months as he followed his father, a navvy, around the country. But attendance at school was sporadic for a working-class child—a total of eighteen months to two years of education between ages five and eleven accumulated from a few days here, a couple of weeks there, when the family could afford school pence and help was not required about the house . . . A London street seller, age thirteen, reported that he had been to an "academy" kept by an old man but that he didn't know the charge because . . . "the schoolmaster used to take it out in vegetables." The private school—with its lack of rules governing dress, appearance, and cleanliness; its easy admission and withdrawal procedures; and its unstructured curriculum—was the institutional analogue of this poverty-induced pattern of education.[82]

Laqueur's connection of this type of unsystematic, uncoordinated schooling with poverty is broadly true, insofar as a substantial surplus of income over needs, whether in the domestic or national context, is necessary for the maintenance of continuous full-time education for every child of school age. But poverty does not appear to have been the sole cause of the continued preference in England for the old schools—

which, unlike the new, charged fees—nor was it the main reason why popular education evolved as it did in China.

The sishu answered the needs of a society in which informal, particularistic ties predominated over explicit vertical controls. Through them, the government received an adequate supply of "the talented" without cost to itself; scholars replicated their image in the next generation; and the children of peasants or craftsmen prepared for upward ascent. The tendency for schooling to be identified with the social mores of a particular group rather than with the transformation of the whole people was reinforced by the neo-Confucian stress on self-cultivation rather than mass mobilization as the aim of education. Toward the end of the nineteenth century, these assumptions were challenged.

3
Theories and Experiments

Although Chinese educational reformers were quick to point out the weaknesses of China's inherited educational practices, these defects do not seem to have strained the operation of the system or given rise to irreconcilable tensions. Indigenous institutions were called into question less by their own defects than by the inability of the Chinese polity as a whole to resist Western and later Japanese aggression. In the words of the educational historian Shu Xincheng,

> The changeover to a new system of education at the end of the Qing appeared on the surface to be a voluntary move by educational circles, but in reality what happened was that foreign relations and domestic policies were everywhere running up against dead ends. Unless reforms were undertaken, China would have no basis for survival. Education simply happened to be caught up in a situation in which there was no choice.[1]

Shu observes that had China not been defeated in battle, she might have retained her academies and examinations for centuries to come and offered them as a model to admiring foreigners.

Desperation enforced change; education was placed in the vanguard of change for both philosophical and practical reasons. The Chinese had always given a high place in statecraft to the training and re-cruitment of "men of talent," and the reformers—scholars themselves or men with scholarly leanings—were hardly likely to question its priority. Educational reform appeared to require ideas and willpower, commodi-ties they were not short of, without demanding structural changes be-yond their powers; no new sources of revenue were required and little alteration in government responsibilities. Of all possible Western models for change, that which emphasized education was the most congenial. Western schools could even be given a Chinese pedigree: many recom-mendations for reform opened with the words of the philosopher Men-cius, "In the old days, every village of five hundred families had an acad-emy and every department a college."[2]

Theory

Despite its sheep's clothing, the Western model was slow to gain acceptance; more than thirty years elapsed between introduction and adoption. During this time, a small group of missionaries labored untir-ingly to introduce Western concepts and methods into China. Men like Ernst Faber, John Fryer, Young J. Allen, and Timothy Richard sought not only to save but to enlighten the Chinese, confident that God's mes-sage lay as much in the workings of an electric light bulb as in theological debate. Faber was probably the first to propose a national school system for China. *Xiguo xuexiao* (Western Schools), his first major work, was published in 1873, and his second, *Jiaohua yi* (A Treatise on Education), came out in 1875.[3] Missionaries mediated between their own culture and reform-minded Chinese: Zheng Guanying learned some English at the Anglo-Chinese School run by John Fryer in Shanghai, and Young J. Al-len's journal, *Jiaohui xinbao* (Church News), founded in Shanghai in 1868, served as a forum for debate among Chinese on spiritual and so-cial reform. One of the earliest Chinese plans for universal education appeared in its pages in 1870.[4]

Ideas originating in the foreign-dominated treaty ports had but lim-ited circulation outside them. The architects of the Tongzhi Restoration (1862–1874), the conservatives' attempt to preserve the dynasty by adopting selected Western institutions, were interested in the content, not the forms, of Western innovations, and their wish to reform Chinese education did not extend to altering its social distribution. Popularizers from missionary or compradore circles had to contend with attitudes of the kind expressed in 1861 by Feng Guifen, one of the leading propo-nents of reform within Chinese tradition: "Those who study with foreigners are called interpreters; they are all frivolous townspeople . . . their nature is rough, their knowledge slight, and their motives base." Feng knew of the schools foreigners had started for poor boys but thought them a failure; experience in his home district had convinced him that no talent was to be found in charity or village schools.[5] Feng stood out among his gentry contemporaries in advocating officially sponsored schools for Western learning, but this did not mean that he was prepared to countenance claims of knowledge or status gained independently of official sponsorship or gentry tradition. Until the 1890s, adherents of the self-strengthening movement, the late Qing attempt to borrow from the West while preserving Chinese culture, concentrated on the reform and supplementation of indigenous institutions rather than on their replacement or relegation to a less than dominant position.

Despite the scorn of scholars, proponents of reform speaking from outside their ranks did have some influence within them. Foremost among them were Wang Tao—degree-holder, missionary assistant, and journalist—and Zheng Guanying, an educated and wealthy compradore who had taken but not passed the imperial examinations. Despite Zheng's lack of formal qualifications, such powerful officials as Li Hongzhang, Zhang Zhidong, Zuo Zongtang, and Sheng Xuanhuai appreciated his talents and wealth.[6] Zheng had been impressed by Western institutions operating in colonial Vietnam and Hong Kong. His first work, *Yiyan* (Easy Words),[7] first printed in 1875 and reprinted in 1880, proposed that the government recruit talented men directly from schools, as was done in the West. His travels and reading—and perhaps his failure in the examinations—had given him a notion of "talent" wider than that of most of his countrymen. In particular, he admired the combination in the West of practical training in military and other subjects with theory, in contrast to bookish Confucian education. Zheng first put forward an expanded version of the limited initiatives already taken by reformist officials, suggesting that Western studies be insinuated into the examination system separately from Chinese topics. A supporting system of newly created academies was to follow the Chinese pattern in holding monthly essay competitions, but Zheng suggested a wider range of topics: textiles, banking, coinage, surveying, museums, peace conferences, diplomatic relations. Young men who did well in these should be sent to university in the capital. This segregation of Chinese and Western subjects, however, was only a half measure; Zheng's preferred plan involved more radical change. All schools and academies were to "copy the Western mode" and be converted into a two-stream system of primary, secondary, and tertiary schools for civil and military studies. The classics had no independent place in this scheme. State control would not extend to the primary schools (equivalent to the later higher primary schools) set up at county level, but Zheng emphasized the democratic nature of popular education: "Each district should set up family and public schools, so that rich and poor can all study books and learn skills."[8] Zheng's plan set out the essential features present in Western and absent in Chinese schooling: a fixed period of study, a fixed curriculum, annual promotion from one class to another depending on marks gained in school examinations. In addition, he urged government control of all institutions of advanced study, a control hitherto existing in name but not in fact.

Others in the small circle of Chinese in close contact with Westerners spread ideas similar to Zheng's, most notably Wang Tao, a journalist and Christian convert who had spent some time in Scotland as the assistant of the translator James Legge.[9] In his lucid editorials, Wang, like Zheng, favored the establishment of a national system of schools divided into civil—including the humanities and technology—and military streams.[10] Wang envisioned such schools as primarily training officials, but he cited both Confucian and contemporary justifications for an educated citizenry. In particular, he urged on his countrymen not only the time-honored ideal of equality in education for rich and poor, but also the novel one of equal access for the bright and the slow-witted.[11]

Wang and Zheng had both seen foreign institutions in operation abroad—Wang in Europe, Zheng in Vietnam—and in the colony of Hong Kong, an experience relatively few educated Chinese had enjoyed. Overseas study had faltered after the closure of the Educational Mission sent to America in 1870. Emigration was prohibited until 1894, and in any case was confined mainly to those without hope of bettering themselves in China.

As China set up diplomatic missions abroad, a second group of men with firsthand experience of the West emerged from among the scholar-officials. One of the first of these, Guo Songtao, was in Britain in 1877–1878. Passing through Hong Kong en route, he admired its prison and Government Central School, of which he wrote: "[The master] can see and hear everything; so not a single boy can escape from or gloss over his work . . . the rules are well thought out and severe . . . It would appear that the Europeans have inherited something of the ancients' ideal of forming and nourishing the talents of their pupils."[12] The observation appears to be a spontaneous identification of Benthamite regulation with native Chinese stereotypes of order. Such admiration for the West, understandable in comprador or convert, ranked as apostasy in a member of the gentry, and the publication of Guo's diary led to his recall amid a storm of protest. He died in obscurity.[13]

Another diplomat whose travels began at the same time as Guo's, Huang Zunxian, was prudent enough to defer publication of his impressions until 1895, amid a more favorable climate of opinion. His *Riben guozhi* (Account of Japan), written on the basis of his tour of duty there from 1877 to 1881, includes a dry but detailed description of Japanese scholarship and education. Huang's emotional identification was with Chinese studies. Those seeking a blueprint, however, could find one in his work, which describes everything from the function of Japan's Ministry of Education to the use of blackboard and chalk.[14]

The years between the experiences Huang records and his publication of them saw the continuation of piecemeal reforms in education based on the segregation of Western studies in special schools. Few gentry members were anxious to change the system to which they owed their status, and it was left to Zheng Guanying to sound the tocsin. The reforms were obviously failing in their purpose, the repelling of foreign aggression: Hong Kong had been ceded to Britain, the Ryukyus lost to Japan. "Strong neighbors press in daily, and Tibet and Korea are likely to topple any minute," Zheng wrote in *Shengshi weiyan* (Warning to a Prosperous Age), his most influential work.[15] "And our country's schools have not been developed, our education (*jiaoyu*) is incomplete, and our technology and trade lag behind Japan's."[16]

Many advocates of reform, starting with Feng Guifen in 1861, had called for attention to a wider field of Western learning than that encompassed by military technology, but Zheng appears to have been the first to locate China's salvation in the schoolroom.

> In ancient and modern times, in China and abroad, every country has regulated its education (*jiaoyang*) and gained its wealth and power primarily through schools. Now Japan has taken the West's excellence in education as its model in fostering talent, and the country's power has indeed risen greatly. How can our country fail to bend all its strength to this? In a word, one can say categorically that if we do not set up schools, no talent will emerge and if we do not abolish [examinations on] set literary forms, the schools will be no good to us.[17]

Zheng's proposal for a three-tier school system (tertiary institutions to be set up by the provinces, secondary by the prefectures, and primary by the counties) was the same as that outlined in his earlier work. At the apex of this system he now placed a Ministry of Education on the model of the Japanese system. Money for the schools was to be found through the joint efforts of local officials, gentry, and merchants.[18]

Although Zheng still did not see the state as intervening directly in elementary education ("primary" schools, the first level of government-administered education, were for those with a few years schooling behind them), he gave detailed suggestions for the reform of sishu, whose "stale scholars" "teach what children do not understand and leave out what they do." Lessons should be graduated in difficulty and suited to the child's interests. The local dialect could be used for reading lessons, and writing taught through letters, stories, or news items.[19]

As the concept of education moved from that of an individual, private pursuit to that of an organized, mass activity controlled from above, the language mirrored the change. A new word, or rather an old one retrieved from antiquity through Japan, came into use to describe this phenomenon: *jiaoyu*.[20]

Traditional Chinese discussions of education had used a wide variety of terms, most containing the root *xue* ("learn"). The Chinese spoke of "promoting learning" (*xing xue*), "learning matters" (*xuewu*—an administrative term), "Ministry of Learning" (*Xue Bu*). All these terms emphasized the relationship between the learner and the thing learned. They continued to be the most widely used terms in the 1890s, but alongside them was growing up a different concept of education reflected in a different vocabulary. Zheng Guanying's terminology was still fluid. He entitled the section on education in *Shengshi weiyan* "Learning" (*xueshu*), subdividing it into sections on "Schools" (*xuexiao*) and "Western learning" (*xixue*), but in the context of the state's organization of and duty to its subjects he several times used words containing the root *jiao* ("teach"): *jiaoyang* (literally "teach and nourish"), *jiaohua* ("teach and transform"), and *jiaoyu* ("teach and rear"). These connoted benevolent state activity. They had a long history of use in reference to the state's duty to scholars and people; they were now called in as translations of the foreign concept of "education." The title of a work by Li Jiazhen published in Shanghai in 1893, *Taishi jiaoyushi* (History of Western Education), reflects the emergence of both term and concept. Henceforth, "education" referred not merely to concrete methods of study but to an abstract process. It had a life of its own.

Zheng's views on education were repeated privately, in Sun Yat-sen's 1894 letter to the reformist governor-general of Zhili, Li Hongzhang, and publicly, in the petition of lower-level degree-holders to the throne in 1895. (These proposals were not exclusive to Zheng, but until the emergence of Liang Qichao as a propagandist of reform, Zheng was their most influential and coherent exponent.) Sun and Zheng came from the same county in Guangdong, and Zheng's literary influence was complemented by personal acquaintance. Sun had lived under British administration in Hong Kong and, like Zheng in Vietnam, was impressed by the orderliness and prosperity of colonial rule.[21] In his letter, Sun reiterated Zheng's points, adducing both the West and China's classical age, the Three Dynasties, as evidence of the benefits of widespread schooling. He pointed out the need for more schools to avoid the present waste of talent and for more specialization to provide training for civil, military, agricultural, technical, and commercial occupations. The only hint of Sun's revolutionary fervor is his praise of the heroic temper, which, though in a commoner's breast, takes the charge of the empire on itself and finds a way to achievement with or without government recognition.[22] Li ignored Sun's plea that talents of this type should be encouraged. A few months later, Sun established the revolutionary Xing Zhong Hui (Revive China Society) in Honolulu.

China's humiliating losses in the Sino-Japanese War of 1894, which made plain the inadequacy of previous attempts at self-strengthening, gave force to arguments for change. Hitherto, spokesmen for fundamental change had come mainly from the fringes of Chinese society, from new occupations—journalists, compradores, diplomats. They had no political base of their own and, for the implementation of their schemes, relied wholly on the more progressive scholar-officials, who were themselves reluctant to move with undue speed both for reasons of temperament and expediency.[23] The defeat brought to the political stage a body of disaffected scholars who disregarded the prohibition on private discussion of government affairs and sought to replace the present unsatisfactory policies and officeholders with their own men and plans. In one way, their actions were those of an outside group—scholars out of office—seeking a voice in policy matters controlled by insiders—high metropolitan and regional officials. From another perspective, however, they acted for the self-preservation of the scholar-gentry as a whole in claiming as part of their rightful competence all expertise in government, including those skills and policies at present monopolized by Western-oriented Chinese in the treaty ports. The reformers did not regard the emerging bourgeoisie as natural allies against die-hard officials on the opposite side; Liang Qichao, for example, expressed considerable scorn for those Westernized Chinese without a background in Chinese learning who mixed with foreigners and picked up their habits.[24]

The voice of this group was first heard in the Gongju petition to the throne, drafted by the iconoclastic Cantonese scholar Kang Youwei and signed by several hundred other candidates gathered to take the metropolitan examination of 1895. It invoked much of the rhetoric familiar from Zheng's work, asking for changes in the method of selecting talent for office and for extension of learning to peasants, craftsmen, and merchants. ("Talent" had by now lost its original exclusive connection with scholarship and government service.) The petition's concrete proposals were conservative, even anachronistic. It would have maintained the existing structure of state education fed by students from academies who received their basic education under private auspices. Universal education was an optimistic afterthought. The main proposal was the replacement of the military examination system (in which no Confucian scholar had any stake) with examinations in technical subjects, to be prepared for in technical academies parallel to but separate from those teaching the classics.

The petition combined the structure of Western school systems with that of the three levels of state examinations: different grades of technical schools were to be set up at the county, provincial, and metropolitan levels. The proposed curriculum was likewise a hybrid: each student was to be as competent in one of the classics as he was in his specialized field of study. The influence of Western schooling was most evident in Kang's insistence that each stage require a specified period of time, that quotas be abolished, and that degrees be awarded on the basis of examinations held in the schools. He also suggested reforms directed toward freeing the literary examinations of empty formalism.[25] These propositions were not novel, but their implementation would have constituted a government commitment first to Western studies and second to direct intervention in the educational process (as distinct from assessment of the end results of a basically self-regulating system).

Over the next three years Kang and Liang Qichao wooed a wider constituency for reform through three progressive journals: *Shiwu bao* (The Chinese Progress) in Shanghai, *Xiangxue bao* (Hunan Studies) in Changsha, and *Zhixin bao* (Knowledge of the New) in Macao. At the height of their respectability, Governor-General Zhang Zhidong subscribed to 288 copies of the *Shiwu bao* on behalf of academies and yamen in Hubei, an action followed by officials in Zhejiang, Jiangsu, Hunan, Zhili, Shanxi, Jiangxi, and Guizhou.[26] The joint readership of the three journals was probably in the vicinity of 100,000[27]—an impressive figure, albeit only some 5 percent of the number estimated to be sufficiently educated to attempt the examinations.

The expansion of journalism in the late 1890s was accompanied by an increase in the translation and composition of books on Western institutions. The range and quantity of information available to the authors of the *Xiangxue bao* is impressive. By 1898, a student of foreign education could read *Japan's Present Education, An Outline of Education, Prenatal Education, Japan's School Regulations, Prospering the Country Through Humane Studies, Curricula in Western Subjects,* and *An Introduction to New Learning in Seven Countries,* most of which had been published since 1895.[28] The *Shiwu bao* sold out an edition of 2,000 guides to the new learning and printed a further 3,000.[29]

Missionary works leaped suddenly in popularity. For their part, the missionaries were ready. The Society for the Diffusion of Christian and General Knowledge (SDK) had been founded in 1887, the Educational Association of China in 1890. Timothy Richard was to recall with pleasure that whereas previously "the booksellers of China refused to handle, on any account, any Christian books for sale, considering it a transaction disloyal to their country and unworthy of honorable men . . . in 1895, after the appearance of Mackenzie's *History of the Nineteenth Century* and other books of the SDK, a great change came over the booksellers."[30] Over the six years from 1893 to 1898, sales revenues from SDK publications increased more than twentyfold, and millions of pirated copies of its works circulated.[31] Believing that the time was ripe for intervention, the Educational Association of China appointed an Educational Reform Committee to prepare a national education system for China.[32] The missionaries had, however, misread the reasons for their publications' popularity. The Chinese gave little credit to the missionary contribution, and reformers attempted to minimize whatever personal connections existed between themselves and the missionaries. Zheng Guanying cites Young J. Allen as a *xi ru*, or Western scholar (*ru* normally refers to a Confucian scholar), not as a missionary;[33] Wang Tao suppressed his conversion to Christianity in his publications;[34] and Liang Qichao, who had worked for Timothy Richard, made hostile references to missionary writings and converts and downplayed the role of Christianity in the formation of Western civilization.[35]

By 1896, Liang had abandoned foreign tutelage and was independently engaged in planning the future of Chinese education. Works by Westerners and Japanese had answered the question of how to set up an educational system on the Western model. The editorials of Liang and his fellow reformers addressed themselves to the why. "The preservation of what would otherwise be lost, the maintenance of what would otherwise be done away with, making the ignorant knowledgeable and strengthening the weak . . . all rest on schools," Liang wrote in 1896. Marshaling statistics from foreign countries and imaginative deductions from China's past—which yielded education for women, teacher-training institutions, the division of schooling into primary, secondary, and tertiary levels, and technical training for merchants, peasants, craftsmen, and soldiers—he recommended the integration of examinations with government schools at the county, prefectural, and provincial levels as the best policy. Primary schools should be established immediately for 400,000 pupils, middle schools for 11,840, and universities for 1,850 odd (the exactitude of these figures derived from computations based on current Western statistics for attendance at different levels, scaled down to China's capacity). This would yield a minimum of 8,000 university graduates, more than enough to "place in high and low positions, to change every system." [36]

Those already in power were less enthusiastic than Liang at the prospect of a new contingent of men and policies. A vitriolic retort charged that "Kang and Liang and their ilk . . . get together and form cliques . . . calling it a struggle between old and new, they use 'opposition to the new policies' to entrap those whose views are different." [37]

Whether or not one gives credence to such protests, they serve as a reminder that the conflict between the reformers and their opponents was one of interests as well as ideas. In terms of rhetoric, Liang's skill as a publicist had his opponents on the defensive; but rhetorical victories by an outsider could not alter established government policy. Change had to come through the correct channels. The first memorials asking for an increase in the number of schools met with a cautious reception. When reformist metropolitan official Li Duanfen (in a memorial that may have been written by Liang Qichao and certainly expressed ideas similar to Liang's) asked that schools be set up at county, prefectural, and provincial levels, with a university at Beijing at the apex,[38] the Zongli Yamen (the office in Beijing in charge of foreign relations and, by extension, modernization) agreed to the university but declined responsibility for provincial schooling.[39]

Among high officials, Zhang Zhidong was most active in urging the new schools on the court and the public. His *Quanxue pian* (Exhortation to Learning), published shortly before the Hundred Days' Reform of 1898, was read by the emperor, who ordered it distributed to provincial officials. Manuscript copies circulated in Beijing, while in Shanghai pirated editions appeared in rapid succession.[40]

The *Quanxue pian* repeated the proposition that the strength of the West derived from its schools. Like previous advocates of a school system, Zhang used both ancient precedent and Western example to buttress his proposal that primary, secondary, and tertiary schools be established at the county, prefectural, and provincial levels and in Beijing. The new schools were to use the material base of the old, taking over the premises and other property of academies and charity schools. This was to be supplemented—Zhang's Confucian disregard for popular religious feeling and entertainments is especially apparent here—by appropriation of 70 percent of Buddhist and Taoist temples and by diversion of money spent on religious festivals and operas.[41] The remaining costs were to be raised from wealthy local people, supplemented with official grants where necessary. The government would thus be relieved of the major part of the financial burden of setting up new schools, but would retain control through a Ministry of Education of curricula and text-books.[42] Zhang suggested other proposals such as sending students abroad (especially to Japan), translating Western works, and reforming the examination system.

The *Quanxue pian* exhibits Zhang's characteristic style and concerns. It is a work of polemic and propaganda, directed to winning over followers of the old learning and reining in enthusiasts for the new. Zhang's eagerness to reconcile Chinese and Western knowledge did not lead to acceptance of everything Western: he sharply dismissed Liang Qichao's claim that the restrictiveness of the examination system was designed to weaken the people vis-à-vis their ruler[43] and inveighed against "the disorder-fomenting policy of 'people's rights.'"[44] Where Liang Qichao fought uninhibitedly on behalf of the new, Zhang foresaw the demise of the Confucian order and struggled to prevent the erosion of the old.

Despite differences of emphasis, proponents of educational reform had several arguments in common. Loyal to their heritage, they harked back to the golden age of the Three Dynasties for a prototype school system. They adduced as proof of the beneficial effects of schooling on the Western model the power and prosperity brought by reform to Japan (a favorite example after the Sino-Japanese War), Prussia, France, and Britain. For many, the introduction of a school system was a panacea, a talisman that would transform weakness into strength. They retained a Confucian faith in the government's need for talented men, but were eager for a wider recruitment and more specific training. The common complaint that scholars learned what they could not apply and applied what they had not learned reflects contemporary dissatisfaction with officials' lack of training either in administrative skills or the broader fields of government, history, and current affairs. Advocacy of practicality combined with appreciation of those Western sciences and techniques absent in China led the reformers to applaud educational specialization as they understood it to be practiced in the West. There, in the words of Liang Qichao, "farmers have scholars in farming, craftsmen have scholars in craft, merchants have scholars in commerce, and soldiers have scholars in soldiery,"[45] as distinct from the traditional Chinese conception that confined scholarship to one walk of life, that of the scholar-gentry, and to preparation for one career, that of an official. The question of a future oversupply of educated men did not arise—a country could never have too much talent. China's current difficulties stemmed not from having too many educated men, but from their being educated to no purpose.

In attacking Chinese ills, advocates of reform on both sides assumed axiomatically that the wealth and power of Western countries lay not in guns and soldiers but in schools. But the deeper such beliefs penetrated the Chinese social fabric, the remoter they became from firsthand experience. Wang Tao and Huang Zunxian had both seen foreign institutions operating *in situ*, and Zheng Guanying was familiar with them in the colonial context. Until the suppression of the Hundred Days' Reform, however, Kang Youwei and Liang Qichao had never been out of China; nor did Zhang Zhidong ever travel abroad. Carried along by contemporary Western ideas, Kang and Liang and their followers accepted a worldview of inexorable historical progression from a lower to a higher stage, the latter represented by the "civilized" institutions originating in the West and adopted by Japan. Timothy Richard's translation of Mackenzie's *History of the Nineteenth Century*, "a crude glorification of progress in the nineteenth century," became very popular in the mid-1890s.[46] Liang Qichao recommended it as an "excellent book" in his bibliography on Western learning [47] and included it in the reading list for the Shiwu Xuetang, a progressive Hunanese school.[48] There is some justice in the accusation of one of Liang's opponents: "As Mr. Liang admits to never having traveled in the West himself, how does he know about the virtues of their laws and the thoroughness of their testing of officials? He has simply been moved by the exaggerated claims of the Western books he read and thus taken up the thesis that pedants are the ruin of the empire and examination essays the ruin of China."[49]

The secondhand nature of the reformers' experience and the limitations of the medium through which they received it led in many cases to a simplistic and one-dimensional view of the operations of Western society. The *Shengshi weiyan* and the reformist press did not raise such questions as Was mass literacy the cause, concomitant, or product of industrialization? Nor did they analyze the presumed relationship between productivity and enlightenment. Western institutions were taken at face value, and flaws in nineteenth-century industrialization—such as child labor in British factories—were merely unfortunate accidents.[50] Missionary persuasion reinforced Confucian tradition in attributing transforming powers to education. Reformers believed not that education itself had failed China, but that China had suffered from the wrong kind of education. Once the examinations were reformed and new schools set up, China's ills would right themselves. The reformers appear to have had no concept of the problems or changes that would spring from the importation into China of institutions tailored to the mores of industrial capitalism. Once again, conservatives sounded the alarm, either rejecting Westernization as proposed by Liang and Kang on the grounds that it would "level monarch and subject and reverse the roles of male and female,"[51] or fighting a rearguard action, as did Zhang Zhidong, to maintain the benefits of reform and guard against its attendant ills. The eventual establishment of a national school system in 1902–1904 was to bring less predictable but more far-reaching changes than either party foresaw.

Practice

Until 1898, when the short-lived reform edicts decreed the establishment of a three-tiered school system, the government made no attempt to implement any of the proposals discussed above. Chinese education, however, was not wholly unaffected by the West. Certainly, those enclaves of Western learning set up from 1861 on to train a handful of men in the skills of defense and diplomacy "were generally regarded by the Chinese as completely outside the regular concept and system of education"[52] (although they did accustom a section of the official world to the idea of state promotion of education in Western subjects). Much the same applied to missionary schools. Neither had sufficient prestige to mold the remainder of Chinese education in its image. Enlightened missionaries hoped that the neutral values of Western knowledge would sweeten their proffered faith, but the tendency was rather for the taint of "foreign religion" to discourage attendance at mission schools and even, by analogy, Western-style schools established by Chinese. Yet Western contact gave rise to many transmutations and modifications in Chinese schools, and schools modeled on those of the West assumed varying forms in the Chinese setting.

Western-influenced changes in Chinese education occurred in a sequence less chronological than categorical: each new form coexisted with a number of previous ones. The rate of change was neither constant nor uniform; it varied between one province and another, between town and country, and between one social group and another. Any student could reverse the sequence by moving from a "modern" institution to a traditional or transitional one (as late as the 1930s a few graduates of normal schools chose to teach in sishu). In general, however, the adoption of Western-style schooling proceeded in three phases.

In the first, reforms were bounded by the traditional content and forms of Chinese education. This phase began with the reformed academies of the Tongzhi Restoration. In the second, which spanned the 1880s and 1890s, the traditional forms were maintained but a new, semi-Western content injected into them; at the same time, the technical schools teaching Western studies began to broaden their focus and offer an education more suitable to a gentleman. They retained, however, the severe discipline derived from their Prussian models. In the final phase, in the late 1890s, both form and content were Westernized, although no uniformity was achieved until the issuance of school regulations in 1904. By the late 1900s, all institutional traces of China's indigenous institutions of higher education—the examination system and the academies—had vanished. The same three phases are discernible in the development of elementary education, with a time lag. With one exception, it appears that (besides mission schools) no elementary schools on the Western model were started till the late 1890s. The indigenous type of elementary schooling, the sishu, persisted into the late 1940s and possibly the early 1950s.[53]

The first phase began with adoption of a change long discussed in scholarly circles: the abolition of the eight-legged essay from the curriculum of certain academies. In the Chinese context, it was part of a trend toward *shixue*, or solid learning as opposed to the ornamental or empty, and toward the practical rather than the speculative. The concept *shi* provided a bridge between Chinese and Western learning. It was, for example, incorporated into the Chinese neologism for industry, *shiye* (literally, "solid undertaking"). As enshrined in the ambiguous but authoritative wording of the 1906 statement of educational goals, *shang shi* ("respect for *shi*") could refer equally to respect for useful technical studies or to serious work on the classics.[54]

Two famous academies that banished the eight-legged essay were founded before the threat from the West became apparent: the Gujing Jingshe, set up in Hangzhou in 1801, and the Xuehai Tang, established in Guangzhou in 1820. These were renowned centers of Han learning and the models Zhang Zhidong followed in establishing, during terms of office as a provincial educational official, the Jingxin Academy in Hubei in 1869 and the Zunjing Academy in Sichuan in 1874, and subsequently as governor of Shanxi, the Lingde Academy there. In doing so he was impelled not simply by philosophical preference, but by the wish common to statesmen active in the reforms of the Tongzhi Restoration: the restabilization of the state in the face of internal and external enemies. Over the same period, language schools were set up in Beijing, Shanghai, and Guangzhou, naval schools in Fuzhou and Tianjin, and a telegraph school in Tianjin. Although some eventually expanded into wider areas of study, the narrowness of their original conception indicates the restricted role allocated to Western learning by the majority of Chinese officials, who were still seeking the answer to Chinese problems within their own tradition. Their attitude contrasts with that of the reformers of Meiji Japan, whose creed was that "knowledge was to be sought for throughout the world"[55] and who introduced a highly Westernized system of schooling in 1872.

Further modifications of the established pattern came when Zhang Zhidong set up the Guangya Academy in Guangzhou in 1887 during his term as governor-general of Guangdong and Guangxi. Students could study in one of four departments: classics, history, neo-Confucianism, or government.[56] This again was an example of the mingling of Confucian precedent and Western practice. The famous Song educator Hu Anding had divided the prefectural schools he headed into departments of classics (*jingyi*) and government (*zhishi*), which was subdivided into military studies, water transport, mathematics and the calendar, and other subjects.[57] Hu had few followers; normal Confucian practice subsumed all branches of learning under the study of the classics. Late Qing educators usually associated subject divisions with Western learning.

Zhang Zhidong was not, of course, the only patron of the reformed academy. One of the most prolific sponsors was Huang Pengnian, who in the course of official posts in the early Guangxu period (1875–1908) resuscitated the Guanzhong Academy in Shaanxi, the Lianchi Academy in Zhili, and the Zhengyi Academy in Suzhou. The ancient Yuelu Academy in Hunan, Nanjing in Jiangsu, and Luoyuan in Jinan were also renowned centers of scholarly inquiry that maintained or renewed their reputations during this period.[58]

The considerable adaptability of the traditional framework of the academy is evident in a list of topics set for the monthly essays in Suzhou in the early 1890s. In addition to questions on the Five Classics, "subjects concerning current affairs are also frequently given out, as for example, the Best Methods of Military Defence; the Conservation of the Waterways; China's Relations with Foreign Countries, etc., etc."[59] The continued vitality of a revivified Confucian scholarship can be seen in Shu Xincheng's account of an academy in Hunan that he attended in 1907. "Luliang Academy belonged to what was called the 'new school.' We composed elucidations of the classics and topical dissertations instead of the examination forms." Shu found stimulating and inspiring the example of the head, who expounded the classics and history in a way new to Shu and shared with the students his notes. The college was filled with a spirit of diligent emulation.[60] From Shu's account of his own reading while at the academy and from the head's background as a teacher of numerous successful examination candidates, the stimulus appears to have derived from Chinese historiography and classical studies, with little Western influence. This academy was among the last to continue functioning: in 1909 this center of advanced study was made into a lower primary school.[61] The academy apparently provided an equally satisfying environment for Li Zonghuang, who attended one in Yunnan from 1898 to 1903. He speaks with affection of his friends and teachers, and of the "excitement" and "enlightenment" he received from lectures on the Four Books and Five Classics.[62]

Parallel to the reformation of academies was the elimination of the eight-legged essay from the examination system. Although favored by numerous advocates of reform in the late Qing—among them Xue Fucheng, Li Ciming, Zhang Zhidong, Chen Baochen, Yan Fu, Kang Youwei, and Liang Qichao[63]—change was slow in coming. Whereas alterations in the course of study or essay topics of an academy could be achieved by the injunctions of its official founder or benefactor or through a change of heart or personnel among the scholars and officials who set the topics, the examination system could not be reformed piecemeal; as a unitary system, it had to be altered from the top. The abolition of the eight-legged essay was among the unrealized reforms of 1898; it was not until 1902 that the topical dissertation was finally substituted.[64] Some students had difficulty coping; much hilarity was caused by the incompetence of those who, for example, replied with an essay on defective wheels, complete with classical allusions, when asked to write on Napoleon (whose name written in Chinese characters is almost identical with the characters for "taking a broken wheel").[65] Others made a smooth but superficial transition, concealing ignorance with the linguistic deftness born of their training in the eight-legged essay.[66] Nonetheless, the new system made possible the acquisition and display of a broad range of knowledge on domestic and international affairs. Had the reformed examination system achieved the conjunction of stimulating topics, intelligent students, and enlightened graders, it might have become an avenue for the synthesis of Chinese and Western statecraft.

The second phase of the transformation of Chinese education, the incorporation of Western content into indigenous institutions, began with the introduction of mathematics into the curriculum. Mathematics encountered less resistance than other new subjects since it was not only the mother of all Western sciences but possessed an indisputable Chinese pedigree. It was included in the curriculum of apparently the first academy to incorporate Western learning, Weijing in Shaanxi. In 1885, two scholars at the academy set up a department teaching astronomy, geography, the classics and history, government, neo-Confucianism, and mathematics, hoping thus to "bridge East and West, making use of the works of our predecessors, to deliver us from present dangers." The last words indicate the common motivation of such enterprises, the sense of urgency that gripped those aware of the encroachment of the powers and of China's defeats.[67] Mathematics was also one of the six departments envisioned for Zhang Zhidong's planned Lianghu Academy in 1890. Indeed, the first concession to Western learning in the examination system came in the allocation of places to students of mathematics who had also achieved a high standard in the normal examination subjects.[68] This ruling, important though it was in principle, had little effect in practice.

Schools, or *xuetang*,[69] teaching Western techniques developed parallel to and separately from the reform of indigenous institutions. The Self-Strengthening School (Ziqiang Xuetang) set up by Zhang Zhidong in Wuchang in 1893 appears from its name to have been intended as a further development of such schools. In its original conception, however, it was both broader in scope and more traditionally Chinese in organization—three of its four departments (mathematics, science, and commerce) were to offer monthly examinations to external students rather than to have fixed courses. Mathematics, however, was transferred to the Lianghu Academy; science and commerce were never started; and the school ended by teaching languages only.

The regulations Zhang drew up for the students' conduct consisted mainly of prohibitions. He was particularly anxious lest they be seduced from their studies, either temporarily by the examinations or permanently by "following base occupations, even to the extent of so far forgetting self-respect as to take employment with a foreign firm as an interpreter."[70] His strictures illustrate the dilemma facing the promoter of Western studies who would steer a course between entrenched scholasticism and defection to the enemy.[71]

Zhang's next attempt at a modern school was the School for Gathering Talent (Chucai Xuetang), set up in Nanjing early in 1896. As with the Self-Strengthening School, Zhang's ambitious plan to expand the curriculum—to include international affairs, agriculture, industry, and commerce—was defeated; his successor confined the school to training translators. Regulations were a blend of military discipline and Confucian decorum. Students had to rise at seven on four strokes of the gong, assemble for breakfast at half past seven on two strokes, and so on throughout the day. They were not to leave the grounds or receive visitors (in contrast to the freedom of academies, where a student might leave for days or months or simultaneously hold a job elsewhere).[72] "The school being a place of decorum, students should behave as befits their junior position . . . in meeting their teachers they should stand with arms at their sides and answer respectfully if addressed . . . for foreign teachers they are to raise their hands to their foreheads [that is, to salute] as a greeting."[73]

Although half of the students' time was spent in Chinese studies, the Chucai Xuetang was basically following the tradition of schools that provided specialized technical training. The same applied to the other schools Zhang founded that same year, the Military School (Lujun Xuetang) and the affiliated School of Mining and Railways (Kuanglu Xuetang) in Nanjing and the Military Preparatory School (Wubei Xuetang) in Wuchang. The peculiar ethos of such semimodern schools was later satirized in a passage of novelist Lu Xun's reminiscences. Lu had attended the Jiangnan Naval School (Jiangnan Shuishi Xuetang, founded in 1890) and the School of Mining and Railways in Nanjing between 1898 and 1902. Of the first school, he recalls a swimming pool filled in after two students drowned in it. A temple to Guan Di, the god of war, was set up on the site to placate their ghosts, and Buddhist masses were said annually in the gymnasium for the repose of their unquiet souls.[74] His brother's comments on the school were less astringent but equally critical.[75]

Like the School for Gathering Talent, the Naval School attempted to maintain an unfamiliar discipline. Students were supposed to regulate their lives by whistle blasts, although some recalcitrants lay abed till the school servants brought breakfast to their dormitories. In some respects, however, the school's organization was old-fashioned. It lacked that cardinal feature of the modern school, a succession of different subjects during the day. Instead, a whole day or half-day was devoted to one subject. In Lu Xun's time, students spent four days on English, one on classical Chinese, and one on the composition of classical Chinese. Although the 1904 Outline of Educational Principles (*Xuewu gangyao*) had accorded "deep meaning" to hourly changes of subject, the Naval School apparently persisted with its own method until the end of the dynasty in 1911.[76] Other aberrations from the new school system were the allowances paid to the students and the custom of having both a "regular" and a "supplementary" intake of students.[77] The persistence of such anomalies illustrates the variable rate of change in Chinese education.

The innovations of the late 1880s and early 1890s—reforms in the examinations and a few academies, the founding of a few new schools—were the work of a handful of men contending with public indifference and the hostility of court and provincial factions. China's shattering defeat in the Sino-Japanese War of 1894 revealed the inadequacy of their labors. The war discredited the segregation of Chinese and Western studies, but Chinese officials made no plans to adopt wholesale the Western institutions that the victor had made its own. Rather, a further period of uncertain but optimistic experimentation in synthesis occurred. No fixed model existed. Mission schools had by then been operating in

China for over half a century and enrolled tens of thousands of students, but the comments of educationalist Kuo Ping-wen were true of the majority:

> The schools thus founded, though not strictly confined to the children of Christians, remained chiefly as the place where new converts were educated and preserved from too intimate contact with the unbelieving world . . . They had no well-established educational policy. Each school was opened as the exigency of the occasion demanded and the funds of the home board permitted. Their schools were, moreover, confined to the children of the humbler classes.[78]

China was carved up into educational territories by 32 different missions, most of which ran village day schools for a score or so of pupils.[79] Although Protestant groups had founded five colleges by 1894 and several boys' boarding schools offered instruction in Western subjects, total enrollment was relatively small.[80] For most Chinese, missionary education was indelibly associated with Christianity and therefore suspect (although individual missionaries might be called on to play an advisory role or help staff Chinese schools). The Chinese founders of reformed schools took an eclectic rather than an imitative approach, combining as they wished features of Chinese and Western schooling. In the words of a historian of education, between 1894 and 1900 schools "were opened on the initiative of individuals, setting their own fashions, completely devoid of system; the gradation of levels was incomplete, and such names as higher, middle, and primary school had not been formally adopted."[81] At one end of the spectrum, one finds the self-discipline and freedom from restraint of the traditional academy; at the other, the rigid external regulation imposed in the specialist schools for Western subjects. The new institutions of the late 1890s take their place at varying points within this range.

One tending more to the academic model (though it claimed to be following the example of Zhang Zhidong's Ziqiang Xuetang) was the Dongshan Jingshe, set up by reformist Hunan scholars in early 1896. They proposed the same four divisions as Zhang's school but, owing to lack of funds, limited themselves to mathematics and a student body of twenty. As in academies, regular students were to receive monthly allowances based on scores in the semimonthly examinations, and the head of the school held the title of *shanzhang*. The rhetoric, however, was modern: the school's founder invoked the example of Japan and planned to purchase reformist journals and newspapers.[82]

Other academies were set up or reorganized to teach both Chinese and Western subjects in Guizhou, Zhejiang, Guangdong, Fujian, Jiangsu, Hubei, and Shaanxi. In Shaanxi, the pioneering Weijing Academy appears to have passed the torch of innovation to its younger offshoot, the Chongshi Academy, whose title signifies its respect for solid learning.[83] One Chongshi student later remembered Weijing as being headed by an opium-smoking devotee of the eight-legged essay who kept a donkey in the middle of the rival academy's courtyard—a sad testimony to the Confucian belief that institutions are no better than the men who run them. Chongshi, like the Naval School, alternated instruction in Western subjects by the day. It followed the practice of traditional academies in holding monthly examinations and semimonthly lectures. Teaching appears to have been poor; students wrote satirical verses on their teachers.[84]

At the same time as these transitional academies were set up, "modern schools" or xuetang, of an equally transitional nature were founded. The most famous of these was the Shiwu Xuetang, or Current Affairs School, in Hunan, at which Liang Qichao taught. Shu Xincheng has aptly characterized its spirit as that of "the learned expositions of scholars of the old days";[85] essentially, it offered a course of guided reading supplemented by lectures and essays in which scholars shared their perceptions of the meaning of classical works. The problem was Liang's interpretation of the latter; neighborhood gentry were incensed by the implication that Liang's party possessed the only valid interpretation of Confucianism, other scholars being base examination hacks.[86] Apart from such partisanship, study at the academy was undertaken in the spirit of such orthodox academies as Suzhou's Zhengyi, where students similarly kept a record of their reading, commented on their perceptions and doubts, and were assessed monthly on their achievements.[87] Because of its close association with the reform party, the Shiwu Xuetang closed with its fall. Its successor, however, was also prepared to countenance the new learning, though not heretical interpretations of the old; even the name of the new school, the Qiushi Academy, indicated that it had joined the popular pursuit of solid learning.[88]

The same name was borne by a new school set up in Anhui in 1897, the Qiushi Xuetang. This institution tended toward rigidity of discipline, but retained many of the organizational features of the academy. It bore all the expenses of 60 regular students, who were carefully drawn from different counties (the emphasis on equitable geographical representation recalls the examination system) and in addition gave allowances on the basis of monthly examination results. In return, students had to agree to stay the four years required for graduation or repay all costs. Anyone who left to take a job elsewhere was required to repay five times what had been spent on him.[89] Such stringent requirements made many families hesitant about sending their sons to new schools. Especially when overseas education came into vogue, this unusual and enforced separation was sometimes feared final.

Among the new educational institutions, two founded by Sheng Xuanhuai, at the time a customs circuit intendant, foreshadowed most closely the hierarchy of the modern school. These schools were the first fruits of the third phase of the assimilation of Western schooling. The Tianjin Sino-Western School, set up in 1895, had a first (higher) and a second (lower) division. Each took four years to complete; "skipping a level" (*liedeng*) was not allowed. As dean of the school, Sheng appointed Charles D. Tenney, an American who had come to China as a missionary fourteen years earlier and was then serving as American vice-consul in Tianjin.[90] Sheng, then director-general of the Imperial Railway Administration, established a second school, the Nanyang Gongxue (Nanyang Public Institute), in Shanghai in 1897. Among the contemplated improvements was a system of four sections (*yuan*): an outer or primary school (*waiyuan*), a middle school (*zhongyuan*), a higher school (*shangyuan*), and China's first normal school (*shifanyuan*). To this institute, too, Sheng appointed an American missionary-educator, John C. Ferguson. It may have been partly at Ferguson's instigation that Nanyang Gongxue published the first textbooks specifically for use in schools, a series of readers based on English and American models.[91]

The pace of change was uneven. Even after the government ordered the incorporation of academies into a three-tier school system in 1901, many institutions persevered in their accustomed practices, as the content of the edict was sufficiently vague to allow for a certain leeway in interpretation. In Anhui, for example, the provincial university, formed by amalgamation of the Qiushi Xuetang and the Jingfu Academy, enrolled all scholars at the provincial capital as supplementary students and conducted monthly examinations on topics set by provincial officials; in short, it assimilated to itself the functions of an academy.[92]

Educators' freedom of action was circumscribed by the 1902 regulations and restricted even further by the detailed prescriptions of 1904. Although the setting up of a model by no means assured universal compliance—inexperience and inadequate resources meant that many new schools were such in name only—variations were henceforth illegitimate departures from a fixed system rather than valid forms of experiment.

The changes discussed above had their greatest impact on advanced education. Elementary schooling exhibited similar changes—from a remaking of indigenous forms and content, through the introduction of

Western content into Chinese forms, to the setting up of a prescribed Western model that outlawed all others—but the time scale was later and effects less easily achieved.

The first school founded by Chinese to move beyond the traditional scope of elementary education was the Zhengmeng Shuyuan in Shanghai, founded by Zhang Huanlun in 1878. It was divided into grades and taught both Chinese and Western subjects; among other innovations was the introduction of games. Texts in classical Chinese were translated into the vernacular. Like Weijing in Shaanxi, Zhengmeng was set up out of a sense of national need (its aims were to "understand righteousness and principles and gain a knowledge of current affairs"),[93] and like Weijing it was in advance of its time: statesmen and scholars did not interest themselves in founding similar schools until some twenty years later.

The lag is explicable partly in terms of the traditional autonomy of elementary education. The concept that schooling was primarily for producing "men of talent" for government service and was therefore sufficiently monitored by the examination system had left the government with relatively little interest in the schooling of the masses, and thus with little voice in it. Scholars who had themselves come to Western studies in their adulthood tended to regard them as qualifications for administration and thus irrelevant for young children and the mass of people. It was commonly believed that Western learning could be acquired by a few months spent reading new books. Furthermore, Western studies undertaken too young were a hindrance to Chinese learning, still the gauge of gentlemanly status, and involved the additional danger of the child's picking up foreign ways. Thus the educational reforms initiated in 1898 had as their base schools enrolling boys from twelve up; elementary schooling was still not conceived as a matter for the state.

This is not to say that there was no interest in how children learned to read or write. The principle that *xian ru wei zhu*—what is learned first is dominant—had directed the attention of generations of scholars to early childhood education.[94] Like opposition to the eight-legged essay, criticism of meaningless rote learning had long been a counterpoint to the prevailing practice. To the Qing educator Wang Yun (1784–1854), "Pupils are human beings, not pigs or dogs; if what they read is not explained, it is like reciting the Buddhist scriptures or chewing wood shavings."[95] He also criticized the use of corporal punishment as a spur to diligence, recommending instead that the pupil's interest be aroused and that he be led according to his mental development.[96]

Such views, originally confined to the unusually enlightened or indulgent, combined around the turn of the century with Western views on child development to produce a gradual change in attitudes on mental and physical discipline. The new attitude among educators was a compound stemming partly from a sense of national priorities, partly from ideals of the kind Wang Yun expressed. Children should not start studying too early or be supervised too strictly. When they were slightly older and their minds more receptive, the teacher should skillfully entice them along the path of their inclinations.[97] For the Confucian educator, however, the child's inclinations were a means, not an end; education remained text-centered rather than child-centered.

Besides Zheng Guanying (see above), another to interest himself in the reform of elementary education was Wu Rulun (1840–1903), head of the famous Lianchi Academy in Zhili and subsequently dean of studies (*zong jiaoxi*) at Beijing University. Wu was familiar with foreign educational practice from his reading (which included Zheng's *Shengshi weiyan*, specialized works on foreign schools, and the press) and from conversations with Japanese authorities. A plan that he drew up in 1901 combined elements of Western education, such as the teaching of arithmetic and the distribution of approved texts to schools, with proposals made by Wang Yun and reinforced by Western example—teaching reading through simple classical poetry and character recognition through familiar objects and concepts. The words he suggested for the latter show how deeply ingrained was the concept of education as training in ethics and statecraft: after words like "sun," "moon," "father," "mother," and "teacher" came "filial piety," "loyalty," and "good faith," followed by "peace" and "danger," "good order" and "disturbance," "change," "promote," and "retrieve," all before the child had learned to read a single sentence.[98]

Parallel with the movement for reform on traditional lines was an attempt to introduce Western subject divisions and knowledge of the West at the elementary stage. Wang Kangnian, a colleague of Liang Qichao's on the *Shiwu bao*, founded a public association for elementary studies in Shanghai in 1897. The association published an illustrated paper for children containing lessons in English (see illustration 2), Japanese, and Chinese, Western and Chinese history and geography, arithmetic, morals, and science. No field was too remote; articles were printed on the races of Europe, geology, and early Chinese dynasties.[99] The pedagogic utility of this magazine is uncertain, but it is significant as one of the first attempts within China to divide the child's world from the adult by writing specially for children.

Few elementary schools on the Western model were opened during the first period of reform. Even after the state decreed their establishment in 1901 and regularized their structure in 1904, the young child's contact with Western knowledge was most likely to come within the familiar framework of the sishu, or to be precise, the family school. New ideas were slow to percolate down to the village school. Many writers recall their early lessons as a mixture of old and new. Chen Guofu, the Guomindang politician, was taught rhymes about astronomy and geography (which "left absolutely no impression" on him) in Zhejiang in 1899.[100] Such jingles fitted easily into the existing curriculum, alongside or replacing time-honored primers of general knowledge such as the *Three Character Classic*. The young Hsiao Kung-chuan was nourished by a heterogeneous selection of ancient and modern texts: in 1902, he was studying a historical reader composed by a deceased ancestor, a manual for writing couplets and a selection of classical poetry (both common sishu texts), and the modern "Song of the Globe."[101] The mysterious syllables of the latter, with its recitation of unknown continents, impressed the infant minds of many of Hsiao's generation. Novelist Ba Jin recalled that he and his sisters found the new verses as incomprehensible as the old ones.[102]

The replacement of the eight-legged essay by the topical dissertation necessitated alterations in the curriculum of those sishu that prepared pupils for the examinations. These changes varied from the reshuffling of traditional elements, such as the teaching of the Five Classics before the Four Books (from which the eight-legged essay questions had been taken),[103] through the reading of collections of topical dissertations as models and the study of Chinese history[104] to utilization of such technological advances as the newspaper. One teacher even set his students to composing newspaper items for publication.[105]

The most wholehearted espousal of Western methods was that of the family school started by the Hanlin scholar Yan Xiu in Tianjin. In 1898, he hired a young graduate of the Beiyang Naval School to give lessons in English, mathematics, science, and games to five boys from his family, who were subsequently joined by ten from outside.[106] This was the seed of the famous Nankai Middle School, Zhou Enlai's alma mater; a later expansion created Nankai University, still one of China's premier institutions.

One writer who spent his boyhood in Shanghai successively attended three sishu ranging from enlightened to ultraconservative. The first, in 1902, used a modern-language primer and taught grammar as well as recitation of the classics. The second, in 1904, "was more conservative and used antiquated texts," but at least taught the author to compose topical dissertations. The last of the three was taught by "a reactionary

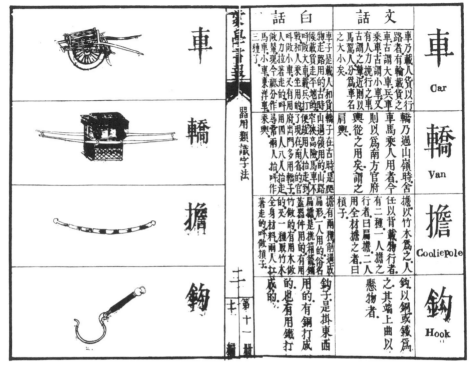

2. An Early English Lesson (*Mengxue bao*, no. 11 [1898])

old pedant who believed that Western learning was heresy."[107] This writer's progress backward through different stages of the educational reforms of the late Qing is a reminder of their fragmentation and disunity.

Reception

At the turn of the century, the new schools were very much a tiny minority. If each of the over four thousand academies in existence at the end of the nineteenth century had several score scholars—associated through essay competitions, in most cases, rather than through resident tuition—this means that approximately half a million men supplemented their income and their learning through the academies. In contrast, semimodern schools and academies were numbered in tens rather than thousands, and their instruction was normally confined to a few score resident students.

The new schools were not only in a minority, they were unpopular. Although the "public opinion" (*yulun*) formed by the *Shiwu bao* and other reform journals and by the writings of Zhang Zhidong and Zheng Guanying favored the new education, "popular opinion" (*sulun*) was apathetic or hostile. Neither conservative gentry nor the unlettered masses had a high opinion of the new schools.

Most students attending schools of the Western type did so because they were free. They were the sons of gentry fallen on hard times or entrepreneurs disinclined to waste good money on schooling, with a sprinkling of the rich and idle who could not be bothered to study for the examinations.[108] The first government school to teach Western subjects, the Tongwen Guan in Beijing, was at first filled with the dregs of an old official school for Manchu bannermen. The students and their families were ostracized by friends and relatives for surrendering to the West. Some even had difficulty in finding wives.[109]

Prejudice was dissipated in one place by official support and approval of the new institutions only to return in another. By the late 1890s, the Tongwen Guan was attracting more students than it could handle;[110] in Guangzhou, however, students at the city's first nonmissionary Western-style school, Shimin Xuetang, were jeered in the streets. A former student recalled that

> the Cantonese gradually ceased to look down on Shimin only when the new school system was fixed [in 1904] and private and public schools opened up one after the other. I still remember how, before there was an education minister (*xuewu dachen*), Cantonese gentlemen would say we belonged to Kang Youwei's party, or if not that, then they'd call us Christian converts. If we chanced to cross the town, behind our backs would rise the derisive sound of curses and spitting, and when we met relatives and friends they would repeatedly urge us to leave the school.[111]

Resentment against the schools had both a cultural and a material basis. Many groups had a stake—of property, prestige, or profession—in the preservation of the old educational institutions and were reluctant to accept the new.

Among the threatened groups was the Buddhist priesthood, whose temple holdings were to be transferred in part to the new schools. Alarm was felt both among Buddhist priests at the court and at the local level: Ma Xulun recalled seeing in 1898 two agitated nuns carrying a bodhisattva away by night to avoid the threatened confiscation. Their alarm was premature but not groundless.[112]

Sishu teachers and the staff and students of academies made their living and owed their status to traditional education. For both ideological and financial reasons, many were reluctant to take their chances with the new system, which was tainted by associations with commerce, with barbarians, with Christianity. One sishu teacher rejected with scorn a proposal that he teach geography on the grounds that "*he* had not converted to the foreign religion."[113] As late as 1907 sishu teachers in Guangxi were apparently spreading rumors and discouraging attendance at the new schools.[114] It is evident that the new schools had no popular constituency: the demand for their establishment came from above, from a section of the elite that could make its voice heard in Beijing.

At the turn of the century, the future of schooling on the Western model must have seemed precarious. On one side was ranged progressive public opinion; on the other, popular indifference or aversion, expressed in concentrated form by the destruction wrought by the Boxers in North China. Indigenous institutions were showing considerable powers of regeneration and demonstrating a capacity for absorption of the new learning without fundamental structural alteration. The balance was tipped in favor of foreign imitation by the foreign powers' defeat of the Boxers. Policies of naive chauvinism, or even of constructive reform within the Chinese tradition, were outdated: they could not compete with the allurements of modern school systems, blazoned with the successes of Germany and Japan and promising China equal strength.

The period of experimentation in Chinese education, when it seemed possible to marry Chinese reforms with Western innovations, was cut short by the wholesale adoption of Japanese prescriptions in 1904–1905. The tension between native and foreign, *tu* and *yang*, was thus sidestepped rather than resolved. Shifting definitions of and ambiguous attitudes toward the two continue to characterize educational debate in China under the People's Republic. For decades, indigenous practices flourished alongside imported ones: illegally, where banned sishu continued underground; illegitimately, where schools nominally new were conducted with sishu or academy organization and methods; and tacitly accepted, where students ignored technical studies to pursue abstract statecraft or looked on schooling as the stepping-stone to a government job.

4
The Role of the State in the New School System

The role of the central government in traditional China, as outlined above, was that of an arbiter—a judge, a setter of standards, holder of the balance between conflicting regional or local interests. Direct supervision went no lower than the county magistrate. The examination system was one expression of this concept of central power, for which ideological control was primary, administrative secondary, and direct fiscal control—as opposed to a percentage of the take—relatively unimportant. When defeat by foreign powers made this view untenable, Qing statesmen sought in the constitutions of the victors a clue to their success. From Germany and Japan, they derived an understanding of the center as initiator, as activator, with powers of compulsion and regulation unknown in China, yet gladly accepted by the ruled as representing their own best interests. Men such as Zhang Zhidong saw in this type of government an unprecedented opportunity for the realization of ideological control. They were slower to grasp the need for a new type of administration to carry it out and almost oblivious to the need for a new fiscal structure to support such an administration; their perception of Western state structure was filtered through their own dominant preoccupations. This was to prove a severe weakness in their attempt to implement foreign institutions in China.

The Japanese Model

Among the institutions singled out as responsible for the achievements of Germany and Japan was the educational system of the two nations. To Chinese observers, defeat or the threat of defeat had spurred both mentors to great efforts in the field of education. Prussia's victory over France, its former conqueror, attracted much retrospective attention, and the statement that it owed victory to its primary school system was often quoted. Wang Tao's work on the Franco-Prussian War, for example, recorded the educational reforms that preceded Prussia's regeneration.[1] Japan's rise provided an even more apposite example of a country with an antiquated social system, haunted by "the fear of possible encroachment by Western powers who were already protected by the unequal treaty of 1858,"[2] that had been able to transform itself into a powerful industrial state. The Chinese attributed Japan's victories to its educational system. Scholars had always believed that their country's greatest wealth lay in educated men. The reformers now went a step further; from being father and mother to the people, the educated were to become begetters of factories and modern armies. In modeling the Chinese educational system on that of Japan, China hoped to duplicate its achievements.

The belief that China's best policy was to copy Japan rested on two dubious assumptions. The first was that Japan owed its rise to its educational system. On this point, the historian Herbert Passin reminds us that "it is . . . necessary to avoid the *post hoc, ergo propter hoc* fallacy: Because Japan succeeded in establishing universal education quickly, *therefore* she quickly achieved self-sustaining economic growth . . . Economic growth might very well have been achieved without a successful system of compulsory modern education—through the talents and enterprise of entrepreneurial elements, the general skill level of the population carried over from premodern times, and many other factors."[3]

British experience emphasizes this moral. The first industrialized nation had in the nineteenth century an educational system similar to that of contemporary China: a "combination of restriction to a wealthy elite of access to the higher educational process, of a classical, formalistic, literary, moralistic curriculum, and of competitive entry into the bureaucracy by examination in familiarity with this body of literature."[4] Chinese reformers, trying to reduce the rigidity of their own classical education, were not attracted to the British model; they were aware that British education lagged behind German. They do not, however, appear to have considered the implications of Britain's commercial and colonial empire: that education, while not irrelevant to the pursuit of wealth and power, is not the most important and certainly not the only necessary precondition.

The second dubious assumption was that what had worked in Japan would work in China. In 1898, Zhang Zhidong adduced four reasons for sending students to Japan to study rather than to Europe: savings in fares, ease of supervision, similarity of script, and Japanese success in garnering the best from Western writings. In Japan, "circumstances and customs are close to ours and we can copy it easily."[5] Zhang's choice of the Japanese model was based in part on Japan's rapid rise to military and industrial strength rivaling that of Western nations, in part on his admiration for the conservatism of late Meiji Japan, the emphasis, especially in elementary education, on patriotism and loyalty, and the preservation of the "five relationships" of Confucianism (between subject and ruler, parent and child, elder and younger brother, wife and husband, friend and friend) in the 1890 Imperial Rescript on Education.[6] It seems unlikely that he would have chosen the Japanese system as a model had it continued along the liberal, American-influenced path followed in the 1870s, with its devolution of educational responsibility to the local level. Direct American or British influence was still less acceptable, for political as well as strategic and social reasons. Qing officials suspected the many eager missionary-educators of divided loyalties,[7] and governmental coolness frustrated their desire to "secure and retain control" over the coming educational changes.[8] So concerned was the government that the new education should be secular and independent that it ruled out organized missionary participation in the national school system.[9]

With official approval, Japanese influence grew rapidly during the early years of the century. Contacts took place at both the formal and informal levels. Wu Rulun, head of Lianchi Academy and later dean of Beijing University, discussed with Ito Hirobumi, one of the masterminds of the Meiji reforms, the relative place of moral, intellectual, and physical education.[10] In 1902, Wu was sent to inspect Japanese education and its effect on Chinese students studying abroad.[11] Zhang Zhidong himself, while governor-general of Hunan and Hubei, actively promoted contact. In 1901 he sent two provincial delegations within six months to report on Japanese schools;[12] other provincial leaders followed his example.[13] In the reverse direction, Kanō Jigorō, head of Tokyo's Higher Normal School, visited China in 1902 to inspect its educational reforms.[14]

In addition to direct contact, an increasing number of Japanese works on education were available in China.[15] Many were publicized through Luo Zhenyu's *Jiaoyu shijie* (Educational World), which was at first wholly devoted to translations. Luo had been one of the party sent by Zhang Zhidong to examine Japanese education in 1901. When, in 1903, a triumvirate headed by Zhang Zhidong revised the first, incomplete regulations, Luo's ten-volume translation of Japanese regulations on education was almost certainly in their hands.[16]

The regulations promulgated under Zhang's direction in 1904 reveal detailed study of Japanese practice both in letter and in spirit. Departures from it were painstakingly justified: two pages, for example, were devoted to explaining why Chinese children should learn poetry instead of singing songs like their Japanese counterparts.[17] The closeness with which the Chinese regulations followed the Japanese may be seen in a comparison of the aims of primary education in each country. The ordinance promulgated in Japan in 1890 stated that its aim was, "while paying attention to children's bodily development, to lay the foundation of education in morality and citizenship education, and also teach them the ordinary knowledge and skills necessary for the conduct of life."[18] The analogous Chinese regulations of 1904 run: "The lower primary school . . . is to inculcate in [its students] that knowledge necessary for the conduct of life and to lay the foundations of morality and patriotism, while caring for their bodily development."[19]

Zhang hoped in transferring a simulacrum of the Japanese system to China to strengthen the nation both morally, by reaffirming Confucian values, and materially, by creating conditions for a modern army and industry. Yet the school system he designed to strengthen the center assumed its strength, its ability to promulgate laws that would be heeded. It assumed a nonexistent parallel with Japan. In reality, the symbolic value of the ruler, the responsiveness of the elite, and the powers of the center differed fundamentally in the two countries.

Powers and Priorities of the Central Government

The Meiji emperor, symbol of Japanese unity, had come to power with his hands clean, heading a government of men who had resisted foreign aggression and overthrown the signatories of the unequal treaty of 1858. In China, the court had for decades yielded one concession after another to foreigners, culminating in an ignominious retreat from the capital before foreign armies in 1901. With the exception of the revolt of Saigo Takamori in 1877, no great division had riven the Japanese elite, whereas many would-be modernizers in China had bitter memories of the execution of the Six Martyrs in 1898. Although comparatively few scholars and officials had been involved in the reformers' attempted takeover of power, Liang Qichao's *Xinmin congbao* (The Reno-

vation of the People) published in exile, was almost compulsory reading
among those interested in the West. Liang's condemnation of the Empress Dowager obtained wide circulation, contributing to the growing
alienation between the reform-minded and the Manchu court. Attempts
by Chinese officials to identify the interests of the dynasty with those of
the nation were vitiated by Manchu distrust of the Chinese and unwillingness to make concessions.

In Japan, the elite inhabited a common world of discourse, despite
variations in politics and beliefs, and with the centralization of government, they often inhabited common territory literally, all being resident
in Tokyo. This was not the case in China. Its size—more than twenty
times that of Japan—poor communications, and the devolution of
power to regional leaders (of whom Zhang Zhidong was one) meant that
the elite did not respond as a unit to the national crisis. Throughout
most of the nineteenth century, the threat posed by the West had caused
dissension rather than unity, being perceived differently or not at all in
different parts of the country, by different levels of society, and by different groups within the government. During the Taiping Rebellion in
the 1850s and 1860s, the restoration of internal order had taken priority
over external irritations experienced directly by only a small number of
people. Even the Japanese victory over China in 1894 was the subject of
confused reports: popular ballads had it that China was the victor and
the enemy fleet almost totally annihilated.[20] In 1896 the Zongli Yamen
circulated a memorial calling on officials in the coastal provinces and the
Yangzi Basin, the areas most affected by foreign intrusions, to establish
modern schools, while allowing those in the interior provinces to use
their discretion; response by the former was considered both more urgent and more likely.[21] In the last decade of the Qing, the rise in number
and circulation of newspapers and journals, by nature advocates of modernization, created a community of informed subscribers, but they were
not equally accessible to all: in 1907 the *Dongfang zazhi* (Eastern Mis-
cellany), for example, had 49 outlets in twenty cities and towns in the
coastal province of Jiangsu, but in the interior provinces of Henan, Jilin,
Shanxi, Shaanxi, Gansu, Yunnan, Guizhou, and Guangxi it was on sale
only in the capital cities.[22]

The powers possessed by the Meiji government in Japan were in
China to a large extent delegated to regional and provincial leaders.
Men like Zhang Zhidong derived their authority from the central government, but had almost total discretion in wielding it. The court played
a balancing game, playing off against each other court factions and provincial officials, reformers and conservatives. It took the allied armies'
entrance into Beijing during the Boxer Rebellion to tip the balance in

favor of reform. The new school system, decreed in 1901 and given its first regulations in 1902, grew from provincial consultation and advice. The process of its formation illustrates the interplay of bureaucratic procedure with personal, racial, and local interests.[23]

The court's first action on its return to the capital after the allied occupation was to circularize high metropolitan and regional officials, asking for their proposals on reform. Memorials on educational reform were sent by Tao Mo, governor-general of Guangdong and Guangxi, Yuan Shikai, governor of Shandong, and jointly by Zhang Zhidong, governor-general of Hunan and Hubei, and Liu Kunyi, governor-general of Jiangsu, Anhui, and Jiangxi. In accordance with their suggestions, the court ordered in August 1901 that dissertations on current affairs replace the eight-legged essay, the bane of reformers, and in September that a three-tiered school system based on the conversion of academies be set up. Both measures were simply a repetition of those enacted but not carried out in the Hundred Days' Reform of 1898.

The newly established Bureau of Government Affairs, in conjunction with the Board of Rites (still at that time in charge of educational affairs) and regional leaders, was to set regulations for the new schools. Yuan Shikai was the only regional leader to respond, with limited proposals that in their first stage amounted only to an expansion of the curriculum of provincial-level academies to include Western subjects and the provision within them of training at different levels. His suggestions, though moderate, afforded conservatives a pretext for attack.

Yuan's regulations, essentially no more than a modest supplement to the examination system, were replaced in 1902 by those drawn up by the official in charge of education (*guanxue dachen*), Zhang Boxi (who had replaced Sun Jia'nai, whose duties had been light since the court had countermanded the school system planned in 1898 a few months later and the Boxers had destroyed its sole fruit, Beijing University, in 1900). Zhang was conscious of the limited power of his office. His report on the university opened pessimistically: "At present, despite the fact that all provinces, prefectures, circuits, and counties have been ordered to set up schools everywhere, up to now few places have reported the opening of schools. Thus there are no suitable entrants for university study at present. It will take time for each province to set up schools, and one cannot say when they will all reach a uniform stage, nor when students will finally graduate in sequence."[24] Under Zhang's regulations, administration was carried out through the school system itself, with Beijing University at its head.

Like Yuan, Zhang became the target of conservatives' accusations of incompetence and insincerity. The Manchus, alarmed at Zhang's success in building up a band of talented men, suspected a connection between rebellious Chinese students in Japan and the visit there of Wu Rulun, dean of the university, who had been appointed by Zhang.[25] A Mongol bannerman, Rong Qing, was placed alongside Zhang Boxi. The two did not get on well together, producing a deadlock broken only by the arrival in Beijing of Zhang Zhidong. Political as much as educational considerations resulted in the setting up of a three-man commission, consisting of Zhang Zhidong, Zhang Boxi, and Rong Qing, to draw up a new set of regulations. The result, promulgated in 1904 and nominally a joint work, bore the strong imprint of Zhang Zhidong's ideas.

Like Zhang Zhidong's earlier *Quanxue pian*, the regulations were fighting on two fronts: trying on the one hand to convince conservatives that the new scheme had a point and on the other to curb its already apparent dangers. The *Xuewu gangyao* (Outline of Educational Principles) devotes several paragraphs to the former cause, testifying to the lack of acceptance of the commonplaces of modern education: "The subjects of the different schools are really not complicated and difficult . . . The sequential teaching of different subjects is established practice in all countries and has a deep significance."[26] Many more paragraphs are devoted both to the active preservation of China's threatened heritage (including several pages of arguments for studying the classics and literature) and to the prevention of sedition and unruliness.

Zhang was concerned more with ideological than with fiscal or administrative centralization. He hoped to ensure that the school system was a channel for the pure stream of Confucian teachings, unsullied alike by outworn pedantry and modern heresies. Schools had a regulatory function; they were to "set our course straight." "Starting from a boy's entrance into lower primary, his teachers should give him constant guidance during his lessons, enlightening him on the meaning of respect for family members and bringing him into conformity with correct ways. All heresies and biased views should be strictly opposed and reproved."[27] To this end, the Outline added three years to school attendance to enable mastery of the classical curriculum[28] and banned girls from public schooling.[29] (Zhang's successors modified both measures.)

Perhaps because administrative control was secondary to ideological in the priorities of Zhang Zhidong and his colleagues, the administration of the new school system remained a makeshift anomaly until 1906.[30] The 1904 school system replaced the vague and general duties of the officer in charge of education, who had had responsibility both for the university and for the school system as a whole, with a *zongli xuewu dachen* (director of education). The new officer was charged with "controlling the educational affairs of the whole country," including "directing

3. The New School Curriculum Depicted as a Heavy Weight
Crushing a Young Child (*Xingqi huabao*, no. 30 [1907])

schools in the provinces, formulating a school system, examining school
rules, certifying . . . textbooks, appointing teachers, selecting graduates,
coordinating school expenditures, and all matters connected with education."[31] This plethora of tasks was to be handled by six departments,
each with a head and several assistants. Among their tasks were tours of
inspection and reports on the provinces.

The proposed tours (none were undertaken during the office's brief
existence) were the only evidence of Zhang's concern with the implementation in practice rather than the regulation in theory of the new
school system. The central educational office had no direct administrative contact with its provincial equivalents; indeed, the very existence of
a provincial equivalent was left to the discretion of each region's governor. In the words of Duan Fang, a member of a five-man mission sent by
the government in 1905 to report on foreign countries and a critic of
this laissez-faire method, "people could do as they wished on all things."[32]
The only educational officials sent out from the center to the provinces
were the traditional *xuezheng*, or director of studies, deputed by the

Board of Rites to serve three-year terms in the provinces. Their main duties concerned supervision of the examinations, although Zhang probably hoped that new appointments to this position would also busy themselves with modern education.[33]

The Ministry of Education

The abolition of the examination system, announced in 1905, appeared an opportune moment for the rationalization of educational administration. A Manchu memorialist proposed the abolition of the Board of Rites and the establishment of a Ministry of Education like Japan's.[34] The latter part of this proposal was taken up, and the Xue Bu—the neologism *jiaoyu* was not used in the ministry's title till 1912—came into existence in December 1905. It was headed by Rong Qing, the Mongol bannerman who had assisted in the drafting of the new school system, with the experienced educationalist Yan Xiu as second in command. Luo Zhenyu, who joined the ministry in its early days, has left a picture of a rather casual mode of functioning: "When the Ministry of Education was first established, it had no offices and conducted its business in a rented dwelling. Few of the personnel who had been transferred had as yet arrived . . . at that time the ministry's regulations had not been drawn up, and there was no division into departments and sections. [Rong Qing] had all members of the ministry attend each afternoon for discussion."[35]

In May 1906, the staffing and organization of the ministry were decreed, the anachronistic office of xuezheng (which had outlived by some months the examination system) abolished, and an administrative hierarchy reaching to the county level set up. Provincial education was to be headed by *tixueshi*, or educational commissioners, appointed from the center. There appears to have been some debate between conservatives and professionally oriented educationalists within the ministry over appointment of these commissioners, who ranked second to the financial commissioner (*fansi*) and ahead of the judicial commissioner (*niesi*) in provincial administration. According to Luo Zhenyu,

> Vice-President Yan at first suggested that they would have to have an understanding of education, meaning that they should be former schoolteachers or administrators. He had already transferred a number of Tianjin primary school headmasters and teachers to the ministry. I raised the point that since the position of commissioner of education was a very distinguished one, at the same level as the financial commis-

sioner, someone of commensurate standing should be chosen . . . the only thing to do was to appoint them as the former xuezheng were appointed, from the Hanlin Academy.

Yan disagreed, but Luo pointed out that the juren and shengyuan who staffed the new schools did not necessarily know much about education and certainly knew nothing of official life. A compromise was reached— the Hanlin scholars appointed were to be sent on a tour of inspection overseas for several months before taking office. When it came to the selection of particular men, Yan Xiu again proposed a "modern" method, selection by secret ballot, but was overruled by Rong Qing. Some of the ministry's employees objected to one of the men chosen, on the grounds that he was "corrupt and reactionary, an impossible choice," but as Luo dismissively observed, the protestors "were all former primary school teachers, so their words had no effect."[36]

Records of the ministry's internal politics are, unfortunately, scarce, but it is evident that the ill-feeling between cultural loyalists and those who threw their lot in with modern institutions was repeated within the ministry. In particular, there was a conflict between men who identified with the scholar-official class and those who saw themselves primarily as professional educationalists. Despite Yan Xiu's background as a xuezheng, he championed the point of view of the latter group. The conservatives appear to have won many of the early battles, although their published statements were usually couched in language intended to disarm rather than antagonize their opponents. For two years, from 1907 to 1909, Zhang Zhidong returned to the capital as head of the Ministry of Education. The obituary notice published in *Jiaoyu zazhi* (Educational Review) on Zhang's death illustrates the rift between the two groups. It gave due praise to the Zhang Zhidong of ten years earlier, who "created a change in the temper of the times and was the hope of the educational world," but deplored the influence of his conservatism and gradualism on education. "Some may ask" the writer continued, "why Zhang's earlier and later behavior differed from each other. There is no difference. Zhang Zhidong was a politician, not an educationalist; he was an educationalist of the old days, not what is called an educationalist today . . . there was not one of his acts but was counter to world trends . . . he specialized in flouting public opinion."[37]

If by "world trends" the writer meant "Japanese experience," he was a little unfair to Zhang. Over the preceding thirty years Japan's school system had evolved as a conservative reaction against and selective exclusion of the wholesale foreign borrowings and accompanying liberal philosophy of the early Meiji period. One of Zhang's problems was that, unlike

Japan, where conservatism and patriotism could be linked, in China the two seemed antagonistic. By seeing what was Chinese as essentially moral and cultural—the study of classical texts and the practice of classical virtues—Zhang left the field of nationalism to those who favored Japanese-style modernization, some of whom were able by opposing the Manchus to reconcile patriotism with abandonment of ancestral custom.

Some of the dilemmas of the conservatives can be seen in the ministry's reports on textbooks submitted for its approval, particularly those on modern history. The sorry record of repeated Chinese defeats by foreign armies could not be suppressed; indeed, shame at defeat could fulfill a positive function in the inculcation of the last three of the five aims of education announced in 1906, the exaltation of the public good, martial spirit, and solid learning (*shang gong, shang wu, shang shi*).[38] At the same time, undue emphasis on China's weakness and foreign strength might undo promotion of the first two aims, loyalty to the emperor and veneration of Confucius. The department entrusted with the certification of texts had to guard not only against factual but against political errors. Although there were some professional educationalists on its staff, their presence was negated by old-fashioned scholars who felt free to chop and change texts as they liked. Their superiors were even more conservative.[39] The result was a careful casuistry: a geography text came under censure for stating that the Manchus had upheld Confucianism simply to win over ethnic Chinese.[40] This statement was suspect not only because it cast doubt on the universal validity of Confucianism but also because it raised obliquely the issues of racial differences between Chinese and Manchus and the basis of the latter's rule. No such delicate questions of historical interpretation plagued the Japanese educationalist. The 1908 rescript, one of two that "guide us in the education of the young" has an almost hearty tone: "Civilization is advancing day by day and progressing month by month, and the nations of the whole world, East and West, through mutual dependence and help, alike share in its benefits . . . The precepts of Our Sacred Imperial Ancestors and the facts of our glorious history shine like the sun and the stars."[41]

Charges that gradualists such as Zhang had slowed the development of Chinese education arose partly from a lack of historical perspective among educationalists. Looking at the Japan of their own times—which had achieved universal compulsory education—they ignored or were unaware that in its first decade of operation, the Japanese school system had encountered the same problems as they saw at home—peasant riots against schools, public lack of appreciation of their benefits, untrained teachers, irregular attendance, unsuitable buildings.[42] Nor did they compare China's geography and population with Japan's. Many educationalists apparently expected that the Japanese achievement could be replicated in China in a third the time with a population some ten times larger spread over a land area twenty times as great. They considered the failure to attain this as evidence of China's unfitness for the modern world and blamed the inevitable consequences of poor communications, inadequate finances, and inexperience on the stubbornness of conservatives or the shortsightedness of peasants.

The administrative changes of 1906, following on the abolition of the old examinations, put the finishing touches to what was on paper an extensive, highly centralized administrative hierarchy, well-fitted to carry out the tasks involved in government control of education. Only one point was omitted in the flood of detailed regulations: money. Attempted centralization merely revealed the weaknesses and limitations of the central government, which was a client of the provinces on which it was financially dependent. As historian Albert Feuerwerker has pointed out, "in contrast to Meiji Japan, where the land-tax revision of 1873 brought the major revenue sources of the country under the direct control of the new central government, the late-Ch'ing government was politically incapable of extending its control of the revenue."[43] After five years of rule, the Japanese had succeeded in the former Chinese province of Taiwan in raising the land tax to 5 or 6 percent of what the land produced. In China, however, the amount collected had fallen by 1900 to 2 percent of production. The central government's main source of revenue was fixed if not contracting and was in any case not remitted directly by centrally appointed agents but indirectly through a tax-farming network responsible to local officials.[44] De facto fiscal autonomy remained with the provinces and lower levels and was indeed increased rather than lessened by the need to raise money from new sources to finance schools. The central government was in no position to make grants to provincial or local schools; rather, metropolitan educational institutions such as Beijing University and the Ministry of Education itself depended on sums remitted from the provinces. Each province had been assigned a certain contribution to the expenses of the center, but a memorial of 1906 indicates the extent of their delinquency. The 50,000 tael budget of the Xuewu chu (predecessor of the ministry) depended, with the exception of interest on money with the Sino-Russian Bank, entirely on provincial contributions, but these had never amounted to more than 10,000 taels. This sum had been inadequate even to support the schools and the university under the Xuewu chu's direct control and would be even more inadequate after adoption of a policy of universal education. The disparity between income and necessary expenditure "was a source of anxiety day and night." Discussions with two of the provincial leaders most interested in modern education, Yuan Shikai and Duan Fang, had elicited a promise of 50,000 taels from each annually; would the court order other provinces to make similar contributions according to their size?[45] The court acceded, and eighteen provinces were assessed a total contribution of 710,000 taels. According to the following year's statement of income, about a third of this amount reached the ministry.[46] In 1910, some provinces asked to be excused their share on the grounds that they could not afford to pay. Other provinces simply retained their payments without the formality of asking permission.[47]

Problems of Control

Lack of money had not hampered the examination system, which had determined the objective and course of study for students throughout the empire simply by setting standards and rewarding achievement. As long as the examinations were held, the education that led up to them was self-regulating. Proponents of the new system wished to take over education at all levels, but in attempting to do so they overturned the consensus and coincidence of interests that had characterized the old system without being able to enforce new norms.

The examinations were not abolished immediately on the establishment of the school system of 1904 since conservatives still strongly favored them. Their claim to continued existence lay in their previous reform: in 1902 the government had abolished the eight-legged essay and given disquisitions on politics and history equal weight with classical essays.[48] But the proponents of modernization viewed even reformed examinations, like reformed academies, as inimical to the new schools; the examination degrees, as Zhang Zhidong observed bitterly in 1903, were regarded as easier to obtain and as a surer path toward "benefits and emoluments." He repeated his objections in a second memorial the following year: the gentry and the rich were unwilling to put their money into schools while the examinations lasted, and students did not commit themselves wholeheartedly to their new course of study because negligence could be repaired by a lucky stroke in the examinations.[49] Zhang and his colleagues finally succeeded in getting the examinations abolished in 1905. (From 1905 to 1910, candidates sought government office on the basis of school qualifications confirmed by re-examination by a magistrate. This new system had to be abandoned because of a surplus of graduates from the new schools.)

The Ministry of Education, then, supposedly presided over a school system with no competitors. In actuality, however, the highest and lowest reaches of education—study abroad and sishu schooling—tended to lie outside the ministry's scope (although it did made attempts to bring these errants into the fold), and its influence even on schools nominally established in accord with the regulations was tenuous when such schools lay outside Beijing or provincial centers.

Geographical Limitations

The ministry in Beijing was isolated, impotent, and ill-informed. Beijing and the metropolitan province of Zhili were familiar territory, but not the regions beyond the ministry's headquarters. Provincial tours of inspection by ministerial officials were exploratory. Reliable information, of the sort needed to monitor the operations of an extensive centralized system, was rare. Even the statistics on schooling in different provinces, which the ministry made a great effort to collect, were untrustworthy. Its statistical compilations of 1907, 1908, and 1909 each ran to several hundred pages.

Figures for the number of schools and students for 1909 indicate that in relation to total population Zhili ranked first, followed by Sichuan, Yunnan, Shaanxi, Shanxi, and Guangxi, with the Yangzi Valley and coastal provinces well down the list. Anhui recorded the worst ratio,

Number of Schools and Students, 1909

Province	Schools	Students	Province	Schools	Students
Zhili	11,201	242,247	Zhejiang	2,165	76,114
Fengtian, Jilin, Heilongjiang	3,240	125,621	Jiangxi	1,262	30,428
			Hubei	2,886	99,064
Shandong	4,396	60,765	Hunan	1,437	52,229
Shanxi	2,333	57,291	Sichuan	10,661	345,383
Shaanxi	2,953	59,196	Guangdong	1,794	86,437
Henan	3,773	90,824	Guangxi	1,328	51,097
Jiangsu, Jiangning	2,462	80,947	Yunnan	1,944	57,808
			Guizhou	1,811	27,036
Anhui	865	24,674	Fujian	678	29,653

SOURCE: China [Qing], Xue Bu, *Xuantong yuannian: Disanci jiaoyu tongji tubiao* (Beijing, 1911), Gesheng, pp. 1–2.

probably justifiably, since floods and famine hindered its recovery from the Taiping Rebellion. It is intriguing that, with the exception of Zhili, the provinces claiming the highest rate of attendance were among the most remote from Western contact. Shaanxi, a poor and backward province, recovering from a severe famine, did better than Jiangsu, center of educational innovation. Educational statistics for Japan in 1895 appear to tell the same story. "Before I went into the question," wrote a contemporary observer,

> I was sure that I could have painted those provinces which contain the treaty ports black [to indicate 70 percent attendance of school-age children], and have triumphantly called attention to the presumptive fact that the presence of the foreigner had brought with it the inevitable enlightening result . . . The figures show us that Yokohama and Kobe are only in second-rate educational districts, whereas Nagasaki is in one of the worst educated provinces . . . I can only come to the conclusion that, as far as the masses are concerned, education makes more effectual progress in some of the quiet and outlying districts which are practically undisturbed by the foreigner . . . and where the only modernising influence which is now making itself felt is occasioned by the Government regulations.[50]

The cynic may wonder whether a possible explanation for the apparently high attendance in remote areas is that officials charged with reporting the progress of such areas found it easier to invent statistics than to obtain them. I have not checked the Japanese figures, but the Chinese ones show certain inconsistencies. Tables for Yunnan and Shanxi, for example, in the 1909 survey purport to show percentage attendance of school-age children. Both take a base population much lower than the lowest estimate and conjure from it a number of schoolchildren in excess of that given elsewhere in the survey: Yunnan has added a mere 5,000 to the total shown in the table, but Shanxi boldly claims an attendance of over 200,000, a 400 percent increase in the space of a few pages.[51] The inflation of one set of figures does not directly discredit the others but does nothing to assuage doubts about their reliability. Yunnan's good showing may be explicable in terms of the persisting influence of its indigenous educational base—the province reportedly had 30,000 charity schools in the 1730s.[52] On the other hand, this figure may simply be an early example of official hyperbole. The statistics Sichuan sent to the Education Ministry in 1907 were too confusing and contradictory to be used;[53] Does Sichuan's inclusion in the 1909 survey bespeak greater accuracy of reporting or greater care in rearranging?

A report on the "true state" of education in Shandong, where a number of counties had claimed a rapid increase in publicly supported schools in 1907, commented that in one area

> scores of schools had only one student . . . for the others, Huimin county claimed 186 lower primary schools, En county 364, and Lingying department 321 elementary schools. Some of them had no schools in 1906, or only one or two, but in one year they have climbed suddenly to over a hundred or to several hundred. I am afraid this cannot be the true state of affairs. Even if the figures are genuine, they must refer to the common people's sishu, which have been twisted into schools for the purposes of the survey.[54]

The Persistence of Sishu

The comment above indicates the sishu's tenacity. Many educationalists write as though the period from 1902 to 1911 saw the end of all traditional education.[55] In fact, during the last years of the dynasty and probably for at least a decade afterward the majority of those receiving any schooling acquired it in sishu. Under a superimposed structure of modern schools and a thin layer of reformed sishu, the old sishu continued in their wonted style, an independent, parallel form of schooling, little affected by government decrees or the theories of educationalists.

One reason for their continued predominance was the relatively small number and limited distribution of the new schools.[56] Sishu filled the gap when modern schooling was not available. Another element in the persistence of sishu even among the elite was the sense that the sishu taught Chinese learning and modern schools Western; thus in some areas "each major family had both a new school and an old-style family school. My own clan at the time [in 1909] had set up the Zizhi School, but we still had four or five family schools. Those who went to Zizhi were the ones whose families were less well-off. As late as 1920–21, when Zijin School was founded, some people still stood out on their own and had their own family schools."[57] Many persons now in their fifties started their schooling in sishu or studied at them temporarily between attendance at modern schools.[58] The coexistence of the two can be seen from the many educational administrators and school sponsors who continued to hire a sishu teacher for their own children and from the ease with which teachers and graduates from the new schools turned to sishu teaching as a career.[59]

In addition to those with a foot in both camps were many who wanted nothing to do with the new schools. Those in humble circumstances simply wanted their sons to have a bit of culture and good behavior knocked into them; there was a feeling that the new schools were "not for the likes of us" but only for those of high social position. (This at least was an excuse for nonattendance proffered to anxious educationalists.) Others felt that the abolition of the examinations was temporary and the classical education given by the sishu was a better preparation for their return than the fancy subjects of the new schools. Both the poor and the conservative found the sishu "convenient."[60] They taught decent, familiar subjects, not games or singing (the latter had a disreputable association with singing girls), and had a flexible schedule, easily bent to community or individual needs. Uniforms or even good clothes were unnecessary.[61] These virtues were particularly appreciated in the countryside, where foreign influence was less strong.

A further cause for rural reluctance may have been the attitude of those associated with the new education toward country people. From Liang Qichao's witticism in 1896, that having talked to the stupid, mean, ignorant sishu teachers of his home district, he knew why country people stayed country people to the end of their lives,[62] to the comment of an educationalist in 1913 that "country people don't know much; one can't talk about educational principles with them, and yet they manage to obstruct the progress of education in a variety of ways,"[63] educators conceived of themselves as bringers of light to the benighted. This attitude was not new among Confucian reformers, but had not previously impinged on relations between the villagers and their schools.

The sishu persisted in the town as well as in the countryside, assisted by the association of the new schools with foreign and therefore undesirable ways. In Yangzhou in 1909, for example, parents, fearful that their children were picking up foreign habits, removed them from the new schools and sent them back to sishu. Reportedly, in the ensuing resurgence, fifty new sishu opened.[64]

To the educational authorities sishu were anathema. Although Zhang Zhidong's regulations had charged the new elementary schools with promotion of literacy and virtuous conduct—the sishu's traditional tasks—the majority of sishu were banished from the system by a clause stating that only those with thirty or more pupils were eligible to participate. The task of bringing sishu into the fold was left at first to private educationalists. A movement for sishu reform, beginning in Jiangsu in 1904, spread to other parts of China and was finally taken up by the central government in 1910.

The founders of the Society for the Improvement of Sishu regarded the native practices of the sishu as "dark and base," but were prepared to cut the new schools from old cloth. Sishu were allowed to keep their traditional organization—small classes and one teacher—but had to offer a basic curriculum of ethics (taught from the classics), Chinese, mathematics, and sports, with drawing and music as options. Other desiderata were textbooks, maps, blackboard, and chalk, to be furnished by well-wishers, and the pursuit of a graded sequence of study fixed by the society.[65] If strictly adhered to, these criteria would have meant that very few sishu qualified as improved.

Interest in the reform of sishu spread from private bodies to public ones. In 1906, Duan Fang, then governor-general of Liangjiang, ordered the provincial education officials under his jurisdiction to see that branches of the society were set up.[66] When county-level educational officers were appointed in all provinces in 1906, the encouragement of sishu teachers capable of reform was among their duties.[67] The sishu, which had been characterized for centuries by distance from officialdom, began to feel the weight of bureaucratic dictates. In Beijing, the city's educational authorities launched an elaborate program for the conversion of sishu teachers through registration, training, examinations (for the pupils), and prizes. They claimed a success rate of slightly over a fifth of registered sishu (102 out of 481) by the end of 1908, but many sishu teachers may have avoided detection.[68]

The national government, harassed by calls to prepare for constitutional government, turned its attention to the sishu for the first time in history in 1910. The regulations issued that year were based on programs conducted in Beijing and Henan for the improvement of sishu. They demanded slightly lower standards of reformed sishu—physical education was not compulsory, and the teacher could decide the timetable and length of course—and emphasized using texts approved by the Ministry of Education and understanding rather than rote learning. The preamble to the regulations exhibited a budding sociology: the sishu was explained as the product of the family system (*jiazu zhuyi*), the new public schools as the product of the system of military citizenship (*junguomin zhuyi*). China was about to follow the world's advanced nations into the latter, but for the present limited resources meant that the traditional private schools had to complement the public schools.[69]

A corollary to the attempt to reform sishu was the attempt to close down those that did not reform. Conscientious modernizers thrust registration, certification, and inspection on the sishu in an attempt to weed out the bad from the good. In one county in Shandong, as early as 1904, the local magistrate planned to institute an examination of the county's two thousand sishu teachers to prevent the ignorant ones from teaching.[70] Jiangsu scheduled a similar but even more draconian examination. Young and capable sishu teachers were to teach in government schools after a period of training; the elderly or ignorant would be "provided for" in unspecified ways. Henceforth no sishu teachers were permitted to set up their own schools or accept appointments.[71] These methods were open to abuse; a memorial of 1909 objected that opportunistic officials increased their own incomes by heavily fining families who appointed sishu teachers.[72] The supposedly impartial procedures of bureaucratic regulation were easily corrupted when implemented locally.

The Revolution of 1911 afforded sishu no respite: by 1912, under the Republican Ministry of Education, Anhui, Hunan, Guizhou, and Beijing had committed themselves to closing sishu that did not conform to governmental standards for improvement. An article written in 1914 described, with overtones of farce, the progress and tactics of a campaign in Beijing the previous year: attempted investigation (frustrated by the sishus' lengthy New Year's holiday), followed by compulsory registration (evaded by sishu that falsely claimed to have closed) and retraining for sishu teachers (who declined to attend). The anticlimactic result of all this activity was the shutting down of several sishu, whose pupils, to the surprise of the educationalists in charge of the program, were unable to find places in the new schools since these were already full. New schools, taught by unauthorized, self-appointed teachers—ex–sishu teachers?—sprang up to take advantage of the situation.[73] In rural areas, the prohibition was a dead letter. Liao T'ai-ch'u describes with relish the flourishing of "underground" sishu in rural areas of Shandong in the 1930s.[74] Moreover, sishu influence lingered on in new schools. An American observer of the same province a decade earlier noted: "Today, whenever people are freed, by one of the frequent turnovers in government, from the recent educational restrictions, they return to the classics and the old methods of study. Even when new-style schools are opened, the old ideas and practices dominate."[75]

In view of the traditional autonomy of elementary education, it is not surprising that, especially in rural areas, it was often beyond the control of both the Qing and the Republican Ministries of Education. Sishu teaching, declared or disguised, continued as it had for centuries. It was the government's demands that had changed, leaving sishu and their kin lagging behind, irrelevant to the race for wealth and power.

Study Abroad

The Qing government encountered precisely the opposite problem with Chinese students abroad, especially in Japan. Here it was not a question of whipping up the laggards, but of holding back overeager spirits and preventing shortcuts. From entry to higher primary school (equating a classical education with lower primary school since both furnished a knowledge of reading and writing) to graduation from university required, under Zhang Zhidong's regulations, a total of fifteen or sixteen years; a man who started studying the new subjects in his twenties might be forty by the time he had finished. Optimistic students hoped to telescope lower and higher stages by studying abroad for a few years or even months; re-examination on return to China could lead to the awarding of degrees, whose holders were commonly known as "foreign juren" (*yang juren*) or "foreign jinshi" (*yang jinshi*), though these were obtained by relatively few.[76] The majority of the several thousand students supported in Japan by heavy expenditure of government or private funds (annual fees ranged from 300 to 650 yen per student) were taking short courses in schools such as the Kobun Shoin, specially set up in 1902 for Chinese students.[77] Their peak appears to have been reached in 1905–6, when there were some 13,000 Chinese students in Japan.[78]

Over 90 percent of students lived in Tokyo, chiefly within a radius of one and a half miles in the city's northwestern section.[79] They attended the same schools: the Kobun Shoin alone had graduated 1,959 students by the end of 1906 and had another 1,615 taking courses.[80] To a large extent they governed themselves through the Chinese Students Union, which had a membership of 4,500 at its height.[81]

Both the Japanese and the Chinese governments attempted to control this state within a state. In 1905, much to the students' indignation, the Japanese government issued regulations to curb their freewheeling life-style.[82] The Qing government was more concerned with restraining political activity. In 1902, after a student demonstration forced the resignation of the Chinese minister to Japan, the court appointed an educational minister to keep dossiers on Chinese students;[83] the institution's lack of success is apparent from the resignation in 1907 of a second commissioner over disputes with his charges.[84] The Qing government did, however, manage to obtain the closure of the revolutionary *Min bao* (The People), which enjoyed wide circulation among students, and the expulsion of Sun Yat-sen from Japan, where he had made many converts.[85] In 1906, the Ministry of Education went to the root of the problem, issuing regulations aimed at curtailing the flow of students. In the future, only graduates of Chinese secondary schools with a knowledge of Japanese could study in Japan. Those entering short-term courses had to be over 25 years old (the average age for all students in 1904 was 23).[86] Together with a 1909 order making four- or five-year courses compulsory, these actions reduced the number of students in Japan to under 4,000 by 1910.[87]

The problem the Qing government faced was not simply one of rowdy or even revolutionary student behavior. These were merely symptoms of its loss of control, of the breakdown of symbiosis between scholars and government. The examination system had provided an effective means of "getting the heroes of the empire into one's net," in the words of a Tang emperor. The scholars did not forsake the system: even after the changes of 1902, it remained their preferred channel of advancement. Rather, the government did, convinced by the example of Japan that schools could strengthen central state power. The framers of the 1904 educational system attempted to borrow the prestige of the old degrees by keeping their nomenclature for those awarded to graduates of Chinese and foreign schools and by continuing to tie government employment to possession of the higher degrees (most striking is the provision made for graduates from higher technical schools, whose expertise was to be dissipated in administrative tasks for which a knowledge of the classics had hitherto been sufficient qualification).[88] But however graciously the emperor might confer jinshi or juren status on a returned student, it was evident to all that the man had actually won his colors at Waseda or Tokyo Imperial University or Yale or Harvard, that the ministry was simply subscribing to the assessment already made by these institutions—an assessment made, moreover, with no obligatory nods to dynastic glory or Confucian propriety. Even within the country, the schools rather than the central government controlled the new degrees. Provincial and county officials were supposed to re-examine school graduates, but they frequently had no knowledge of the new learning and marked students at random. The protests of indignant students could lead to the overturning of these judgments and the issuance of marks closer to their school grades.[89] The only residual exertion of the government's authority was its refusal to grant degrees to graduates of mission schools, a refusal that apparently did not greatly affect the popularity of colleges such as St. John's in Shanghai, which had built up an independent reputation.

In giving up the examination system, the government had also given up its claim to be the arbiter between different regions. Japanese degrees jostled with European and Chinese: no artificial quota system could balance them as geographic quotas had done under the examination system.[90] The examinations had also tied a scholar to his native place in the sense that he could not take them elsewhere. (One candidate had been turned away when he tried to take the examinations in the county in which his family had lived for generations rather than in its place of original registration.)[91] Abolition of quotas weakened particularism by making one's place of origin less important where schooling was concerned. At the same time, it removed an obstacle to the victory of particularism; the center no longer determined the balance between differently endowed regions.

In short, in abolishing the old examinations the central government had unwittingly done away with a large part of its spiritual authority. The Ministry of Education played with the regalia of power, preoccupied by the question of eligibility for the new degrees and with the bestowal of other honors at its disposal: ranks, memorial arches, inscribed tablets, tokens of imperial favor for those who had endowed schools. These were incentives with a small market since they required the possession of a large fortune and the willingness to give most of it away. The majority of those involved in setting up and running the new schools received no recognition from the central government and reciprocated by treating its directives casually.

Although the Ministry of Education presided over the building of a school system that, with the new army, was among the most successful attempts at remolding Chinese institutions to conform to a Western model, the ministry itself played relatively little part in this transformation. The role of the central government as a whole was that of a facilitator of the new education—it removed obstacles such as the old examination system that stood in the way of the new schools' expansion and provided degrees and the hope of office to their graduates. The much-trumpeted views of educationalists and other liberal ideologues on the value of education to China's regeneration do not appear to have swayed most members of the central and provincial governments: the Ministry of Education was starved for funds both in the last years of the Qing and the early decades of the Republic. Its lack of monetary power was not compensated by an abundance of moral authority. The ministry's failure to match performance with expectations fueled the frustrations of different groups in society. Cultural loyalists were not reconciled to the abolition of the examinations, patriots were examining alternative forms of government, and both conservative and modernizing gentry found in the new schools invigorating corroboration of their powers of independent action.

5
Local Implementation
of the New School System

The school system as decreed in 1898 and 1901 and amplified in the regulations of 1902 and 1904 made relatively slight demands on provincial and local officials. Its minimum requirements were modest: one higher-level school in each provincial capital, one middle school in each prefecture, one higher primary school in each department or county. A certain amount of latitude was thus permitted each locality. At the same time, the court made it clear that it was "keen to promote education" and that officials should set up more schools if possible.

Although educators perceived the new schools as a foundation for universal and compulsory education as practiced in the West and Japan, the nature and degree of official involvement in their establishment were an inheritance from the indigenous system of academies and official school-temples. The regulations envisaged that, as before, private persons and community organizations would be responsible for education leading up to that provided by the state. They were urged to set up lower primary schools and allowed to set up higher primary and middle schools, but not higher schools.

Official Sponsorship

The basis of the government-school network was to be the converted academy, whose buildings were to be transferred to the new institutions. Since most academies had their own lands and revenues, the first obstacles to the setting up of prefectural and county schools were ideological rather than financial. Once the new school system cast off its academic chrysalis, its demands for revenue rose sharply. Higher-level and technical schools were particularly expensive to maintain since they needed to hire highly paid foreign teachers. Even middle and higher-primary schools, if run in accordance with regulations, required expensive texts, equipment, and specialist teachers. Nowhere in the extensive instructions to educational authorities was the question of financing the new system discussed in detail. Those in charge of education had to steer a cautious route between apathy and extortion.

The provincial government acted as a clearinghouse for instructions from the center. Depending on the zeal of individual governors and governors-general, these would be pressed on subordinates or pigeonholed. Whether a province directed its main efforts to higher education in the provincial capital or attempted to spread the new schooling to rural areas also depended on the disposition of its leaders. In Hubei, Governor-General Zhang Zhidong at first concentrated on *rencai jiaoyu*, or the training of an elite of talent. By 1902, he had established in Hubei's provincial capital, Wuchang, one civil and one military college, a normal school, a language school, an agricultural school, an industrial school, and two other advanced schools, as well as one civil and one military middle school.[1] Among them, these consumed 657,920 taels that year. Only 22,131 taels were spent on primary education in the city, and no grants appear to have been made to educational institutions elsewhere in the province.[2] Funds were thus flowing in one direction only, with no visible benefits to the localities whence they came. This should have been no novelty to the people of Hubei, who had been financing Zhang Zhidong's ambitious industrial schemes for years. There was at that time no provincial budget and thus no possibility of an allocation for education from it. Rather, schools were financed from different sources in an ad hoc manner. (Lest it be thought that such disarray is peculiar to backward Asian societies attempting to imitate the West, I would point out that public secondary education in England at the end of the nineteenth century was funded partially by ancient endowments, partially by the "whiskey money", a tax "intended originally to compensate publicans whose licenses had not been renewed.")[3] The greater part of the money came from revenue from the salt monopoly; additional sums were supplied by the consolidated tax bureau, the railway bureau, the lottery bureau, the provincial treasuries of Hubei and Hunan, a tax on suitcases, a contribution from a retired provincial commander, and fees paid by Hunanese students attending the schools in Wuchang. The money was transferred either directly from bureau to school or indirectly through the provincial administration.[4]

The educational accounts for Jiangxi province in 1907 show the same concentration on urban education and similarly varied sources of revenue. The main difference was that these had been sufficiently systematized to be presented in a table in the Ministry of Education's gazette. Revenues, of 68,160 taels and 100,000 strings of cash, came mainly from the land tax and other traditional sources. An education tax (*xuewu juan*) had been instituted, but the amount it would bring in was "still difficult to estimate." A small sum derived from former academy property and the cessation of ceremonies connected with the old examination system. The land tax receipts were to be split in a two-to-one ratio between the provincial capital's schools and those in the prefectures and counties. The remainder went toward financing Beijing University (no mention is made of any contribution to the expenses of the Ministry of Education), to the education of Jiangxi students abroad and in Beijing and Wuchang, and to educational administration and schools in the provincial capital. The figures given belie their formal presentation by internal contradictions and inconsistent totals, but are sufficient to indicate that a large part of governmental expenditures on schooling was concentrated on the provincial capital's higher schools.[5]

Not all provincial leaders emphasized *rencai jiaoyu*, in effect the training of a small elite, over the more recently fashionable *guomin jiaoyu*, or education for all citizens. In Zhili, Yuan Shikai and his lieutenants C. D. Tenney (an ex-missionary educator) and Yan Xiu laid the groundwork for widespread primary education. Although little of the Zhili Education Office's budget went directly to primary schools, 35 percent of the 1906 school allocation, or 102,490 taels, was spent on teacher training.[6] A small but significant item of expenditure in the same year's budget was 1,300 taels for publications using Wang Zhao's phonetic alphabet. Both Yuan and Yan, its first promoter, were convinced of the alphabet's merits through experience with their own households. Declaring the unity of the written and spoken language to be the basis of extending education to all citizens, Yuan ordered the alphabet taught in all elementary schools and included in the curriculum of higher primary and normal schools, a measure in which he was far in advance of the central government.[7] The Zhili Education Office also issued its own textbooks; here again, Yuan realized the new schools' potential for welding citizens together long before the Ministry of Education. A 1906 advertisement in the office's journal, founded before the Ministry of Education's bulletin and Shanghai's *Jiaoyu zazhi* (Educational Review), lists 35 titles for sale, including *Minjiao xiang'an* (The People and the Churches Should Be at Peace with One Another) and *Guomin bidu* (Basic Reading for Citizens).[8] The latter, a patriotic primer written by two returned students from Japan, appeared in a first edition of 100,000 copies.[9]

The vigor of Yuan's administration meant that by 1906 he could claim an average of twenty primary schools per county, with some thirty students in each.[10] Quality was not uniform: according to two inspectors, local authorities eager to comply with the letter of their instructions but indifferent to their spirit often sacrificed quality to quantity. After a disappointing visit to two sishu-like primary schools that had not responded to a personal demonstration of blackboard technique and modern teaching methods, the inspectors could only conclude that such schools were no better than nothing: "If it is fixed that a large county must have thirty [lower primary schools], a medium county twenty, and a small one ten, then departments and counties will fob off the provincial authorities with them, and the villages will fob off the departments and counties. Officials will not know how the people are managing, and the people will not know what officials are after. Some even wish to buy exemption, looking on schools as a kind of labor service."[11]

In Hubei, Zhang Zhidong had been converted by 1904 to the cause of primary education. He managed to fund it through an ingenious sleight of hand. Hubei's contribution to the Boxer indemnity extorted from China had been fixed at 1.2 million taels. Zhang had brought together the provincial governors, prefects, and county magistrates, who, in conjunction with gentry leaders, had settled the proportion of the burden to be borne by different localities and the means of raising money. The bulk of this came from land and poll taxes, supplemented by taxes on contracts and levies on shopkeepers. In September 1904, Zhang concluded that the indemnity could be paid from three recently developed sources of income: lottery profits and taxes on opium decoction and on minting. Magnanimously, he excused counties and prefectures not from raising the previously agreed on sum but from forwarding it to the provincial government. Instead, the tax money was to be used locally for schools, which would not only enlighten the people but would lead to unprecedented prosperity for agriculture, industry, and commerce.[12] Zhang thus achieved, albeit temporarily and in one region, what was to be an unfulfilled yearning of Chinese educationalists for decades: the allocation of a fixed sum for schooling, free from dependence on the whim of often unresponsive powerholders. (After months of unpaid salaries, staff at Beijing government schools led a movement for the independence of educational funds in 1920; in 1928, Shu Xincheng commented that since that time funding had fallen even further in arrears, in the provinces as well as in Beijing.)[13] In 1907, Hubei had the highest educational revenues of all the provinces. Zhang was so proud of his achievement that he incorporated a reference to it in one of the songs he wrote for Hubei schools:

> All provinces were busy raising the indemnity,
> The charge came down to the people and the merchants.
> Hubei province gave up its levies,
> And used this money to build up schools.[14]

The move met with widespread approbation. One statistic reveals the extent of the previous imbalance: educational revenues for the prefectures and counties were less than one-tenth that of the provincial capital in 1904. By 1905, when the remission had taken effect, the localities and the capital were nearly equal. The majority of educational funds, however, continued to be spent on Zhang's higher-level schools in Wuchang.[15] Moreover, whether funds were collected by the province or the locality, whether obtained by direct or indirect taxation, they were paid by the same people. In the short run at least, the foundation of the new schools and the heavier tax burden on craftsmen, shopkeepers, and peasants probably decreased rather than increased the prosperity of commerce, industry, and agriculture.

Even in Zhang Zhidong's own terms, the remission of tax revenues was not an unqualified success. Prefectural officials tended to follow Zhang's example and establish a prestigious middle school in the prefectural capital rather than a network of primary and normal schools.[16]

Lacking the financial leverage of the Hubei government, provincial officials elsewhere had to rely even more on exhortation as a means of prodding those responsible for local schools into action. Active provincial education offices sent out forms to prefectures and counties under their jurisdiction asking for truthful progress reports, but got back little reliable information. The powerlessness and lack of information that characterized the central government's dealings with the provinces were frequently repeated in provincial governments' dealings with the admin-

istrative divisions beneath them. The provision in the 1904 regulations
that "any official who deliberately delays the setting up of a school for
which funds and staff have already been obtained or who fobs off responsibility with a makeshift arrangement should be investigated by the
provincial educational office and reported to the governor with a request for punishment"[17] was an indication of concern over delinquency
rather than a realistic procedure to curb it.

The Ministry of Education attempted an administrative reorganiza-
tion to enlist the support of the local elite; in 1906, the ministry provided
for local educational exhortation bureaus (*quanxuesuo*) on the model of
those founded by Yan Xiu in Zhili. The provincial commissioner of education appointed the chief executive officer from among the local gentry; this officer, in turn, chose his own assistants, also from the local gentry.[18] Their duties were to win over local folk with arguments designed to
appeal to them (the school as a promoter of health, wealth, and virtue,
and as a replacement for the examination system), to calculate a locality's
need for schools and the funds available for their establishment, to
spread knowledge of educational principles, and to struggle against the
influence of bad gentry, foolish commoners, degraded sishu teachers,
and distracting brothels and gambling houses. The bureaus were less
successful than had been hoped: one observer commented that their
establishment

> means only that the localities have acquired another new word . . . the
> provincial education office cannot deal directly with officials who treat
> educational matters lightly, but must ask the governor to give them a
> black mark and dismiss them. But crafty officials and clerks . . . will say
> "I've discharged my responsibility adequately by setting up one or two
> primary schools." If pressed further, they end the matter with just two
> words, "inadequate funds." Moreover they use the name of the educa-
> tion tax to fool the common people and enrich themselves.[19]

Official apathy was difficult to combat; even worse was official corruption. The *dongcao* levy imposed by Jiangsu county officials was meant
for schools, but the more covetous officials held on to the money themselves.[20] As early as 1902, educational authorities in Sichuan had com-
plained that the founders of most new schools were either out to feather
their own nests or to make a name for themselves to advance their private ends and that teachers got their places by pulling strings.[21] In
Guangdong the following year, a magistrate was investigated for embez-
zlement of the 120,000 taels he had been permitted to levy for educational purposes.[22]

The Gentry Takeover

During the early years of the new school system, the foundation of schools was undertaken largely by officials. Zhang Zhidong's account of the allocation of responsibility for the raising of the Boxer indemnity and the injunctions in the 1904 regulations on the procedures to be followed in setting up schools make it clear that the authorities attached considerable importance to consultation and cooperation between the relatively isolated and dispersed local officials and the native gentry families. Several press accounts refer to a prefect's or a magistrate's calling together local gentry to discuss the founding of a new school. At first, gentry cooperation was not always forthcoming. The gentry often stood by with folded arms while officials discussed setting up schools, intervening only to obstruct the conversion of academies.[23]

The decision to change an academy into a school could be made unilaterally by an official. Once academy revenues had been used up, however, further funds had to come from increased local taxes and levies. These could be either indirect commodity taxes and likin or direct compulsory or voluntary levies. For the former, the agreement of the gentry was needed, for the latter, their active participation. The 1904 regulations provided that "local officials may select gentry members from their area and charge them with responsibility for the management of educational affairs. But in selecting such members of the gentry, only honorable and enlightened men with a reputation in their home district should be chosen. On no account should one let evil gentry and local bullies mix in among them, to perpetrate ill deeds and pursue private advantage to the detriment of educational progress."[24] In Zhili, "the key to the success of educational reform . . . was the support of urban and rural elites because it was not Yuan's administration, but they, along with local magistrates, who funded the new school system" through public contributions and increases in the land tax.[25]

Cooperation between officials and gentry in the promotion of education ranged from consultation on the disposal of county taxes, through deputation of gentry members to collect local levies, to cases where the initiative in fund raising from local sources was taken by gentry members and rubber-stamped by officials, to a nadir of unauthorized exactions by local bullies. The wheel turned full circle when overambitious gentry ventures had to apply for subsidies from county coffers or, if their own funds were exhausted, were taken over by the county or prefectural government.

From 1904–1905 on, there was a sharp rise in the number of community-funded (*gongli*) schools. Some were merely sishu under another name, but many appear to have been new foundations sponsored by members of the gentry. (See figure.) By 1909, the predominance of community-funded schools was established in all provinces except Hubei, where government schools had been dowered by Zhang Zhidong, and the remote and backward Xinjiang, Gansu, and Guizhou. Although the exact figures are suspect, they indicate growing gentry activity in the field of education.

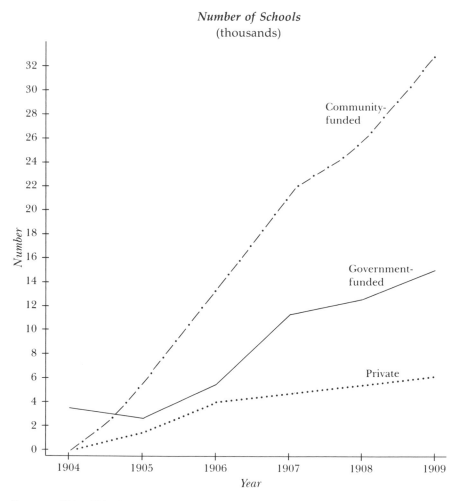

Number of Schools
(thousands)

SOURCE: China [Qing], Xue Bu, *Xuantong yuannian, disanci jiaoyu tongji tubiao* (Beijing, 1911), Gesheng, pp. 9–10.

The first year in which the number of community-sponsored schools exceeded the number of government schools was 1905, the year the examination system was abolished. It appears that the gentry, finding its normal path to advancement blocked, finally reconciled itself to using the new schools. Such an explanation may be an oversimplification. A 1904 article claimed that 60 or 70 percent of scholars had ceased taking the examinations when the topical dissertation replaced the eight-legged essay in 1901 and that attendance at prefectural and county examinations had fallen by two-thirds. Schools had failed to produce the expected results not because of the positive counterattraction of the examinations but because of their own defects. The aim of a school career was far from certain, unless it was to learn a little English in order to get a job with a foreign firm.[26] The concept of the new school was unfamiliar to most members of the gentry. Educational authorities in Beijing had not outlined the plan of the new system until 1902, and examples of its operation were at first few and slow to spread. It may have taken gentry members some time to realize that the wealth and power promised by the new schools were personal as well as national.

One scholar, writing in 1906, commented sarcastically on the gentry's takeover of the educational field. "If simply being a member of the gentry qualifies one to be in charge of education, I am at a loss to know what the difference between gentry and officials is."[27] An earlier article, published in October 1904 at the outset of gentry aggrandizement, was even more outspoken about "the 'dictatorship' of the gentry," who taxed shopkeepers and confiscated temple property in the name of education.

> Seeing monks fed without ploughing and clothed without weaving, rich though not officials . . . with gentlemen and women from the four quarters flocking as their benefactors, they think "Why is it that they can live like this and we can't?" and think daily of twisting their arms and snatching [their wealth] from them. Then they see the shopowners of all trades raising money in summer and winter for theatrical performances that are nominally to thank the gods but in reality are for their own enjoyment: music and singing pierce the clouds, the odor of wine and food hangs heavy. In the space of several days, they run through thousands and tens of thousands. And the gentry wonder "Why is this not ours but theirs?" and daily think of extracting the wealth from their purses.

Schools gave them an excuse for extortion approved from all sides, by the press, by officials, by foreigners.[28]

From the other side of the fence, the matter looked different. One early advocate of the new schools left a spirited account of a battle in a county in Guangxi between the dominant gentry family "representing feudal forces" and his own group of would-be school-founders "representing the forces of enlightenment and progress" over whether temple accommodations and locally raised funds were to stay with the militia or be taken over for a school. The militia leader, a juren named Huang,

> urged on men of the eighteenth militia unit to bring a suit against us for not respecting the temple of the God of Literature [the premises at issue]. We weren't afraid of him and brought an accusation against him of obstructing the progress of schools. The lawsuit was taken to Guilin [the provincial capital]. The head of the militia bureau shielded them, but the educational exhortation bureau and the commissioner for education were on our side. We won the lawsuit, and the militia were told to hand over the school site and the money. But Huang kept resisting and wouldn't give it up. We found out that Huang and his son ran gambling places . . . and again took the ill deeds of the pair to Guilin in a lawsuit. This way we finally overthrew their power and solved the question of the site and expenses of the new school. But Huang was still not content. In secret, he tried unceasingly to undermine us, slandering us by saying that our setting up a school was to spread the foreign religion, so that the peasants did not dare send their boys to school. We dealt with him by making house-to-house visits to exhort people and enroll students.[29]

Mobilization of Resources

However one assesses the motivation of those members of the gentry who busied themselves with education, it is clear that their chosen sources of revenue did not conflict with their own interests. Zhang Zhidong, a staunch Confucianist, had suggested as early as 1898 the expropriation of 70 percent of temple property to finance the new schools. He argued that in any case Buddhism and Taoism were entering a period of decline; Buddhism was already halfway into the last period of the law, and Taoism's spirits had lost their divinity.[30] Temples received a temporary respite when the Empress Dowager rescinded the edicts of the reform party in 1898, but were again in jeopardy when the founders of new schools cast about for sources of income.

The location of schools, particularly elementary schools, in temple premises was a time-honored tradition. It appears that such schools occupied the temple's spare room, while worship proceeded uninterrupted. The Japanese school system had begun in similar circumstances: an 1875 survey showed that 40 percent of new schools were housed in Buddhist temples.[31] In Britain in the 1870s, school boards organized "temporary schools in mission halls, chapels, and even under railway arches."[32] In China, such accommodation seems to have scandalized educationalists but been accepted with equanimity by the faithful. The ire of the latter was aroused only when temple property was wholly taken over for the schools. Gentry educationalists saw themselves as converting private religious property to public uses; the people saw them as taking property out of the public domain—temple worship, fairs, and theatrical performances were open to all comers—and converting it to the private interests of their own segment of society. The people did not believe their gods had "lost their divinity" and were distressed by their desecration. Guo Moruo recounts with zest his career as an infant iconoclast. His higher primary school had been converted from a temple. At first, he and his friends simply played in the hall of worship, but growing bolder—and incensed by the discovery of a hollow image formerly used by the monks to trick worshipers out of their money—Guo "started pushing over those idols, and then pissing on them. Afterwards the temple benefactors protested, and a wall was built outside the wooden railings and we had no way of getting in."[33] Protests could take a stronger form. Between 1904 and 1911, local mobs indignant at the confiscation of temple property destroyed twenty schools.[34] Such incidents continued into the Republican period. One case, in Hunan, had tragic consequences—a school was set on fire and two pupils thrown into the flames.[35]

Local gentry, who were "close at hand and better informed" than officials, led the way in the inventory and confiscation of temple property. After receiving official approval of their plans, they would take over property with estimated values of up to two or three hundred thousand taels.[36] Some monasteries and temples fought back, even affiliating themselves with Japanese counterparts to gain the protection of extraterritoriality. Others anticipated seizure by opening their own schools, either for the public—a praiseworthy move—or, in a more transparent subterfuge, for young monks.[37]

Another common method of funding new schools was "extra levies" (*paijuan*). These were part of a long tradition of cooperation between local officials and local gentry to raise money for public works such as roads, bridges, irrigation, and grain storage, the burden being borne chiefly by shopkeepers and tradesmen. They were now imposed on the same people on an ad hoc basis to fund one new school after another.

> Without the extra levies schools might have nothing with which to get started; without the name of the schools, one might not be able to collect the levies. But instead of urging education on people, they urge

taxes; indeed, not urge, but impose. Those on whom the taxes are imposed do not know what schools are, but because of the threats of officials and local gentry they contribute money they begrudge to a cause with which they have nothing to do. The people squirm under the accumulated authority of dictatorship. They may not resist, but if they don't hate officials they hate the gentry, or if they don't hate the gentry they hate the schools.[38]

"Voluntary contributions" (*lejuan*) were nominally distinct from extra levies, but in practice there seems to have been little that was voluntary about them. Like extra levies, they were raised freely to support particular schools.

Puritanism mingled with covetousness in the desire of Confucian gentry and officials to acquire money wasted, in their eyes, on such festivities as processions for the gods.[39] In at least three instances, the suppression of these activities caused riots against the new schools that benefited from the expropriation of funds.[40]

Whether gentry or official or a mixture of both, the financing of the new schools was an anarchic race to reach available sources of income before others carried them off. The composite nature of revenues can be seen in four examples from the Hangzhou prefectural gazetteer.

1. Public Benefit (Gong Yi) Combined Higher and Lower Primary School . . . Founded by Lu Jiarang and others. Opened Guangxu 32.4 [1906]. Annual income 1,500 yuan in voluntary contributions from the clerks of the finance and grain departments, 900 yuan in voluntary contributions from five silver ships, 252 yuan in voluntary contributions from the clerks of the finance department's general relief store . . . thirty odd pupils.

2. Qiantang Yuhang Tiaoxi Combined Higher and Lower Primary School . . . [Founded by] Zhong Yizhong and others . . . The opening expenses were met from voluntary contributions. Opened Guangxu 33.10 [1907]. Annual income approximately 300 yuan from transferred public property, 360 yuan from voluntary contributions, 1,100 yuan from extra levies, 32 yuan taken from fines, 528 yuan from students' boarding fees . . . 40 students.

3. The Tea Trade Combined Higher and Lower Primary School . . . Started by the Tea Trade's Wan Yun Pavilion in the winter of Guangxu 31 [1905]. Put a tax on bowls to provide income. Approved by the provincial office of education. Subsequently stopped several times because of disagreements. In the summer of Guangxu 33 [1907] switched to jointly borne indirect taxes (*gongren*). Raised

300,000 cash per month. Reopened in the eighth month. Income 245 yuan per month in jointly borne voluntary contributions from the tea trade . . . 24 pupils.

4. Qixi Combined Higher and Lower Primary School . . . in the old Qixi lecture hall. Opened in Guangxu 32.6 [1906]. Founded by Yao Shouci and others. Income transferred from the funds previously belonging to the lecture hall—taxes on silk, pawnshops, and rice, charity school fees, and temple property. In 33.9 [1907] added a tax on tea. In 34.10 [1908] added a contribution from Yang Dingqing. In the first year of Xuantong [1909] added a tax on the town's cooks. Receives a thousand-odd yuan annually from rent and taxes . . . 62 pupils.[41]

With money from so many different sources and no responsibility to account for it publicly, it is not surprising that among the founders of new schools were men who "built their fortunes through managing schools."[42] In April 1907, less than a year after the educational exhortation bureaus had been set up at the county level to encourage schooling, the Ministry of Education pleaded for more care in choosing their members: "Recently we have heard that some gentry members in the bureaus of the different provinces have used their office to detain the common people, some have had local officials pursue them with punishments, some have imposed harsh fines of large amounts. Of course they were motivated by the hope of raising large sums early and daily increasing the numbers of schools, not knowing that this is just what former sages called 'More haste, less speed.'"[43]

As this quotation indicates, many of those who promoted the new education were impelled by cupidity or the desire for power. Often they had no knowledge of or interest in education except as it served their own ends. One jaundiced observer, possibly putting the point of view of the professional educationalist, wrote, "They take the name of education in vain in order to manipulate public monies. They clash over power and compete over influence. Probably 90 percent of the middle-aged and older scholar-gentry who run schools and set up societies belong to this group."[44] Another objected that schools were regarded as a variety of yamen: their principal "does not need ordinary learning or a knowledge of teaching or discipline. The only question asked is whether he can call himself an expectant circuit intendant." When such a principal tears himself away from his drinking companions or the mahjongg table to visit the school, an army of retainers and school officials springs into action, only to melt away again on his departure. The only one at all assiduous in his duties is the bursar, who pores over abacus and account book working out his percentage of the provision bill or the school building materials or textbooks fund. "From the inner sanctum of the principal right down to the gatekeeper, everybody gets his cut."[45]

Government schools often maintained an official grandeur of establishment. In Hangzhou in 1903, six schools employed among themselves some 140 servants, approximately one to every three students.[46] A middle school in Zhili was even more luxurious, with ten servants for nine pupils.[47] Shu Xincheng, who entered a modern school for the first time in 1908, recalled the air of gilded youth that differentiated it from the academy and sishu he had previously attended: not only were there gatekeepers, messengers, cooks, and kitchen hands, but also a servant to every two bedrooms and studies. Students were even waited on at mealtimes.[48]

Political Consequences

As members of the gentry extended their operations into areas previously the preserve of officialdom, they began to demand political power commensurate with their responsibilities. Although much locally raised money went into local schools, there was no clear demarcation between funds to be retained by the locality and those to be remitted to the county or provincial center.[49] A somewhat hyperbolic statement of gentry grievances is given in a 1909 article on "local self-government and education": "In the years since our state, seeking strength, changed its laws and began running schools, each prefecture, department, and county has scraped off the flesh and blood of our kith and kin, and somehow or other, under pressure of orders from above, set up one or two schools . . . they have sought out the funds of each locality and carried them off to the city," where a good education was enjoyed by "officials and one or two urban gentry."[50] The cities benefited not only from the presence of prestigious colleges and other government schools but from their position as a locus of educational endeavor for private persons and public bodies. "In Shantung the schools that received the subsidies usually were located in [the provincial capital of] Tsinan. This meant that aspiring educational modernizers from all over the province were drawn into Tsinan in hopes of obtaining official monies to support their new schools."[51]

The educational exhortation bureaus were originally intended to enlist gentry support for the promotion of education by local officials.

4. Peasants Ransacking a School (*Xingqi huabao*, no. 1 [1906])

Though not holders of official positions, members of the bureaus owed their position to official appointment. The institution thus lagged behind gentry demands for control of their own affairs. The government finally acceded to these demands under pressure from a growing constitutional movement supported by gentry and rich merchants who "saw in the assemblies an even more effective means than the examinations for assuring their own status and power."[52] In 1908, regulations for local self-government at the city, town, and district levels were promulgated, followed in 1909 by regulations for self-government at the prefectural, departmental, and county level. The first provincial assembly elections were held that same year.

Education and self-government were overlapping areas of gentry influence. One could qualify for election to provincial assemblies by having held an educational position for three years or by being a middle or higher school graduate. In local self-government, too, "the majority of those involved were educationalists."[53] Under the regulations, educational institutions up to the level of middle school and their concomitant fund raising came under the jurisdiction of the local assemblies. Since the educational exhortation bureaus had not been relieved of responsibility for educational fund raising, areas that had set up both local assemblies and the bureaus experienced some confusion until the powers of the latter were redefined at the beginning of 1911.[54]

Self-government bodies institutionalized the gentry's right to raise funds from the local population. The gentry extended the experience gained in extracting money for schools to funding a variety of projects, not least the local government offices themselves. Local government demands coincided with pressure from the center for increased tax revenues to service foreign loans and pay indemnities. In neither case were new sources of revenue tapped or old ones rationalized; the method was rather to pile a few cents here, a few cents there, on every possible commodity or service. The total tax burden was heavy, as the British consul in Changsha noted on the eve of the 1911 Revolution:

> The various districts in the province also seem to find great difficulty in making both ends meet, chiefly on account of the expense involved by the introduction of numerous reform measures. Much ingenuity is shown in devising new forms of taxation to meet expenditures on local self-government, police and education. Among these are additional levies based on the land tax and the tribute rice and land transfer fees; taxes on shops and houses and on rentals; on the slaughter of pigs and oxen; on iron, paper, hides, timber, coal, beans, salt, tobacco leaf, oil and steamer tickets; on the export of rice, pigs, pottery, tobacco and wine; on wheelbarrows and brothels; and on cases submitted to arbitration. There is little doubt that taxation is advancing by leaps and bounds; and it is much to be deplored that the money raised is expended to so little good purpose, thus rendering the new taxes doubly unpopular.[55]

The people were not passive under these exactions. New taxes for the schools sparked 43 out of a recorded 120 instances of peasant riots against schools.[56] Riots against local self-government were often closely connected with education: out of 37 incidents in Jiangsu in 1910 and 1911, 13 involved the destruction of schools. In Haizhou, rioters threw the teachers into a cesspit—a far cry from the respect supposed to be accorded to the scholar.[57]

In these conflicts gentry and officials were often at odds. One researcher characterized the struggle as one between the new emerging forces—self-government personnel—and the old forces—local bullies, monks, and officials. Since the growth of self-government eroded the power of local officials, the latter allied themselves with opium smokers, the illiterate, the unemployed, and others not qualified to vote in self-government elections.[58] Another observer detected the same divide, albeit with a different allocation of praise and blame: "The gentry became the primary object of popular discontent, and at times the government officials sympathized with the masses. Previously, it had been government officials who collected taxes, embezzled money, and ordered the common people around. Now it was the gentry."[59]

Overall, the decade from the edict ordering the establishment of a new school system in 1901 to the fall of the Qing in 1911 saw a shift to predominantly gentry control of the new schools and to greater autonomy for the gentry in local affairs.[60] In the first stages of this transition, the promotion of schooling was primarily the duty of officials; gentry were consulted on proposed measures and entrusted with their implementation. The delegation of official functions to members of the gentry was standardized by the establishment of county-level educational exhortation bureaus in 1906. Meanwhile, a rapidly increasing number of schools were being set up on the initiative of local gentry. Official delegation and gentry assumption of the power to tax the local population and appropriate public property for educational purposes were among the conditions that led to demands for local self-government. The gentry's unprecedented assumption of a formal political role led to new tensions among gentry, officials, and the central government on the one hand, and between gentry and the mass of the people on the other.[61]

6
Social Implications
of the New Schools

The school systems evolved in Europe and transferred to Japan were universal, compulsory, and practically oriented. Their Chinese propagandists had chosen them for these characteristics, which they assumed would be replicated in China. For Liang Qichao, education could be made universal by fiat. Educational bureaucrats were little more realistic: the 1902 regulations called for a minimum of one school per district (*xiang*) as a preliminary to compulsory schooling, and in 1907 Luo Zhenyu drew up a detailed timetable for implementation of this regulation, beginning with large centers of population and working down to the village level.[1] In practice, fee-paying universal education turned out to be a contradiction in terms for a rural population in a subsistence economy, and the beneficiaries of the new schools were not too different from those who had used the old ones. Like their predecessors, they hoped for government office and, like them, settled for teaching jobs. The chief differences were a rise in the cost of higher education and a change in its content, both of which lessened rural opportunities for advancement.

The Intake of the New Schools

Differences exist over whether the new school system broadened or restricted access to education.[2] My own assessment is that the new schools drew their students largely from those who would otherwise have attended sishu; that is, for some time after their introduction they did not enlarge the educated class, but rather segregated a portion of it in new educational institutions.[3] The common assumption among modern writers that the schools were breaking new ground in terms of enrollment and that no one outside them received formal education is erroneous.

Education and Elite Status

The new system did, however, affect perceptions of educational opportunity. Formerly, the scholar had been a charge on his family while he was being educated, but could frequently expect public support—as a stipended scholar or academy student—once he reached the higher levels. The new system partially reversed the cost structure. There was little or no charge for elementary education, but fees for the upper levels were higher. This change, as well as the abolition of the state examinations in 1905, made it difficult for the "poor" scholar to find a foothold in higher education. The deprivation was especially keen because the rhetoric of the new schooling had raised expectations.

The road to the top had never been an open highway in the past; although it is often assumed that a poor boy could "study with the village teacher" for the examinations, the average village teacher was a byword for ignorance. A family that wished its son to progress would often make considerable sacrifices to send him a distance away to a teacher with a good reputation and correspondingly high fees.[4] Such education, however, involved no long-term commitment, whereas the modern schools insisted on a fixed and continuous period of study, valueless unless completed. For this reason and because the cost of boarding at a modern school was higher than that of studying under a well-known teacher— the overhead was higher—the generalist (nonvocational) stream of the new schools eventually excluded from advanced study the majority of the inhabitants of rural areas. This pattern persisted through the Republican period: the 1932 gazetteer for Wanyuan county, Sichuan, an area with a population of over 200,000, stated that "the cost of living has gradually risen and no one can afford school fees. Those who study outside the province after middle school are rare. Middle-level families cannot even afford to stay in middle schools." Old-style scholars were said to lead a simple life in the countryside, while the younger generation swaggered in the towns.[5]

The changes described above took effect gradually. The 1902 school system took a middle way between charging fees and giving allowances; that is, it drew up a schedule of monthly fees ranging from 30 cents for lower elementary to two yuan for higher schools, but waived the fees for all but the highest levels during the first five years of the system's operation.[6] The suggested fees did not apply to private schools, which were free to set their own, nor did they include the cost of boarding where this was necessary. In practice, the 1902 regulations were largely ignored. In this period, the school system was building on former academies and could indulge in temporary democracy. The new schools acquired not only the academies' property but their ethos. Most continued to offer allowances to those who passed their entrance examinations at a level that admitted them to the school's regular quota of pupils. (Additional students had to meet their own expenses.) Such generous provision was in part the result of custom, in part a deliberate attempt to attract students away from the examinations to the newly founded schools. A county-level school in Zhili remained attractive to its small intake—six regular and three reserve students out of thirteen who took the entrance examination—only by giving every student an allowance of 2,000 cash per month; even then, there was no guarantee that they would turn up when classes started.[7] In Shandong, the Qingzhou prefectural middle school "exhausted every inducement" to attract pupils from the ten counties in the prefecture, but in 1904 had only 60. Recruiting students "was as hard as recruiting soldiers" since the sons of poor families could not afford the time away from the fields and the well-to-do still pinned their hopes on the state examinations. The allowances seem to have attracted students from relatively humble families, as they all took the harvest season off to go home and help in the fields.[8] The Jiangxi Higher School gave its students varying allowances. Places at both schools were allocated according to county rather than through an open entrance examination.[9] Military schools recruited their pupils in a similar fashion. One writer whose elder brother had taken the state military examinations before they were abolished was chosen as one of the quota of two for his county to attend the new Jiangxi Military School. "At that time people were still backward, and those of good family regarded this as an inferior course. Magistrate Peng . . . considered that I was a filial son . . . and had me take the examination [for entry]. After the subject was given, we were allowed to take it home to write the answer there, handing back the paper the next day." The writer came from a family of small farmers that had branched out into the transport business. Since they could not afford the cost of his trips to the provincial capital, he raised it from a former teacher with one of the old military degrees and other friends who went so far as to sacrifice their family jewelry for this purpose.[10]

Study at the new schools remained suspect in places with relatively little Western influence for some time after it had been accepted in more cosmopolitan centers. In such areas, cash inducements were necessary to attract new students; elsewhere, the practice was not uniform. In Hang-zhou in 1903 only the Military School covered expenses and gave an al-lowance. Other government schools—the university (later renamed a higher-level school), the middle school, and two county schools of uncer-tain level—did not charge tuition fees, but collected 2.4 yuan per month from each student to cover the cost of board. The Sericulture School covered expenses but gave no allowances. (These schools appear to have been new institutions rather than converted academies.)[11]

The 1904 regulations made primary and normal school education in government schools free; other government schools could institute charges at the discretion of local authorities. The justification of school fees in the decree points to a change in attitudes toward the relationship between state and scholars. No longer was it a symbiosis in which the state nurtured the talents placed at its disposal. The authors of the new system—principally Zhang Zhidong—believed that students had taken advantage of free education to be idle and unruly; charging fees was thus a political move aimed at restraining student unrest. They could also point to the shortage of funds for the establishment of new schools to say that the remission of fees impeded rather than increased the spread of the new education.

At the start of 1907, the Ministry of Education issued further reg-ulations on school fees, setting them at a maximum of 30 cents a month for lower primary schools and 60 cents for higher primary, one to two yuan for middle schools, and two to three for higher-level schools. Nor-mal schools took a quota of nonpaying students.[12] Military schools, which were outside the regular school system, also subsidized their students. The regulations in themselves did not fix fees—as late as 1908 a county higher primary school in Hunan met all expenses of its students from the academy property it had inherited.[13] Conversely, schools not thus dowered charged fees in excess of those fixed by the ministry: their min-imum was said to range from 50 cents a month to one or two yuan. Sishu attendance was cheaper.[14] Newly founded schools were in no position to offer the incentives that converted academies could provide. At the same time, the number of academies had been too small to furnish anything but the skeleton of a school system.[15] The disappearance of allowances was an inevitable concomitant of the new schools' expansion.

If government schooling was dear, the best private and mission schools were prohibitive for all but the wealthy. Nankai Middle School in Tianjin, founded by Yan Xiu, charged three yuan per month for tui-tion, five for food, and one for lodging.[16] Mingde in Changsha, which achieved fame rivaling Nankai's through its early revolutionary connec-tions and the longevity of its founder, charged 60,000 cash (approximately $70) per annum.[17] Mission schools' fees varied with local demand. Most middle schools in the capital and in provincial centers charged between $30 and $70 a year for board and tuition, with varying arrangements for reduction of fees for church members or scholarship winners.[18] Such fees were a struggle for the poor: a pupil at a Beijing mission school, son of a widow who lived by letting out rooms to dubious tenants, could remain at school only by doing well in term examinations and thus having the next term's fees remitted. The school charged 20 to 30 cash a month for day pupils and two yuan odd for boarders at the primary level. For middle school, the boarding fees were six yuan for nonbelievers and four for converts.[19] In China's great trading centers, headquarters of the foreign presence, schools exclusively for the rich grew up; Shanghai's Anglo-Chinese School stated frankly that it aimed at "providing a good education to Chinese lads of good standing who can afford to pay substantial fees."[20] Schools and colleges like St. John's (annual fees in 1910 $216 plus $27 for uniforms and supplies) and McTyeire's for girls (annual fees $168 plus $25) became the aristocrats of mission education.[21]

In the government system, higher primary schools were the selection point for further education.[22] In practice, it was not necessary to have gone to a lower primary school to attend one of these since they had their own entrance examination. Attendance at a higher primary replaced the old degrees as a claim to educated status; entry to middle school, like a shengyuan degree—which had originally marked its bearer as student at a government school, the school-temple—meant that one's feet were set on the ladder of success. In terms of social mobility, attendance at a lower primary school meant little more than attendance at a sishu. Zhili, with a population of over 30 million, had 209,668 places in lower primary schools for a school-age population of approximately 2.5 million in 1909. There were then 9,467 students attending higher primary schools. In Sichuan, the ratio was similar: 294,650 pupils in lower primary, 13,956 in higher.[23] Japan had deliberately and successfully implemented a two-tier system of education, with mass compulsory schooling surmounted by a highly selective and competitive system of higher education. In Japan, however, access to higher education was seen as based upon academic merit; in China, it was felt that merit came second to money.

As a whole the new school system was not an organ of elite education since only a fraction of those attending the new schools later joined the elite. But it was an expression of elite aspirations in two senses: it expressed the aspirations of an elite—the popular voice in its formation was negligible—and it was seen as a pathway into the elite, however seldom that path was trodden.

Mass Education and Social Reform

Both social and political motives inspired the nineteenth century's leap into mass education. In England the first was predominant: the specter of a "half-naked, savage, and starving population" drawn into the slums of swollen cities gave a powerful stimulus to mass schooling. A London school official went so far as to say that "if it were not for her five hundred elementary schools London would be overrun by a horde of young savages."[24] Japanese educators, though also sensitive to the necessity of keeping the masses in their place, saw universal education chiefly as an instrument for realizing the goals of the nation-state: a disciplined citizenry meant a strong state. Zhang Zhidong, who still thought primarily in terms of the training of talent, did not exploit either the alarm of the propertied or the zeal of the patriotic in the service of mass schooling. Consequently his regulations bear a slightly anachronistic character. Many of his fellow officials, however, were more alert to social problems and political opportunities.

Both Britain and Japan relied largely on the regular school system to inculcate approved values in the mass of the people but used supplementary means to reach the working poor: Sunday schools in England, simplified three-year elementary schools in Japan (unlike the regular four-year course, these were free after 1886). In absolute terms, China's achievement in building a regular primary school system in the last years of the Qing was considerable: some 50,000 primary schools took in nearly 1.5 million pupils in 1909.[25] Relative to population, however, China's showing was less impressive. Japan had 41 percent of its school-age children in school by 1878, the sixth year of the new system; the corresponding figure for China in 1909 was only about 2.5 percent, although the figure would undoubtedly have been higher had the authorities adopted a more lenient policy toward recognition of sishu. In any event, it was clear that regular fee-paying schooling left the lumpenproletariat untouched. Both prudence and charity called for a remedy.

Early Concern. In Changsha, measures were taken by provincial leader Duan Fang, who as early as 1902 ordered that 30 free schools be set up to teach illiterate and semiliterate young men "with a view to their coming to a gradual understanding of principles as they learn to read, so that they will be able to make a living and not break the law." The announcement, written in popular language, emphasized the resulting civil order as a boon to shopkeepers—who had to stand guarantor for would-be students—and promised unspecified but limited benefits to the students themselves, who were not to "have other expectations" than the pleasure of study for its own sake. Duan Fang was trying to dampen rising expectations associated with a higher educational level.[26]

Duan Fang's attempt to establish free schools can be regarded as a continuation of charity schools for the poor. More definitely modern in character were the craft and welfare bureaus (*gongyi ju* and *jiaoyang ju*), inspired by Japanese models, set up to deal with idlers and vagrants in the cities.[27] In Tianjin, the Welfare Bureau tried to rehabilitate young beggars off the streets.[28] Although the discipline and regularity of modern institutions appealed to those who wished to control rootless idlers, it appalled the idlers themselves. In Baoding in Zhili, the poor were unwilling to attend and even more unwilling to work. Wuchang found its Craft Bureau of so little use that it built a normal school on the site.[29]

Vocational Training.   The rehabilitation of vagrants and petty criminals overlapped with training for respectable workmen and apprentices. The 1904 regulations included provision for schools for apprentices, but few appear to have been set up. Statistics issued by the Ministry of Education in 1907 and 1909 do not list apprentice training separately. "Preparatory industrial courses" enrolled slightly over 4,000 pupils in 67 schools in 1909.[30] A report on education in Henan in 1907 records only two apprentices' schools, with a total of 50 pupils.[31] Those set up seemed to be scattered local initiatives rather than part of a national plan.

Competition from Western goods added urgency to programs for training in manufacture. The commissioner for education in Zhejiang linked moralizing over the disreputable poor with national consciousness of Western encroachment: "The recent rise in prices and the declining ability of ordinary people to make a living are due to the influx of foreign goods . . . since most of the poor cannot afford schooling, they discard work in favor of amusement; merchants are dishonest and craftsmen shoddy." His remedy was the attachment of schools for apprentices to existing primary schools.[32]

Despite isolated examples to the contrary, lower-level technical education was not a priority for either school founders or school attenders during the Qing. Many businesses found their old skills adequate for unmodernized trades and continued to use traditional methods of recruitment and on-the-job training. Their conservatism was not necessarily simply the result of China's lack of modern industry (recent work on Japanese technical education indicates that it developed first in small-scale traditional industries in the 1890s).[33] Rather, it was associated with the degree of integration with the foreign world. Thus when the Ministry of Commerce tried to put Chinese firms on a better footing to compete with foreigners by ordering special classes to be set up for apprentices, the best response came from firms in Shanghai. The Shanghai Cotton Trade Association, for instance, started remedial classes to which each member-firm could send two apprentices. In addition to Chinese, English, and arithmetic, students could attend special lectures on such subjects as law and economics.[34]

Some new types of employment necessitated the training of illiterate recruits. In Jiangsu, for example, policemen had to be taught to read the regulations defining their duties.[35] Attempts were also made in the new army to raise the educational level of enlisted men. In the main, however, education continued, as Duan Fang had feared, to be associated with hopes of upward mobility; and this was even truer of the new schools than of sishu.

Half-day Schools.   Another approach to the expansion of education was distinctive not for the nature of its provisions but for its students. In Tianjin, the indefatigable innovator Yan Xiu set up a half-day school especially for poor boys whose families were dependent on their children's labor. Enthusiastically following his example, the local gentry had set up more than 10 of these schools by August 1903 and were planning 30 more, all "leaving nothing undone for the welfare of the poor and the enlightenment of the ignorant."[36] Since, with typical bureaucratic insensitivity to economic constraints, neither the 1902 nor the 1904 regulations allowed for part-time schools, organization and curricula were left to their founders. Subjects ranged from the practical—teaching the three R's, physical education, and morals[37]—to the baroque: one proposed school would have taught the sons of the poor, logic, Chinese, Japanese, morals, foreign and Chinese history and government, geography, mathematics, biology, physics, drawing, sports, and "method of playing."[38]

Chinese philanthropists had long been eager to provide for the education of the poor but promising. In the early 1900s, this commitment developed into a concern for the education of the masses regardless of individual potential. Self-interest and altruism were combined in such enterprises; as one advocate of charity schools stated frankly, the livelihood of the people was the best security for the property of the rich.[39]

The new Ministry of Education (of which Yan Xiu, founder of the first one, was then vice-president) approved half-day schools in 1906, in response to a memorial pointing out that most of those attending the new schools came from rich families and that the poor, who had a living to make, had difficulty in attending. The memorialist proposed as a solution half-day schools for every two or three hundred families, to "inculcate an understanding of principles and form decent behavior."[40] Since half-day schools were cheaper to run than regular ones, his plan was marginally more practical than Luo Zhenyu's timetable for universal education, but it was destined to equal lack of fulfillment; by 1909, fewer than a thousand half-day schools existed in China.[41]

Despite the good intentions of their founders, the half-day schools missed their mark. The working poor for whom the schools were intended were "as yet insensible to their benefits."[42] Their place appears to have been taken by pupils from relatively humble families alarmed by the profusion of subjects and lengthy hours of the regular schools but sufficiently well off to dispense with the labor of one of their members and to prize literacy. They probably came from a group that would previously have attended a cheap, open-entry sishu rather than hired a family tutor; the half-day school won them away from the sishu because it was free.[43]

A partial reason for the failure of part-time schools to win workers to education may have been the attitude of some of their founders, which resembled the mixture of horror and contempt that urban educationalists had for country folk. An article expounding the benefits of night classes for adults conveys equally strongly, if unintentionally, the limited vision of the schools' advocates. The writer expressed the concern felt by promoters of citizenship education that an uneducated populace would be defeated in the international struggle for survival, but most of his remarks dealt with the masses in a domestic context. Remedial education would, he hoped, transform these rumor-spreading, trouble-making malcontents and mobs of country bumpkins into good citizens. Possibly it might even transform the inconceivable squalor of their home life.[44] Among apostles of enlightenment hostility toward the sin moved easily into intolerance of the sinner, a confusion that could hardly have endeared the reformers to the objects of their mission.

Mass Education and State Intervention

The central government came to mass education later than the social reformers of the cities and with different motives: chiefly, the inculcation of mass patriotism and loyalty. It did not fully exploit this motif, firmly established in Japanese education since the 1890s, until plans for a constitutional government were announced in 1909. The Ministry of Education then drew up a preparatory program, including the establishment of simple reading schools (*jianyi shizi xueshu*) for adult illiterates and the children of the poor. They were established primarily for ideological indoctrination, as distinct from the half-day schools that arose from a mixture of prudential and charitable motives. The ministry drew up special readers stressing moral and civic education. They were to be accompanied by the primary-school text *Guomin bidu*, previously used in Zhili under Yuan Shikai, which emphasized the value of education, military spirit, and loyalty to the state, and by that staple of mass education, the Amplified Instructions of the Yongzheng emperor.[45] The government was attempting to ensure that when a constitution was finally promulgated, voters would understand their duties in the same way as their rulers did.

With training in the abacus or arithmetic, these texts constituted the sole subjects of study; the course was completed when they were read. Graduation took from one to three years, after which pupils would be eligible to enter the fourth class of lower primary school. Like sishu, the simple reading schools required chiefly the knowledge of sanctioned texts and allowed a flexible amount of time for their mastery. The ministry recommended that where regular schools already existed, the reading schools be attached to them as night schools.[46] The ministry appears to have preferred this arrangement because it would not siphon off pupils from regular schools, as independent half-day schools would.

Figures for 1911, if reliable, indicate that the program was relatively successful. Zhili had the largest number of reading schools (4,160 with nearly 70,000 pupils), followed by Sichuan and Henan. In addition, Sichuan claimed to have nearly 200,000 pupils studying the same curriculum at "reformed" sishu. The approximate total of reading schools nationwide was 16,000, with an estimated attendance of over 280,000.[47]

The simple reading school appears to have been a successful compromise between the demands of modernists and the inertia of tradition. As the memorial on their establishment stated, they were cheap to set up and demanded little of their teachers. Pupils did not need to buy expensive texts and had sufficient time to pursue a livelihood outside school hours.[48] Their moral content, concentration on reading, and flexible organization placed them in the familiar context of sishu; at the same time, one's bureaucratic superiors regarded their establishment as creditable, they performed the progressive function of preparing the way for a constitution, and their pupils were credited with the equivalent of three years' study at lower primary school. Their dual nature probably accounts for their rapid spread.

Professional educators, however, saw the good as the enemy of the best. In Jiangsu, after the 1911 Revolution, the governor ordered that simple reading schools be disbanded, not because they were inappropriate in a changed political situation but because it was pedagogically undesirable to have the same classes for children and adults and because administrators were taking the easy way out and setting up simple reading schools in place of regular schools.[49]

The reasons given for disbanding these schools and the fate of half-day schools in Tianjin suggest that part-time education competed with lower primary schools for pupils from groups that would previously have attended sishu. Neither appears to have created a demand for education where none existed before. The lines between old-style sishu, reformed sishu, simple reading schools, and lower primary schools were blurred, but it appears that no reform or innovation extended the circle of schooling significantly. Only in one area was totally new ground broken: the government began to interest itself in schooling for women.

The Education of Women

No statutes had barred women from the examinations; the two simply never came into association, the connection was unthinkable outside the pages of a novel.[50] This does not mean that no girl was ever educated. Girls from well-to-do families often attended their brothers' classes at home until they reached the age of puberty; some were even provided with their own tutors. In the 1890s, the popular novelist Bao Tianxiao had given lessons in Suzhou to the young daughter of an educated family in her own home.[51] Public schooling, however, was another matter. South China, and particularly Guangzhou, seems to have been the most enlightened area in this regard. One nineteenth-century woman missionary visited two Chinese girls' schools with 65 pupils between them, "all from wealthy families," and knew of another 31 schools. A survey of missionary education for women in South China concluded that "native schools in South China formed a part of the sure foundation on which Protestant mission schools for girls were established."[52]

In most parts of China, however, girls received an education at home or not at all. When Liang Qichao drew up plans for a girls' school in 1897,[53] the only modern public schooling open to girls was run by missionaries and catered mainly to the daughters of converts and to destitute girls (although the American Southern Methodist Mission had set up, in McTyeire Home in Shanghai, a school "open for the special purpose of getting pupils from the higher class families, who have hitherto refused to send their daughters to an ordinary mission school").[54] The Chinese schools opened for girls in the 1900s continued to cater to extremes on the social scale. In 1902, the Empress Dowager was reported to be considering hiring a teacher for Western subjects for her palace women; in Fuzhou in the same year, a girls' school managed to recruit only prostitutes and the very poor.[55]

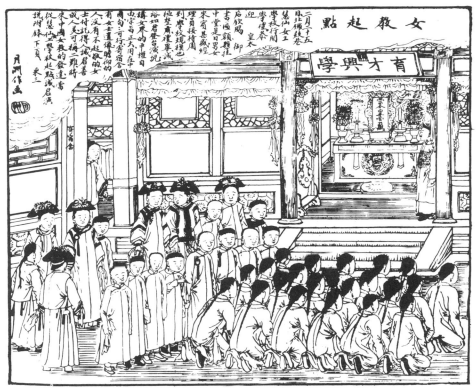

5. Girl Students Combining Piety with Learning
at a Beijing School (*Xingqi huabao*, no. 23 [1907])

Zhang Zhidong's conservatism in social matters is evident in his exclusion of women from public education in the 1904 school regulations.
Female education was to be confined to the home since "in China's present circumstances, the setting up of schools for women would lead to numerous evils"—chiefly, apparently, the desire to choose one's own mate.
Zhang offered a curious compromise: the inmates of widows' homes (a
charitable institution) were to be taught childcare so that they could seek
employment, but all other women were to receive instruction indirectly
through reprints and translations read at home.[56]

On his return from Beijing to Hubei, Zhang disbanded a school for
young women attached to Hubei's only kindergarten, fearing the infec-
tion of dissident ideas and consequent destruction of morality. In its
place, he set up the Revere Chastity School to train governesses for rich

families and another for respectable wetnurses.[57] Both were to be staffed by Japanese women since no Chinese women were qualified to teach and no male teachers were permitted. Zhang's action ran counter to the wishes of the governor of Hubei, Duan Fang, who had set up the school.[58] The incident reveals the extent to which the personal support or enmity of local or provincial leaders influenced the nature of the educational institutions under their jurisdiction. Another example comes from Guangdong, where in 1904 the educational authorities favored schools for women provided they equipped them with the domestic skills necessary for successful motherhood.[59]

Despite the specific interdiction of girls' schools in the 1904 regulations, their numbers and popularity continued to grow. Mission boarding schools for girls in Wuchang were "well filled" by 1906. Those with less money or more prejudices could hire a lady governess to attend for a few hours a day.[60] Some Chinese schools were set up under official patronage, others by women or by the male relatives of educable girls. Would-be educators from outside aroused the greatest suspicion. A magistrate in Changzhou inveighed against unreliable outsiders whose championship of female education ignored Changzhou's past accomplishments in this area. He went so far as to prohibit girls' schools, together with gambling by women.[61] In the south, the Liang-guang commissioner for education emphasized the need for the utmost caution in staffing girls' schools. "Half of those who support this kind of thing," he stated, "are young men, whose boldness makes enemies even aside from the possibility of actual misconduct."[62] Suspected sexual immorality drew moralists irresistibly. As late as the mid-1920s, a lecturer at Chengdu Girls' Normal School had to flee for his life from a lynch mob after developing photographs in a darkroom with a girl student.[63] As in Victorian England, it was heterosexual relations that disturbed the imagination of the pure. Homosexual friendships among boys were not uncommon in boarding schools, but did not attract attention.[64]

Schooling for women was not made a part of the national school system until 1907, when regulations were issued for girls' primary and normal schools (not middle schools, although some had already been established by Chinese; Bao Tianxiao was invited to teach in one in Shanghai).[65] The regulations had little effect, but are interesting as a conservative attempt to grapple with the conflicting goals of enlightening and restricting women. The preservation of morality had first priority: no girls' schools were to be set up unless female teachers and a headmistress could be obtained. Respectable gentlemen over fifty might manage the school's affairs, especially those involving contact with the outside world, but their offices had to be separate from the school building.[66] In the absence of trained women teachers, this was a counsel of perfection; most girls' schools had to employ male teachers. In cosmopolitan Shanghai they were taken for granted; according to Bao, they were often at the mercy of the badinage of their high-spirited pupils.[67] In the interior the proprieties might need to be more strictly observed. The inspector of a girls' school in Wuhu, Anhui, commented approvingly that the head of the school was present in the classroom throughout any lessons given, unavoidably, by male teachers.[68]

Sexual and political radicalism, the twin bogeys for the framers of the 1907 regulations, were to be held at bay by a series of exemplary stories of female behavior from the Zhou dynasty on. Dissolute theories on breaking down the barriers between the sexes or choosing one's own mate were to be firmly repudiated, as were political gatherings and speeches.[69] In 1908, the Ministry of Education asked the governor of Jiangsu to investigate a girls' school in Chongming County whose student body and faculty—several men, a widow, and a Japanese woman— had been accused of stirring up local women with speeches on freedom and equal rights.[70] Despite their rarity, such incidents appear to have colored the public's picture of girl students, giving them a dashing and dangerous image. The word "free" acquired a double meaning. Just after the 1911 Revolution, children in Changsha used to run alongside women with the modern "butterfly" hairstyle chanting "Butterfly head, butterfly head, on about freedom, wants to be free," or "Let's see, are you free?"[71] Respectable schools went to some pains to rid these terms of their dubious connotations. Equal rights, said the speaker at a Beijing school's opening day, meant "an educated woman, able to manage her own household and tasks, and thus the same as a man." Freedom was the self-regulation that ensured that every act accorded with what was right—to be distinguished from rudeness to one's elders and wild behavior.[72] A popular magazine reiterated that true equality would come through study, not through slogans.[73] Carrying on about freedom gave one a certain "air"; an inspector particularly commended a Jiangsu girls' school because its pupils had none of this "air" about them.[74]

The consternation aroused by schooling for girls was out of proportion to the numbers involved. With the exception of those missionary schools that provided free education for the daughters of converts and a small number of charitable enterprises founded by Chinese, schooling for women—even more than for men—was an elite phenomenon requiring both wealth and Westernization. Yang Buwei, whose father and grandfather had both gone abroad on Chinese missions to Europe, took $310—enough to support a family in modest comfort for a couple of years—to Shanghai's McTyeire school as pocket money.[75] Since many areas had no schools for girls, the cost of boarding was often added to tuition fees. (As late as 1918–19, 532 of the 1,819 county-level units had no girls' schools. Coeducation was by then permissible but rare.)[76] The education of daughters was a luxury since a girl would leave her family of origin to serve her husband's. Since many schools forbade footbinding, schooling might make a daughter less rather than more marriageable for those who believed that "buying an ox, you buy a pair of horns; marrying a wife, you marry a pair of [bound] feet."[77] Statistics vary, but it appears that girl students occupied between 1 and 2 percent of the total student body in the new schools. In 1909, 13,489 girls attended schools[78] —roughly 7 of every 100,000 women. Few of these took up the cause of freedom and equal rights. The symbolic significance of girl students was due not to their actual numbers but to the breach they created in the Three Bonds and Five Constant Virtues (*gangchang*)—the basic ordering of state and family, synonymous with Confucianism. The possible emancipation through education of gentry women created far more tension among the elite than the extension of schooling to groups lower in the social scale. Where women of the gentry were concerned, education in the new schools might be part of an act of rebellion.[79] The most spectacular example of this is the revolutionary heroine Qiu Jin, who escaped from a conventional marriage to study in Tokyo and participate in an anti-Manchu conspiracy.[80] However rare such instances were, they broke the elite's control, on paper or in practice, over the rate at which the new schooling spread and the groups that participated in it.

Expedients and Adjustments

Teachers

China's adoption of "education" (*jiaoyu*) as opposed to "learning" (*xue*) led to the need for specialists in this new discipline. As well as the "scholars in farming, crafts, commerce, and soldiery" foreseen by Liang Qichao, the new order required scholars in teaching. No longer was literacy the sole qualification for teaching.

The need was at first met by reliance on foreigners—chiefly Japanese since Westerners wanted higher salaries and propagated suspect values—and on foreign training.[81] Many of the Chinese students studying in Japan took short-term teacher-training courses. The founder of Mingde in Hunan was a returned student from Japan, and after a study tour of Japan in 1904, Yan Xiu and his protégé Zhang Boling set up the prototype of the Nankai Middle School in Tianjin.[82] Japanese influence was particularly strong in the field of educational theory since this area was not highly developed in China. Even sishu teachers were set to using the five-step teaching method worked out by disciples of the German educator Johann Herbart (1776–1841), which had become a standard feature of Japanese teacher training.[83]

Foreign teachers and returned students could obviously not staff every new school in the nation, and since the old degrees were no longer recognized as a pedagogic qualification, the training of new teachers became an urgent matter. One of the shortcomings of the 1902 regulations drawn up by Zhang Boxi was their neglect of teacher training, but this was remedied in the regulations of 1904, which set up lower and higher normal schools parallel to the regular middle schools and higher-level schools. The entrance requirement was graduation from a higher primary school or the possession of the lowest examination degree (itself previously a prized teaching qualification).[84] In theory, all teachers should have been specially trained or at least have studied at the new schools, but in practice the government was forced to compromise. Training centers and short-term courses were set up to answer immediate needs.

The first students were of a relatively low standard. In Zhili, which pioneered teacher training, it was said that of the 140 candidates who took the entrance examination for Baoding Normal School in 1902, "60 or 70 percent were old pedants and village schoolmasters . . . against their will, fearing that their pupils' numbers would dwindle daily . . . they were learning the new methods of teaching as a stronghold for the future . . . among them were white-haired men over fifty trying to pass themselves off as under twenty."[85] In Suzhou, young returned students who had taken courses in teacher training in Japan were set to teach grey-haired sishu teachers. Considerable embarrassment was caused by this inversion of customary relationships, whether personal—being forced to teach an elder relative by marriage or friend of one's father's, or even one's own former teacher—or general—Should these elderly men be made to stand when their young teacher entered the room? Could their names be called for the roll each morning? Were pupils permitted to drink tea and smoke their waterpipes in the classroom?[86] Minor points of etiquette brought out major shifts in status.

Considerable ill-feeling sometimes existed between the newly arrived and those whom they displaced. One old scholar in Sichuan altered the self-congratulatory couplet left by visiting schoolteachers at a famous beauty spot to refer to stinking ignoramuses; the resulting feud was taken to court.[87] Lower down the social scale, countryfolk grudged the change in loyalties. In one county in Shandong, as late as the 1930s, local people were said to place more trust in old teachers, "stubborn and slow to change," who wished for the return of the Qing emperor, than in the

young men at modern schools.[88] An informant educated in a Guangdong village in the 1900s confirms that "the Confucius style" of teacher
was most respected.[89]

Those at the top of the social hierarchy were able to weather changing fashions. Educational theorists might insist on the importance of
specialist qualifications, but to say that professionals regarded profes-
sionalism highly is not to say that they controlled the new schools. The
conflict within the Ministry of Education over the appointment of Hanlin scholars to administer the new school system was repeated in the
provinces, where influence still lay with the juren and their juniors
among the gentry. Of the 24 members of Anhui's Board of Education,
22 held the old degrees. Only two had added modern qualifications to
these. Some had worked their way up within the new educational bureaucracy; others had been on tours of inspection to Japan.[90] For many,
experience of the new education resulted from their position rather
than their position from their experience. On Henan's board, 38 of the
44 members held only the old degrees.[91] In the schools, administrators
were predominantly degree holders without modern training, as were
(despite the regulations) teachers of such "Chinese" subjects as morals,
the classics, Chinese history, and sometimes mathematics. Since the last
degrees were awarded in 1905, their holders had ultimately to yield to
the modern trained, but in the meantime they enjoyed the rewards of
the new education.

By 1909 the ministry claimed more than 89,000 teachers, of whom
some 53,000 reportedly had graduated from the new schools in China or
Japan; 36,000 held no professional qualification. The ministry formalized the position of the latter in 1909, when, bowing to the inevitable,
it admitted that "the need for teachers is great, but normal schools are
few and their graduates even fewer. To provide teaching, we have to
compromise on appointments." Holders of the old degrees "whose Chinese is clear and straightforward and who are thoroughly familiar with
modern teaching subjects (kexue)" were permitted to take an examination to qualify as teachers in primary schools.[92] Like previous regulations, these were more honored in the breach than in the observance;
but throughout all compromises, the state, acting on professional advice,
asserted its right to determine who might and who might not teach.

Perhaps more surprising than the persistence of old-style teachers
was the number of new graduates who turned to teaching.[93] Owing to
the lack of demand for engineers, businessmen, and agronomists, enrollment in industrial, commercial, or agricultural schools tended to be
regarded simply as an alternative form of middle or higher school education, not as a vocational commitment.[94] Modern medicine likewise at-

tracted few recruits.[95] The new schools, however, along with the new army, were an area in which China was expanding: the bureaucratic state could create an army and an educational system, both variations of the organization of manpower, far more easily than it could ensure that mining operations would be successful or railway lines profitable. Thus it came about that the new schools that were supposed to produce budding industrialists and scientists at first produced largely teachers, a result that can be regarded either as a gain for the school system or a loss to the nation or simply a sensible accommodation by graduates to available employment opportunities. Later reformers, taking the least charitable explanation, believed that *lunhuan jiaoyu*, ("circular education")—by which the pupil becomes the teacher teaching pupils who will themselves become teachers—was one of the main evils of Chinese education.[96]

Texts and Tables

The same discovery of specialization and the same frustrated attempts at state control are visible in the supply of textbooks for the new schools. Previously, all that was necessary were the cheap and plentiful "Three Hundred Thousand" (the *Three Character Classic*, *Hundred Family Names*, and *Thousand Character Classic*), sold in thousands by provincial bookstores, and the Four Books. Traveling peddlers had brought paper, pens, and books to the school door.[97] Now, however, schools were to teach texts specially written for a particular age group and subject level, and newness instead of venerable age became the mark of a schoolbook.

In Japan, state authorization of textbooks prepared by others had been superseded in 1903 by state editing of school texts. Chinese authorities at first intended that their state should do the same: in 1902, with the promulgation of the first regulations for the new schools, Beijing University (then head of the school system) drew up a plan for the compilation of texts in the classics, history, geography, ethics, and literature.[98] But little had been done by 1909, when the revised primary-school regulations appeared with lists of prescribed texts for each grade compiled by the Ministry of Education's textbook section. Owing to the section's waste and inefficiency, many of the series named were not yet in existence. Those that did exist were of uneven quality and allocated to the wrong levels.[99]

The gap was filled by the Commercial Press and other publishing houses.[100] The Commercial Press brought out its own series of elementary readers in 1905 and by 1906 had sold a third of a million copies.[101]

At the advanced level, most texts were translations. A survey of the publications advertised by the Commercial Press in 1904 shows that of 153 works, 40 were translated from Japanese and 27 from Western languages. Of the remainder only 27 were original Chinese works rather than secondhand compilations.[102]

Heavy reliance on imported texts was natural when the teaching subjects were themselves importations, but brought problems of unfamiliar concepts and language. These were carried over into books written by Chinese, who used the vocabulary current in Japan to translate terms of Western origin and who assumed their own level of general knowledge in the reader. Even a deliberately popular work such as *Guomin bidu*, written in the vernacular for use in mass education, chose illustrations of its themes from European and American history.[103] The choice of texts for the public lectures that were to replace the rural compact reflects the well-stocked bookshelf of a Western-oriented intellectual rather than the tastes of the illiterate villagers or townsfolk at whom they were aimed. Works to be read aloud included *Robinson Crusoe, Uncle Tom's Cabin*, biographies of Clive and Nelson, and a narrative of a journey through Australia.[104] Not all works, however, were too recondite for popular consumption: the Commercial Press's *Nüzi guowen jiaokeshu* (Chinese Reader for Girls) stuck close to home, with lessons on cats, birds, soybeans, and stoves, little stories on helpful or studious models, and instructions on how to write a family letter.[105] The main problem for its young readers would probably have been that it was written in classical Chinese. Even a Guangdong village sishu, whose head fiercely opposed the new schools, used a set of elementary readers as supplementary material.[106] In general, one should probably not underestimate the degree to which such textbooks were able to transfer simple modern knowledge to the sons and daughters of the middle class.

The new texts were relatively dear (although the cost of each volume was low at the elementary level, whole sets had to be purchased for each of the eight primary school subjects).[107] Distribution was a problem, especially when content kept changing.[108] Nor was the matter ended when appropriate texts were finally in the hands of the students. The women of a Guangdong village insisted on the abandonment of an apparently innocuous primer containing the names of household implements because two of these were used in funeral ceremonies, and the book was thus inauspicious.[109]

Difficulties of communication, in both senses, continued to plague the Republican school system. In 1924, Shu Xincheng, after a tour of four provinces, reported that in his home county in Hunan, people felt

> no interest at all in reading about events in Shanghai. Consequently, in all Hsu-pu, an area of 300 square miles with a population of 300,000, there are only nine copies of a Shanghai newspaper and some six copies

of the *Educational Review* [*Jiaoyu zazhi*]. In the Bureau of Education, Shanghai newspapers [are] always a month late because of slow communication . . . Teachers in Hsu-pu are ignorant of national events. They have heard of the "New Educational System" promulgated by the government two years ago, but they are ignorant of its substance, no detailed syllabus of it having been promulgated in the rural areas. Words like "economical" and "historical background," adopted from Western languages and long in use in the city, are not comprehensible to teachers in rural China.

The situation in Chengtu, the provincial capital of Szechwan, is even worse . . . In Po-tsu-chen, a rural town on the Chungking-Chengtu route . . . textbooks in use are five years out of date and are those that the Ministry of Education in Peking has declared "obsolete" and suppressed.[110]

The old "Three Hundred Thousand" still held the allegiance of many countryfolk. In 1938, the left-wing critic Lao Xiang commented on the difficulty of getting them to accept modern works:

When I was working in the countryside in Hebei's Ding County, I noticed two old bookstores on the northern street. The entrances were so neglected and deserted you could almost "set up a birdtrap" there, and I thought they must have closed long ago. But this was not the case, they just kept on day after day. I only found out after close questioning that they completely relied on the wholesale trade of those outdated old books that still (somehow) survive: the *Hundred Family Names*, the *Thousand Character Classic*, and the *Three Character Classic*. Not only do private, family schools use them but foreign-style, modern schools also use them as supplementary reading material. Many uneducated peasants, in town to trade in their spare time, often buy a copy of the *Three Character Classic* to take home with them. I hardly ever saw them buy a modern, vernacular book put out by the Commercial Press in Shanghai.[111]

Lao Xiang resolved the dilemma by writing modern propaganda in the *Three Character Classic* form; his predecessors, however, were reluctant to make such concessions to a world they believed was disappearing.

Proponents of the new schools condemned the physical as well as the mental furniture of the old sishu. Chen Zibao, an educationalist who had toured Japan, wrote an article contrasting the "civilized" (*wenming*) school chairs used there, adapted to the height of children of different ages, with the "barbarous" (*yeman*) ones he found Chinese children crouching or perching on in a country sishu.[112] School tables or desks, he recommended, should also follow the Japanese design.

Tables and chairs could be locally made, but the truly modern classroom was furnished with some more expensive requisites: maps and charts, scientific instruments, art equipment, blackboards. These were often hard to obtain outside the treaty ports. Ambitious founders of new schools would sometimes send to Shanghai and Tianjin for the more esoteric items, but most went without. Light, airy school buildings, another requisite, should have been obtainable locally, but for reasons of economy most schools were set up in makeshift quarters in converted temples, academies, or private homes. Only the most prestigious had their own buildings. A heavy investment in school buildings was usually made only for higher-level schools in provincial capitals and treaty ports. In such cases, the architecture usually conformed to the prevailing Western style. The ornate ugliness of Shanghai's Nanyang Public School apparently won much praise in its day; a model was sent to the St. Louis exhibition in 1904, where it was much admired.[113] For many Chinese, however, such buildings underscored the alien nature of the new schools.

Subjects

Specialized teachers, texts, equipment, and buildings were all handmaidens of the specialized subject matter that was the raison d'être for the new schools' existence. The long-awaited goals of the nineteenth-century reformers had been achieved: Chinese schools were at last teaching "useful" subjects—foreign languages, mathematics, science, history, geography, sports. Unfortunately for the balanced development of the new curriculum, the people's view of utility was often the opposite of that of bureaucrats and educationalists: they flocked to subjects with an immediate economic market, but were wary of those whose value lay in the promotion of long-term national goals. The careful balance of the claims of old and new subjects in the curricula promulgated in 1904 disappeared in practice, as some subjects outran and others lagged behind the intentions of their inaugurators. The divergence is especially marked in the fate of English courses on the one hand and scientific and technical courses and physical education on the other.[114]

The study of English had long been popular in the treaty port regions as the avenue to a secure, well-paying position in a foreign firm or in the customs or telegraph administration.[115] By the late 1890s, it was losing its associations with unwilling government students and foreigners' clerks and becoming fashionable among enlightened gentry. Shanghai's *Mengxue bao* attempted to teach English through illustrated word lists, largely mistranslated.[116] In Hangzhou at the turn of the century one could learn English in two newly founded schools; in Suzhou, where none had yet been opened, enthusiasts hired private tutors.[117]

By the time the 1904 regulations were issued, Zhang Zhidong and his colleagues wished less to encourage the study of English than to check its dominance. They noted foreign languages as an important item of the curriculum for middle schools, but discouraged their teaching in primary schools.[118] Such was the demand, however, that numerous privately or publicly founded higher primary schools offered English as a subject, often taught by teachers of dubious accomplishments. Competent English teachers could attract high salaries; specialists from the naval and language schools set up in the nineteenth century came into their own.[119] Japanese was slightly less popular. Within the school system, it was taught chiefly in tertiary institutions and technical schools, where instructors were often Japanese.[120]

It is a mistake to deduce from the widespread enthusiasm for the study of English that a new world was opening up before Chinese who could not wait to read John Stuart Mill in the original. A few were certainly impelled by intellectual curiosity, but the majority had more practical motives.[121] A Zhili inspector wrote of Tianjin's prefectural middle school, "There is not too much wrong with its curriculum, except that English is a bit excessive. Students often do not go to Chinese classes, or if they do, they read their English books in the classroom . . . only the supplementary students do this . . . they are mainly from Guangdong, Jiangsu, and Zhejiang. Their sole purpose in coming to school is to learn English with a view to making a living later on." [122] Nankai, which had a native speaker of English on its staff, taught not only English but in English: it was the language of instruction for mathematics, chemistry, and the history and geography of foreign countries.[123] The quality of their English instruction was one of the main attractions of the "aristocratic" Protestant mission schools; Chinese studies often suffered in such an environment.[124] Those with an established social position watched with distress the growing assertion of johnny-come-latelies who claimed educated status on the basis of a few words of English, "with which at best they could get a high position to bring distinction to their wives and children and brag of in the country, or at worst become translators or teachers, either being an improvement on their previous condition." [125]

Even village people were attracted by the opportunities associated with a command of English. A former schoolteacher in a coastal village near Shanghai wrote, "Every parent of a boy or girl with the slightest ambition always hoped to do something in Shanghai. For that, whether in industry or commerce, you needed to understand a few words of English to get your start." The pull of the treaty ports distorted local status structure: the chief ambition of the son of the town's main shopkeeper was to learn enough English to be a waiter in a Shanghai restaurant—a servile career he would not have considered in his own environment.[126]

Scientific and technical subjects had less of a market than foreign languages. They required expensive equipment, often available only from the treaty port cities, and teachers familiar with scientific method and terminology. Even English—written English, at least—could be learned from a textbook more easily than science. Some of Guo Moruo's teachers made ludicrous mistakes. At his middle school in Sichuan, the botany teacher (a graduate of Chengdu Normal School), misread the cursive form of the characters for "natural conditions" (*tianran jingxiang*) as "heavenly dragon conditions" (*tianlong jingxiang*) and proceeded to lecture the class on the difference between the flying heavenly dragons of the skies and the manifest dragons of the fields.[127]

The most glaring discrepancy between popular expectation and educationalists' vision occurred over physical education. This was regarded by parents as an unnecessary frippery at best; at worst, it added substance to the suspicion that schools were a disguised form of military conscription. Old-fashioned scholars thought such activity undignified, whence the apocryphal story of the Chinese gentleman puzzled to see his foreign friend's sons playing tennis themselves instead of "letting the servants do it." For the new educationalists, however, sports were a sine qua non of modern schooling, an inseparable part of the Spencerian trinity of moral, mental, and physical education. The clash between the two views is illustrated in student complaints about the prefectural school in Jiaxing, where "despite the fact that everybody knows that physical education is the most urgent task," the backward head refused to allow appointment of an instructor in military drill on the grounds that drill injured the health.[128] Science and physical education were the two most frequently named omissions in lower primary schools in Henan in 1907; less than half of the schools offered the full curriculum as set in 1904.[129]

Although Westernization of the curriculum alienated rural parents and conservative scholars, it bridged an incipient split by giving the same education to the son of a compradore and the son of a scholar-official. The new learning and its potential national or individual benefits were no longer, as they had been in the nineteenth century, the possession of "marginal men" or rebels out of office. The gentry had successfully outflanked their competitors in the possession of knowledge, although in the process they had left behind their slower members and formed new alliances. Emerging from the initially distant points of court edict and treaty port self-betterment, the new schools were well on the way to merging the interests of all those active in modernized businesses and bureaucracies. In addition, by their monopoly of educational advancement, they drew into their orbit those whose hopes had been deflected but not crushed by the abolition of the old examination system.

The mere achievement of school-based elite integration, however, fell far short of the expectations of educational reformers. They had succeeded in replacing the examination system with schools, but the products of the new institutions bore a dismaying similarity to the products of the old. Education was still not universal, compulsory, or practical; students still aimed at government sinecures, showing little interest in taking up modern trades and technology A paradox arose: the ethos and forms of the new schools were modern, borrowed from centralized industrial states that were examples of "military citizenship," but their concrete operation was suffused by the values and turned to the purposes of a regionally oriented, "familial" agrarian society.

7
The Freedom of Civilization

In retrospect, schools of the modern, Western type were the advance guard of industrial discipline—the discipline that an industrial society imposes not only on its factories but on all enterprises operating on the equation of time, money, and production. Such discipline was an object of admiration to many in China. Chinese observers, however, interpreted it primarily in political rather than industrial terms. The rate of industrialization in China was too slow and the scale too small to utilize the gains of modern schooling, and the bourgeoisie was as yet too small and uninfluential to be able to demand schools producing a large pool of disciplined labor. Rather, the Chinese seized on unison as the outward sign of unity, the secret of Western strength and Chinese weakness. In a 1902 article extolling the virtues of compulsory submission to a uniform system, Liang Qichao contrasted the freedom of civilization with the freedom of barbarism: the latter consisted in anarchy and selfishness; the former in freedom under the law, in which "every action is like the rhythm of a machine, every move is like soldiers marching in step." He went on to relate the necessity for this order to the struggle for survival in a competitive world.[1] *Hubei xueshengjie*, a magazine produced in Japan by students from Hubei, took up Liang's theme of threatened survival in two articles on citizenship education, understood as instruction that inculcated a spirit of nationalism, independence, and responsibility.[2] (Initially the magazine's sales were limited, but they soared after the Hubei authorities banned it.)[3]

Citizenship training combined with universal military preparedness introduced a new concept into Chinese: *junguomin jiaoyu* ("education for military citizenship")—the extension of the discipline and martial spirit found in soldiers to the population as a whole. Like education for citizenship, it arose from a consciousness that China was, in Liang Qichao's words, a lamb among tigers, defenseless amid its enemies.[4] The Japanese educational system appears to have played a part in the growth of this concept. Japanese normal schools, in particular, were run on semimilitary lines, with military drill, severe discipline, and militaristic uniforms.[5]

Views on citizenship and military education gained wide currency among those concerned with modern education in China. They found formal expression in the Aims of Education, proclaimed by the Ministry of Education in 1906 to supplement the 1904 regulations' limited goals of correcting erroneous tendencies and producing well-rounded talents. The preamble emphasized that the training of an elite of talent—the *rencai* centuries of Chinese schooling had sought to form—must today take second place to the education of the whole nation. The new aims summed up the virtues desirable in a modern citizen: continued loyalty to the emperor, respect for Confucius, the ascription of a high value to the public good, martial spirit, and practicality or substantiality (*zhong jun, zun Kong, shang gong, shang wu, shang shi*). The 1906 proclamation recommended that education for military citizenship be inculcated through children's textbooks with stories of battles, pictures of battleships and flags, and songs and poems about the Qing dynasty's prowess in battle (a rather difficult order). In sports classes, young children might play, but older ones should take up military drill to attain "strictly ordered discipline."[6]

Order and Disorder

The freedom of barbarism was, however, not easily eradicated from Chinese schools. A school inspector in Baoding in 1905 deplored the deficiencies of a primary school with only ten students, all "utterly without regulation. Sleeping and eating, leaving and coming in, are all without fixed times, just like an academy." He exerted himself to end this anarchy, bemusing the little school's eight trustees and three cooks by rising at 6:30 to beat the morning gong and composing a code of rules for each room.[7] In one academy in Hunan that reportedly transformed it-self into a prefectural middle school simply by appointing a new teacher, students came and went as freely as before.[8] Attendance was equally casual at another rural school:

> It gave the appearance of an old deserted temple, its three teachers like old monks who had entered Nirvana. No matter what day it was, there was never one when the students were all gathered there together. Although the two sons of the house where I was staying were enrolled in the school, one never went there and the other came and went early or late as he pleased. I used to tell the teachers . . . that they should make an example of specially bad cases, giving them black marks and punishments as a warning to the others. The teachers said that if they did, they would have a student movement on their hands . . . the students, they said, complained all the time that they were restricted by the school and had lost their free amusements.[9]

Such laxity was a transitional but repeated phenomenon, eradicated or muted in one school only to reappear in another. In 1907, an inspector in Anhui was appalled to find that a nominally modernized charity school in Wuhu had no timetable and allowed its pupils to study subjects of their choice at their own pace.[10] As late as 1911, Zhejiang's commissioner for education painted a gloomy picture of the current situation, in which

> teachers do not come to school on time, but take holidays on some pretext; or after the bell has been rung, students trickle in at different times; or teachers are too lenient, and students insult them; or students talk and laugh as they please while the teacher is talking; or groups of students amuse themselves roaming the streets, acting improperly, with absolutely no checks made by those in charge; or students do not study in their study rooms, but amuse themselves as they will, and again those in charge ignore it.[11]

The model school approximated as closely as possible the discipline of its Japanese counterpart. Students who lined up and filed in or out of the classroom at a word from their monitor or who sat at desks in orderly rows charmed inspectors.[12] Clocks and bells regulated activities, in contrast to the self-discipline of the academy. "From the evening [I entered]," wrote Shu Xincheng of the school he attended in 1908, "I lived in the midst of bells for getting up, lining up in classes, calling the roll, for going to class and finishing class, for lining up again, calling the roll again, and going to bed." He did not mind the first and last bells, but resented fiercely the tyranny of the ones that "made you leave aside any occupation, no matter how fascinating, any work you were putting all your effort into, to go to the classroom; and until it clanged again, you had no chance of leaving."[13]

Instances of total nonconformity to the norms of the new school are rare in the reports of inspectors, although they may have been more frequent beyond the purlieus of the cities to which they usually confined their reports. More commonly one reads of imperfections, approximations, misunderstandings. The gap between the minimum demands of villagers and the expectations of a school inspector is humorously rendered in a short story on a village schoolmaster who converts his sishu into a new-style school simply by hanging up a placard, hoping to attract back pupils who deserted his classes to seek modern education. The more informed villagers are not satisfied with the change of name and inquire why (for nearly twenty pupils) he has not appointed other teachers for all the new subjects, a request he attempts to meet by reciting the qualifications of his five sons: one has studied half a book of Palmer and can teach English . . . His students gradually return, but he is exposed by the arrival of an inspector who demands to see his lecture hall, textbooks, scientific instruments, and art equipment.[14]

Attributes of the New Schools

To the popular mind, the primary characteristic of the new schools was the possession of at least two staff members, in contrast to the one-man sishu. Ministry of Education statistics for 1909 show that schools in Zhili averaged less than twenty pupils. The number of teachers (11,921) was only slightly greater than the number of schools (11,201), but the inclusion of 13,508 school officials (*zhiyuan*) (these may have included school trustees) swelled staff numbers. Nationally, schools averaged 27 pupils and three staff members.[15] Newspaper reports of new schools often refer to the hiring of one teacher for Chinese subjects and one for Western. One private school in Beijing boasted eight teachers and three nonteaching staff members for a student body of twenty.[16]

A second readily grasped attribute of the new schools was their division into classes—again unlike sishu, which made no formal differentiation. Uniform progression from one level to another was one of the features of Western schools that proponents of educational reform found most attractive. The emphasis on sequential study found in some neo-

Confucian educators and the Qianlong emperor's recommendation that academies adopt a graduated reading course may have facilitated acceptance.[17] Those educated abroad appear to have seen the principle in terms of advantage for individual cultivation rather than as a means of mass organization. In practice, some confusion existed over the criteria for dividing classes. Those who entered in the same year were generally enrolled in the same class since the lessons were new to all of them, but some schools placed students according to previous attainments or on the basis of an entrance examination. In some schools classes were divided along subject lines. It was rare for a school to have sufficiently standardized its curriculum and enrollment to offer the Ministry of Education's approved progression through five years of lower primary, four of upper primary, and five of middle school. Many schools disregarded the regulations and set the length of their courses independently.[18]

The third innovative feature of the new schools' organization was the adoption of the foreign calendar. The Chinese customarily divided the lunar month into three periods of ten days each; markets would be held or lectures given on, for example, the fifth, fifteenth, and twenty-fifth of the month. This division of time continued in popular life, but within school walls the week, or *xingqi*, was used, with every seventh day a rest day in the Western manner. The school year started in autumn, as in Japan, rather than after the lunar New Year.[19]

For the majority of the new schools, none of these practices were pedagogically necessary or even useful; rather, they were liabilities. The hiring of specialized teachers and the division of pupils into several grades made sense in large middle schools but not in elementary schools with fifteen or twenty pupils. School inspectors, the arbiters of educational correctness, rebuked premature specialization and excessive staff—suggesting, for example, that Jiangxi's Normal School did not really need four physical education teachers.[20] Since inspectors reached only a small fraction of the new schools, they were powerless to adjust requirements that they had in essence sanctioned. Overall, the education system probably suffered less from departures from the mandated standards—from unregenerate shuyuan and sishu—than from compliance with them. To the author of the short story summarized above, it was ludicrous for the old schoolmaster to imagine that his bumpkin sons could teach modern subjects; but the assumption that the reality to which the teacher laid claim was desirable, that his village could and should support a school with six separate teachers of English, history, science, geography, sports, and singing as well as a teacher of the classics, was equally ill-founded.

Persistence of Old Ties

Although the essence of the new schooling appeared to contemporary observers to lie in these organizational characteristics, the social relationships such schooling presupposed were of equal significance. In the schools, new types of relationships defined by new rituals clashed and mingled with existing loyalties and expectations.

The impersonality typical of the modern school's arrangements was tempered in China by the continuing strength of systems of personal relations. Shu Xincheng, it is true, was struck as he crossed from "the sishu and academy produced by agricultural society" to the "school produced by modern industrial society" by the indifference subsisting between teachers and pupils in the latter.[21] Another critic of the new schools' operation charged that teachers and pupils looked on them as temporary lodgings rather than as their life's work.[22] This may have been true of some city schools. Even sishu education had the potential in urban surroundings of becoming primarily a cash transaction with minimal personal overtones. The common practice in the new system of having a single teacher give classes at several different schools must have increased this tendency.[23] Staff appointments, however, were often made through a network of personal acquaintance and recommendation: for example, the prefect of Qingzhou, scion of an old Suzhou family, had a relative recruit teachers for Qingzhou's new middle school from his circle of clients and acquaintances. The man appointed head of the school, Bao Tianxiao, had received no formal modern education.[24] In one Zhejiang village, the primary school was a family affair: the headmaster pressed into unpaid service as teachers his children and several nephews.[25]

Pupils from educated families (as Shu Xincheng was not) would be likely to find kinfolk among staff or pupils even if they attended a city school away from home. Among Guo Moruo's teachers at the prefectural higher primary school, for example, was a relative of his mother's who was also a friend of his elder brother's.[26] In private schools, the initial enrollment often depended on the circles in which the school's founder moved. Beijing's Jifu Primary School, set up by a departmental director of the Board of Punishment, drew its pupils from the upper levels of society. It attracted the grandson of a first-place jinshi and the son of one of the pupils of the famous scholar Wu Rulun, as well as the sons of old friends and family connections and the founder's own son.[27] The founder's son went on to Nankai Middle School in Tianjin partly because his father had been one of the examiners when Yan Xiu, its founder, took the palace examination.[28] With the private school as with the sishu, reciprocal obligation might be implied. Just as sishu teachers were often appointed from another locality for this very reason, so parents to avoid the embarrassment of future claims sometimes preferred a modern private school *not* run by an acquaintance. In Guangdong in the early 1900s, "educated families were all unwilling to send boys to private schools, fearing that the school's founder might seize on this as a favor done to the family, even to the extent of saying that those pupils who got anywhere should be mindful of giving a due return for the care spent on their education."[29] Unwilling pupils at one rural school attended only because their fathers wanted to gain social credit with the school's manager.[30]

The informal and particularistic ties that cut across the supposedly universal relationships of the modern school were evident not only in the persistent influence of personal links but in the continuation of local particularism. This was frequently institutionalized: following the custom of some academies, schools set up from local or provincial funds often limited their enrollment to natives of the areas under their jurisdiction or waived fees for them but charged outsiders.[31] At the prefectural or provincial level, county quotas often governed entry. When the first middle school in Jiading Prefecture in Sichuan opened, it recruited not only students but teachers on the basis of county origin. The attempt failed lamentably, partly because of the uneven cultural standards among counties.[32] Students were divided into classes by county and sought their friends on the same basis. Each county's population was supposed to have its own characteristics: "Luoshan people and those from Jianwei were rather urban, even frivolous, in their ways; people from Weiyuan and Rongxian were very rough; those from Emei and Hongya and Jiajiang were simply country bumpkins."[33] Feeling along provincial lines was also strong. An isolated non-Hunanese in the Hunan Military Primary School was teased and rebuffed constantly.[34] Sometimes both teachers and students would pick on outsiders. One school in Beijing gained the nickname "fellow-countryman school" because of blatant displays of partiality.[35]

Administratively or emotionally based discrimination against outsiders as well as dialect differences and pride of place made it common for extraprovincials to band together and found their own schools in cities where they formed a large community. In Jiangning, for example, where the staff accompanying officials was usually Hunanese, "some of the boys study at the various official schools, but because they do not understand the teachers' accents, there has been a general discussion about raising money to open a school for them with Hunanese teachers."[36] The *huiguan* ("guild hall") was often used as a site. In Baoding, a school for students from the Liangjiang region appears to have been created primary with the aim of restraining juvenile delinquency among the sons of officials and their staff, who were wont to "band together to seek enjoyment, causing a great problem." Such schools were the genteel equivalent of the rehabilitation and training centers for the lower orders, needed because the families of these young men "are unwilling to have them follow a trade. The best follow their fathers as officials and secretaries. The remainder sink into the depths and are heard of no more." The document from which these extracts come, an appeal for official support, draws together the social justifications for mass education with those for education of the upper ranks of society. The appeal was couched in an eloquence reminiscent of the *Xinmin congbao*: "Every unemployed person in the country means one less of use to the country. Every uneducated person means one less who is intelligent. Unemployment breeds poverty and ignorance weakness. To be weak and poor without seeking complete change and the restoration of one's country's affairs is to invite irreparable destruction."[37] Its author thus wove into the theme of national salvation the motifs of provincial solidarity and respectable self-protection. Baoding also had a school for students from Shandong. Another planned by officials and merchants from Hubei was to cut across class boundaries and be open to the sons of "officials, their secretaries, craftsmen, and merchants."[38]

Rituals of Unity

To unity based on place and acquaintance was added that fostered by the borrowed ritual of the school itself. Group activities gave staff and students a consciousness of the school as a distinct organism. Some of them bore a semiofficial character: on Confucius' birthday, fixed as a national holiday for schools in the 1904 regulations, bands of schoolchildren attended the temple of Confucius to pay their respects.[39] Sishu also observed this ceremony. Schoolchildren were organized to observe the funeral of the Guangxu emperor and Empress Dowager in 1908.[40] A display of students was thought to gladden the heart of visiting dignitaries. Bao Tianxiao, head of the Qingzhou Middle School in 1904, organized a show of students at a railway station through which the governor of Shandong's train passed; he was much chagrined to find that the governor had slept through the whole thing.[41]

As well as acting as extras at official public events, schools staged their own. In Tianjin, Yan Xiu arranged the first school exhibition, after witnessing similar events during an inspection tour of Japan. In 1909 a Jiangsu provincial exhibition was held in Shanghai, which had become a center for educational innovation.[42] A more genial affair was a 1907 exhibition hosted by a Beijing girls' training center, which, on the center's anniversary, offered the public films and children's games as well as a display of handicrafts produced by girls' schools.[43] At an exhibition organized the same year by the Ministry of Education, one of the main attractions was a primary school students' band; clad in semimilitary attire, the students sang, drummed, and played the piano and trumpet to an appreciative audience (see illustration 6).[44] Such secular celebrations of learning were perhaps the modern equivalent of ceremonies at the Confucian temple. They reassured educationalists of the value of their activities while serving as public relations exercises. These could, however, go amiss: indignant protests reached the ministry when the girl students of Beijing sold their own handicrafts and put on a performance of songs and dances to raise money for women's education. A circus, advertised as an additional attraction, became an additional offense. The ministry characteristically tried to placate both sides: classical precedents could be found for the sales, but couldn't the girls deliver the articles through others? Singing and dancing were not only against Chinese custom and morality, but would take students' minds off their work. Circuses were even worse. In any case, at this early stage those connected with women's education should be especially careful to give no one any excuse for obstruction.[45]

Schools used their ceremonies both to increase cohesion among staff and students and add dignity to their pursuits, and to forge links with hoped-for supporters from outside. Over a hundred distinguished guests, among them Zhang Boxi, then the official in charge of education, a Japanese professor, and three grandchildren of a Manchu noble, attended the opening of a private higher primary school in Beijing in 1903. The school, which had all the latest equipment and ideology, was dedicated to developing primary education with a view to training citizens first and talent second; in short, "it was in no particular inferior to the schools of civilized countries."[46] The contradiction between the school's prohibitive cost and restricted clientele and its aim of spreading mass education does not appear to have troubled its founder. What illusions veiled the discrepancy between belief and reality? The new educationalists believed in the coming of the Kingdom—a "civilized" China. Ahead of the disorder and poverty around them, they saw shapes of order, rationality, and courtliness, a society that would recognize them at their true worth. The schools were the first earnest of this larger vision. A faith as devout and as contrary to all visible evidence as that of the early Christians assured them of the eventual realization of their goals. Meanwhile, the schools, as elements of that society transferred into the present, bore ineradicably its characteristics of equality and enlighten-

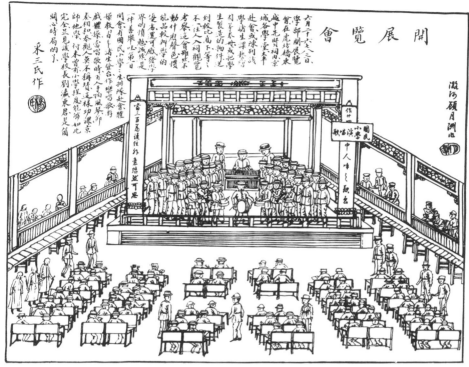

6. A Primary School Choir at an Exhibition Organized by
the Ministry of Education (*Xingqi huabao*, no. 39 [1907])

ment. Any shortfalls were the result not of the institutions but of the
malice or ignorance of those not committed to the new order. To these
this new school, despite its many excellent virtues, duly fell a victim. Few
students enrolled, and it ran into financial difficulties from which it was
temporarily rescued by its founder's fellow Hunanese. It was probably
founded prematurely; the forces of civilization gained a number of recruits when the examination system was abolished.

Within the more modern of the new schools, joint activities, often of
Western origin, formed bonds between staff and students. At several
schools, students acted in "civilized plays," that is, those that used spoken
dialogue instead of the singing of Chinese opera.[47] "Civilized" (*wenming*)
was a term of commendation used of all that came from the West or
Japan, in contrast to what was barbarous or indigenous—striking evidence of the extent to which some Chinese were cleaving to a new way
of life.

The range of informal activities is apparent in photographs printed in the *Jiaoyu zazhi* during the late Qing. Photography, another Western import and itself a group activity, usually necessitated the hiring of a professional photographer. The resultant photograph, however artlessly posed, constituted a permanent reminder of the unity and uniqueness of the school group. The first action of the students who marched out of Nanyang Gongxue after a clash with conservative staff members was to have a joint photograph taken.[48]

Favorite photographic topics, in addition to the standard class group, were excursions and sports meetings. School classes, often in military uniform, can be seen in noted beauty spots, often under a flag bearing the name of their school. Flags were also an important adjunct of sports meetings. An illustration published under the heading "Progress among our citizens" showed the dragon flag of China waving over a mixed assortment of national flags, among them the Union Jack and the Korean flag, on the occasion of a sports meeting held by three Beijing schools on the Empress Dowager's birthday (see illustration 7). In addition to those connected with the schools, a number of schoolmasters from reformed sishu brought their pupils along to gaze at the runners.[49] The first non–mission school sports day was held in Wuchang in 1903 at one of Zhang Zhidong's new schools. Duan Fang, Zhang's successor as governor-general of Hunan and Hubei, was also a patron of sport; at a mission school's commencement ceremonies, he not only watched a game of football but kicked the ball himself.[50]

Sports were seen as closely connected with martial ardor. Physical exercise, compulsory at every school at all levels, often consisted of military drill under the eyes of an officer or a graduate from military school, although calisthenics were coming into use in some schools and were recommended for young children.[51] The stylized Chinese martial arts had no place in the curriculum. They were solitary arts, or at best a paired performance: the new drills and races were meant to toughen the citizens of a nation. The Chinese still felt some hesitation about body-contact sports, but really Westernized schools practiced these as well.

Sports meetings did not always inspire outsiders with the desired martial spirit. Novelist Liu Bannong, writing in 1917, when the new custom was already a commonplace in the main cities, left a comic picture of the milling throng, where the scent of perfume mingled with the stink of sweat and sound of clapping and cheering formed a general hubbub with the Japanese "anata, anata," the Englishman's "Yes, really," the young man-about-town's Shanghai slang, and the women's complaint that "my feet are killing me." Liu called this sports meeting, which ap-

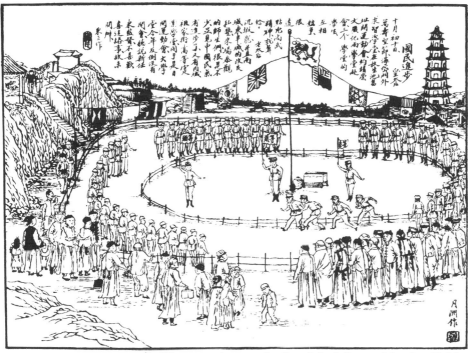

7. "Progress Among the People": A Sports Meeting Held
on the Empress Dowager's Birthday (*Xingqi huabao*, no. 53 [1907])

peared in one of his popular short stories, "Envy-the-West." What educators thought of as patriotism could appear mere imitation to outsiders.[52]

Liu's choice of title emphasizes the foreign origin, both in spirit and equipment, of most of the observances of the new schools. A group of Chinese were eager to import into China the discipline, patriotism, and warlike spirit that they believed the running of races and the raising of flags signified. Unfortunately, the gaze of many of their countrymen remained obstinately fixed on the outlandish accoutrements of these activities rather than the values they were meant to embody.

Troops Marching in Step

Not all martial activity was playacting, however. Radical student activity was the harbinger, if not the determinant, of the fall of the Qing government in 1911 as it was of the fall of the Guomindang government in 1949. The overtly political activities of students occurred in a context of rebellion against both the restrictions of tradition and the restrictions of modernity—on the one hand, against continued enforcement of intellectual submission to the ruling orthodoxy, and on the other, against contraction of accustomed freedom of personal action.

The Conflict of Generations

Zhang Zhidong, the chief architect of the new school system, was keenly aware of the dangers of eating of the tree of knowledge. The Principles for the Control of Schools, drawn up by Zhang Zhidong and his fellow commissioners in 1903, forbade students to concern themselves with matters outside their studies, to strike, or to hold meetings. In the tradition of early Qing proscriptions of scholars' involvement in political activity, students were not to "vent mad statements and strange theories, write wild books, or put out newspapers," take sides in court cases or tax protests, or secretly join political parties. Even their reading had limitations: no novels purporting to reveal the secrets of official life, no "erroneous papers or heterodox books."[53] Despite the studied vagueness of the interdictions, it is evident that Zhang particularly wanted to check the spread of revolutionary propaganda. He and his colleagues even tried to rid the language of such unsightly neologisms as "association" (*tuanti*), "national soul" (*guohun*), "representative" (*daibiao*), "sacrifice" (*xisheng*), "clash" (*chongtu*), "movement" (*yundong*), and other radical catchwords.[54]

Later writers have stressed the government's repression of student activity in the sphere of national politics. At the time, however, students appear to have found even more irksome the petty restrictions of school life. The new system, in boarding schools in particular (that is, in most higher primary and middle schools), had an unprecedented plethora of regulations and supervisory personnel. From the first gong in the morning to the last at night, a student's every waking moment was—in theory—under scrutiny. In a well-run school, the staff kept a record not only of students' academic work but of their conduct. A certain number of black marks could lead to expulsion.[55]

All this was the opposite of most students' previous educational experience. The few academies that had had resident students had allowed them to leave and enter at will and study as they pleased. At traditional private schools, association after the student had passed the age at which corporal punishment intimidated him was on a voluntary basis. A student dissatisfied with one teacher would seek another or study at home, an equally valid preparation for the examinations. With the new schools, private quarrels became public, both in the sense that they were discussed in the press and in the sense that they often took place in public institutions.

While the examination system lasted, the independence of student life was counterbalanced by its strict procedural and ideological requirements. In return for three years' freedom from supervision, the scholar had to provide triennial proof of absolute fidelity and submission. A paper dropped on the floor or failure to elevate a reference to the dynasty above the surrounding text would ruin a candidate's chances. Yet few balked at these restraints. Although only a fraction of those awarded degrees obtained office, the examinations remained the only "regular route" to prestigious and remunerative imperial appointment. Under the new system, the links between graduation and office were not formally broken until 1910, but it was evident earlier that they had been considerably attenuated. In the last part of the nineteenth century, an average of 1,500 scholars became juren at each triennial provincial examination.[56] In 1907, more than 21,000 students were enrolled in China for courses whose successful completion would entitle them to the juren degree; had only half obtained it, the new schools would have produced seven times as many juren as the old examinations, not counting those with Japanese degrees. And this was in the infancy of the system; as a contemporary commentator pointed out, once China had achieved the same level of education as Japan, it would be producing 66,960 juren a year, or forty times as many as the total number of official positions.[57] Students may not have possessed the arithmetical ability or statistical data to enable such an exact calculation, but it was evident to them that their prospects of official employment were uncertain. Their adherence to the rules determining eligibility for such employment was correspondingly weakened.

The poor quality of living conditions increased discontent. Students were often crowded into makeshift dormitories and given poor or insufficient food. Several cooks left Qingzhou Middle School in 1903 after being beaten by dissatisfied students.[58] The authorities at Wucheng Gongxue, set up in Beijing in 1898 on the crest of the wave of reform, had a great deal of trouble with refractory students. An examination question at the school gives an indirect picture of their grievances by listing the sufferings of foreign students, possibly in the hope of eliciting a patriotic response:

> Foreign countries are extremely hard on their students and give them only rank, cold, unpalatable beef for lunch. At night they have to sleep on long benches, as uncomfortable as caged prisoners. Naval and mili-

8. A Comment on the Value of New Qualifications: The traditionally dressed figures to the right carry plaques identifying their achievements in the old educational system. After passing under a gateway labeled "Intensive Course" surmounted by a cloud of "electricity," they emerge dressed in modern student uniforms holding flags proclaiming their degrees in botany, mining, and economics. (*Xingqi huabao*, no. 46 [1907])

tary students are penned up in a most cruel way. But the method of examination is extremely fair; in the Paris Law School, for example, students are examined by drawing lots for questions in their subjects, after which they write answers on the blackboard. Those who pass get three ticks and are applauded by the rest of the class. This is a most august ceremony. But although they are normally treated with such cruelty, no one has ever been heard of as leaving the school. Why do they stay?[59]

In themselves, living conditions and regulations are insufficient to account for the constant eruption of student strikes and walkouts. For this one must look to relations between staff and students. It was not simply the presence of regulations that provoked students, but the question of authority to administer them; not simply poor food, but mishandling of protests about its quality. The schools placed staff and students in a novel situation. It would be an oversimplification to say that the new system represented a transition from a personal to an impersonal mode of teaching; with most post-elementary pupils studying in schools with under 60 students and a high staff-student ratio, there was plenty of room for friendships to grow or grudges to fester. Rather, teachers and students were passing from an area in which personal relationships were, within certain limits, knowable in advance to one in which they were not. This was only in part a question of pre-existing personal acquaintance. Certainly under the new system teachers were less likely to be relatives or family friends, or even to come from the same region. Even so, as indicated above, the network of social relationships based on personal acquaintance, kinship, and local place continued to operate within the new schools.

The problem was not so much the lack of personal ties as uncertainty over their sphere. The new roles of pupils and teachers were not clearly defined, the values on which they were predicated were in flux. Guo Moruo's schoolteacher-relative acted as a mediator between the school and Guo's father after Guo was expelled for being rude to the head.[60] This was the customary method of settling minor disputes, but its validity was uncertain in the changed surroundings of the new school.

No agreement over the principles and limits within which school life should be regulated had been reached. What for one side was a rising against "oppression" and "enslavement" was for the other simply indiscipline and lack of self-control. The pages of *Su bao* are filled with the accusations and justifications of anonymous student correspondents, selecting from the new doctrines on the rights of man and the duties of the citizen such arguments as suited their case.[61]

The authority of teachers over students was brought into question partly because many of the new teachers had themselves cast off the authority of the older generation. It was they who stigmatized as reactionary all defenders of the eight-legged essay, who denigrated the examination system, who attempted to reform or proscribe sishu. Another problem of the transitional period was that school discipline and courses were aimed at children but taken by young men. In one primary school in Zhili, seven of the fifteen pupils were over 29 years old.[62] At fifteen, Shu Xincheng was the youngest in his higher primary class. After the adult life of the academy he had previously attended, he found school a boring imposition: "What the teachers talked about was commonplace, nothing near as interesting as what I found in books."[63]

Clashes were predictable when student adherents of the new ways were placed under their opponents. In Changsha, students appealed to the governor against a known reactionary said to have been made head of the normal school simply to buy off his opposition.[64] In Guangzhou, students protested against the quality of teaching through satirical wall posters.[65] Thirty-two Yangzhou students left school after quarreling with a notorious diehard.[66] In the coastal provinces and the Yangzi basin, such protests often ended with the dismissal or resignation of the unsatisfactory teacher. The situation appears to have been otherwise in the interior: a student was said to have been expelled from a Shaanxi school simply for having included foreign names in his paper, ample evidence that he was a supporter of Kang Youwei and reader of the *Xinmin congbao*.[67]

If old-fashioned staff were sometimes to blame for clashes, there was also the problem of old-fashioned students, who were not going to let a nominal change from independent to subservient status interfere with their customary entertainments. There was no way of enforcing the prohibition of opium smoking in schools. Students would leap over the school wall or make an arrangement with the doorkeeper so that they could spend their nights in gambling dens or brothels.[68] It appears that the establishment of a government school was as welcome to law-abiding townsfolk as the quartering of a detachment of troops or the triennial influx of examination candidates (when, according to Chen Duxiu, shopkeepers were at the mercy of riotous students).[69]

At Wuhu Middle School, the student body was said to be so accustomed to doing as it pleased that the head of the provincial education society graduated it en masse and enrolled new students.[70] The school inspector's fear that even this move would not offset the corrupting influence of the school's location, the treaty port of Wuhu, proved correct when new students, "habituated to wildness," drove out the head of the school and beat up a servant after being served a poor dinner.[71]

More daunting to those with hopes for the unifying power of a modern educational system was the continued frequency of disturbances in schools where both staff and students might have been expected to show a commitment to or at least acceptance of the new system. Commenting on an incident in 1910 in which a headmaster tried to expel his whole school, a writer for the *Jiaoyu zazhi* noted that "when education was first getting under way, the teachers did not understand education and the students did not follow the rules, so the frequency of clashes was understandable. But now almost all scholars are produced by the schools alone, and education has been promoted for years. When the present situation is still like this, what hope can one have for the future?"[72]

Many clashes were not over points of ideology but over trivia. An ink bottle on a teacher's chair, denial of a holiday, chili peppers taken from a teacher's table—all these could set in motion a complex sequence of apologies demanded and denied, deputations and reprisals, intercessions and expulsions. A contemporary writer observed that "all so-called teachers do for their students today is give them a few high-sounding clichés: 'You gentlemen are the talents who will arrest our decline, you are China's future leaders' . . . all vague and groundless . . . and [responsible for] increasing their rowdy ways . . . They are never together for more than a few months without clashes arising, in which teachers regard their schools as temporary lodgings and students look on their teachers the same way as the owner ordering his servants around."[73]

Certainly the ideology of the new school system—the vision of its part in a new China—increased both the confidence and the frustration of students. They were the heralds of a new age, but it was disappointingly slow to follow their summons. In the meantime, they battled real and imaginary relics of the past and slights to the present.

Old-fashioned license joined with a newfound sense of superiority in students at the new schools. Teachers who knew less than they did aroused their scorn. Where moral rather than factual correctness was concerned, they were arbiters of "civilized behavior"—that supposed to be current in the industrialized West and Japan. The attribution of civilization to foreigners and barbarism to Chinese divides two generations. Foot binding was "barbarous"—to the young; the older generation might be roused to fury by such a description.[74] "Barbarous" was used as a stick to beat teachers and superiors. Guo Moruo's recreation of student unrest at his school may owe a little to imagination as well as memory, but renders superbly the attitude of students toward their elders. At an interview with a young student over a dining-hall quarrel, the exasperated headmaster struck the student, who burst into tears. "I could not hold myself back," wrote Guo. "'Mr. Yi, really that was barbarous.' 'Yes, barbarous, barbarous!' the students outside the window all started calling out. 'Barbarous headmaster! Barbarous headmaster!—How could anyone still strike a student in these civilized times!—It's too inhumane, it's despising us!'"[75]

Anti-Manchuism in China and Japan

Resentment and revolt in the schools did not arise solely from internal factors; they were by-products of the Western invasion that had provided both the impulse and the model for reform. When, despite the new school system and the reform of the army, foreigners were still not set to rout, thwarted nationalism turned easily to anti-Manchuism. Here again, the model was a foreign one: China's young intellectuals took up the slogans of "freedom" and "equality" used in the French revolution. ("Equality" referred not to the equality of different social classes but to the equality of generation, race, and sex within the elite.) They were a justification of rebellion not only against the Manchus but against all dictatorial control by the older generation. In the vacuum left by the abolition of the examinations, the government struggled ineffectually to regain its once automatic control over the educated while students sought to preserve their former freedoms from the encroachment of new rules by an assumed superiority to the makers of the rules. The new schools supplanted the examination system as a means of defining the elite; at the same time, they offered young men a vehicle for rebellion against the elite in the persons of those set over them and provided ideal surroundings for conspiracy.

As early as 1900, forbidden works on the Manchu conquest of China had begun to circulate in the schools. At Hangzhou, Ma Xulun came under the influence of a historian on the staff who related the rise and fall of past dynasties to China's current predicament and told his class to read works such as *Mingyi daifang lu* (A Plan for the Prince) by the Ming loyalist Huang Zongxi (1610–1695). These discussions and Ma's own reading, combined with the rout of the Boxers and the flight of the court to Xian, served to inculcate in Ma the beginnings of revolutionary thought. He formed plans to study in a military school in Japan; he himself did not carry out this plan, but two of his friends did. One of them, Jiang Fangzhen, later became military adviser to Chiang Kai-shek.[76]

Study in Japan was the recourse of many frustrated patriots. Increasing numbers of both private and scholarship students found there a new freedom from both political restrictions and social obligations. For the student abroad, "the restraints of his early environment, home, and family (many of them were married) were greatly weakened. He enjoyed a freedom of thought and expression he had not known before. To arrive, as he usually did, with no knowledge of Japanese, and to be placed in a foreign setting required serious mental adjustments. One student said it was like 'being dropped from one planet to another.'"[77] Many found their studies of secondary interest. One observer commented coldly that if there was anything worse than students who pocketed their scholarship money without going to Japan, it was those who went but either did not enroll in a course or "entered any school at all, and after a few months picked a quarrel and left. They hang around for years, and there is nothing they won't do." Most private students were, in his opinion, either aspirants for office hoping to brighten up their curriculum vitae or youths seeking a pretext for dissipation away from home.[78]

Among students' extracurricular activities were demonstrations: on student issues, such as against the Qing attempt, in 1902, to limit the number of private students enrolling in military studies and against the 1905 regulations on the control of Chinese students issued by Japanese authorities; and on national ones, such as the Manchurian crisis of 1903. In Tokyo, students organized a volunteer army with nearly two hundred members. They also published numerous radical periodicals.[79]

The political radicalism fermenting in Tokyo had its counterpart in Shanghai, which was beyond the effective jurisdiction of the Qing government. Several activists who had returned from Japan committed to revolution, including Zhang Shizhao, Wu Zhihui, Zou Rong, Huang Xing, and Zhang Binglin, pursued the task of publicizing the anti-Manchu cause and organizing for revolution from Shanghai. The Aiguo Xueshe, a school formed by expelled students from Nanyang Gongxue with the support of noted scholars Cai Yuanpei and Zhang Binglin, became a model of militant democracy; indeed, students spent so much time at meetings and military drill that they attended few classes.[80] Such organization was supposed to foreshadow the civilized, unrepressive China of the future; but its laxity and reliance on human rather than mechanical discipline—on principled discussion rather than on clocks and bells—show traces of the academic life that several of the older revolutionary leaders had experienced earlier in their careers.[81]

The Spread of Revolutionary Ideas

One student at Nanyang Gongxue recalled being taught from anti-Manchu works such as *Tong shi* (A Painful History). For the most part, however, Liang Qichao's *Xinmin congbao* was the dominant organ of the early 1900s, and it was his picture of an oppressed Guangxu emperor and vicious and corrupt Empress Dowager that gained the widespread sympathy of the young.[82] Zou Taofen, as a student at Nanyang Gongxue, borrowed a complete set of the *Xinmin congbao* from a friendly teacher and "came under the spell" of Liang Qichao's skill as an essayist.[83] Outside Shanghai, the *Xinmin congbao*'s circulation was wider than that of revolutionary propaganda in the early 1900s. One Fujian student learned modern history through its pages, accepting its picture of the piteous deposed emperor, although he did not understand its call for "democracy," "freedom," or a "constitution."[84]

As the events of 1898 receded, the *Xinmin congbao* became relatively respectable. In Guangxi, in 1904, the newly appointed provincial educational officer promoted the reading of the *Xinmin congbao* as well as the works of Ming loyalists and Yan Fu's translations of Mill and Huxley. "At that time," a contemporary recalled,

> most of Guangxi's intellectuals were disciples of Kang and Liang and enthusiasts for reform. Afterward they read *Min bao* and *Huangdi hun*

and other revolutionary writings and came into contact with Tongmeng Hui [Sun Yat-sen's group] people. This, with their perception, through developments in current affairs, of the Qing court's incurable reaction and corruption and of the imminence of the dreadful day when China would be carved up by the foreign powers, led them to realize that reform proposals aimed at ameliorating the present system could not save China from perishing. Thus they gradually broke with reformism and, taking a further step along the revolutionary road, joined the Tongmeng Hui.[85]

The "intellectuals" referred to by this writer did not include all of China's educated men, nor even the total product of the new schools; rather, he was speaking of a small number of the Japanese-educated and those whom they influenced on their return directly or through their propaganda.

Anxiety over China's possible dismemberment had marked calls for reform since Kang Youwei and Liang Qichao had sounded the alarm in the 1890s; it was to prove a fertile field for the revolutionaries. Government-approved texts included some material on China's recent history, but much more was added by patriotic teachers dissatisfied with the present conduct of affairs. Indeed, the liveliest part of the curriculum appears to have been that with direct relevance to China's current plight. A geography lesson in a Guangdong village came to life when the teacher had the pupils color the provinces of China according to their future masters: England, in red, would take Guangdong and Guangxi, Tibet and Sichuan, and Shanghai; and so on through the spectrum— France would have Yunnan and Guizhou, Japan Fujian, Germany Shandong, and Russia the northeast, until eventually only China's barren heartland, Shaanxi province, remained.[86] Even young children picked up something of their country's danger. The writer Cao Juren recalled the deep, though to his infant mind inexplicable, emotions produced in the audience at his country primary school in Zhejiang by a speaker on something called "partition," which meant that all Chinese were going to become foreigners.[87] At the Guangdong village school mentioned above, some of the older boys were kept back after school and asked if they were ready to overthrow the Manchus: an Australian Chinese, the first to speak up, was given a new name, "First," in commemoration of his readiness.[88]

Men who had been willing to give the Qing qualified support were alienated by its reluctance to proceed with constitutional reform. Among them was Xu Teli, who later influenced the young Mao Zedong: "My knowledge of the different subjects was greater than that of my teachers" at the Changsha Normal School (Xu had been studying the new learning on his own), "but what I learned there was new, especially with regard to revolutionary theory."[89] Xu went on to teach and work for constitutional reform. In November 1909, fearing that the provinces' petition for a parliament would once again be fobbed off, he cut off a finger in front of his class and wrote a petition in his own blood.[90] The act shows both a willingness to allow the government one last chance and a pessimism amounting to desperation about its capacity to take it.

The reaction of provincial and local officials and of school authorities to revolutionary propaganda in the new schools varied. Such propaganda was treason, but just because of the magnitude of the crime, such cases were troublesome to deal with. Few magistrates wished to have members of local gentry families executed. Their dilemma is illustrated by an anecdote recounted by Ma Xulun. In 1906, Ma was teaching in a new school in a Zhejiang county. Opponents of the new school—those who had relied on the emoluments of the academy it replaced—accused its founder of writing disrespectful words on the Empress Dowager's photograph, and the case was taken to the magistrate. Though aware of the accusers' motives, he was afraid that lenience would incur the wrath of the Manchu prefect above him; at the same time he was being menaced by Ma and his colleagues, who paid a nocturnal visit to warn him of the consequences of a harsh judgment. The matter was eventually settled through the good offices of the circuit intendant, who happened to be from the magistrate's home county, and the offender escaped with a fine.[91] A similar pattern—of accusations brought by outsiders with a grudge being nullified by the intervention, on grounds of personal acquaintance, of high officials who were not themselves revolutionaries— appears in an incident involving Huang Xing and the Changsha school, Mingde. When a powerful conservative accused Huang Xing, who had filled in his spare time at the school making gunpowder in its science laboratory and planning an uprising, of being a revolutionary, the headmaster was able to call on a vice-president of the Board of Punishment. The latter assured the provincial governor of Huang's good character and introduced Huang to the head of the Office of Educational Affairs, with whose connivance all evidence was destroyed.[92] Huang escaped to Shanghai.

Whether from a justifiable doubt of students' revolutionary capacities or from unwillingness to stir up a hornet's nest, school authorities often turned a blind eye to the political proclivities of their charges. Periodicals such as *Min bao* were passed from hand to hand among students and sympathetic teachers. In Hubei, "in the years before 1911, a number of forbidden books became very popular in our school, but the school authorities never took notice of it. In their view, the forbidden books advocated only anti-Manchu revolution and presented no direct threat to their own position. Consequently they did not interfere."[93] A playlet in a popular magazine gives an entertaining picture of a search by conscientious officials for forbidden literature; forewarned students tucked copies of *Min bao* into their trousers and jackets and found only amusement in the fruitless search of their rooms.[94]

To say that retribution was by no means certain is not to say that making revolution was "a dinner party." Sedition was still a capital crime, and the threat of execution hung over offenders and warned off the fainthearted and the law-abiding. In general, however, officials were reluctant to deal harshly with anyone who had not openly advocated the overthrow of the dynasty; at least within school walls, flirting with revolution might bring only a pleasing notoriety.[95]

How far did student politicization extend? In 1909, China had 147 tertiary schools, 692 secondary schools, and a number of military schools.[96] Tertiary and military education was concentrated in provincial capitals, which usually also had the best middle and higher primary schools. Many teachers at this level were returned students from Japan.[97] Even if a school's staff and students did not actively espouse revolution, they had access to newspapers, books, and journals from Shanghai and Tokyo containing the latest theories. Stories of school strikes and protests were written up by professional journalists or sent in by part-time student contributors, thus contributing to students' self-image. The mixture was an explosive one.

In Sichuan, for example, Chengdu had the province's only higher-level school, four schools of law and political studies, an upper normal school, an industrial school, and a police school, and three army schools, as well as secondary and primary schools.[98] When the movement against nationalization of the province's railroads broke out in open defiance of the authorities in 1911, "the students at all the schools were foremost in enthusiastic support." A branch of the newly founded Society of Comrades for the Protection of the Railroads was set up among them: its head came from the higher-level school, his deputy from the upper normal school. Other schools sent delegates.[99]

Although large cities and treaty ports were the headquarters of student activity, every student was a potential propagandist for reform or revolution in his own hometown. Letters or visits home made elders familiar with, if not enamored of, new concepts and approaches and provided a model for younger family members. Although many local schools remained sunk in the rustic oblivion of their traditional ancestors, in a few, the graduates of higher institutions sought to apply their ideals for a new society or, on a more prosaic level, simply to make a living.

The Sichuan railroad rights recovery movement provides another example of the nature and limitations of such influence at the local level. Personal ties were all-important. To Dazu county, for example, the movement's Chengdu headquarters sent two emissaries: one a juren, former head of the county's academy and later of its higher primary school, now a provincial assemblyman, the other his former pupil, now studying at the Chengdu Upper Normal School. The younger brother of the latter recalled:

> Since [the assemblyman] had a great many pupils in the county and a very high reputation, and since my brother was also one of his students, the work of setting up a county-level organization was smoothly carried out in a short time. They also sent people to the market towns and districts to organize people there. Our talk moved from the county society to the provincial one, and thence to the noble behavior [of the movement's leaders] at its opening meeting, and the traitorous crimes of Sheng Xuanhuai . . . our conversation concentrated solely on these topics, which were all fresh to me.[100]

Revolutionary organizations also had a foothold in provincial and prefectural schools. Sun Yat-sen sent a fellow revolutionary from Tokyo to teach in Guangdong's Huizhou Prefectural Middle School in 1907; by the following year, more than eighty of its students had joined the Tongmeng Hui.[101] In Hunan, "at least ten schools in Changsha had revolutionaries on their staff."[102] A reading of the memoirs collected in *Xinhai geming huiyilu* (Reminiscences of the 1911 Revolution) shows that almost every province had its cadre of Tongmeng Hui members scattered through middle and higher-level schools, a potential audience of some 90,000 students.[103] Less was probably achieved by direct conversion, however, than by familiarization: few espoused revolution, and fewer still put their ideas into practice, but many gained an idea of what revolutionaries meant by the new terms in their vocabulary—"revolution" (*geming*), "organize" (*zuzhi*), "representative" (*daibiao*). (Even in 1911, many older scholars found "revolution" indistinguishable from "rebellion.") The infiltration of these concepts into the everyday usage of the educated was an achievement the schools would share with that other new institution, the press. But the new knowledge circulated and recirculated in limited channels. As a later writer observed,

> While educationalists have already introduced the latest methods from Europe and America, the masses, as of old, stand outside the circle of education; while authors have already written cartloads of books, the masses, as of old, will not part with the *Hundred Family Names* and the *Three Character Classic*. The louder we shout our song, the less the peo-

ple dare to join in—it is not that they do not dare, but that they cannot. Our whole culture has lost touch with ordinary people: in the sky there are planes flying about and on the ground, as of old, one-wheeled carts still struggle in the mud.[104]

"The transformation of the people" that both reformers and revolutionaries hoped to achieve through education in the last years of the Qing had to await the future.

Conclusion

At the end of the nineteenth century, China was embarking on the transition from a "familial" society to one based on "military citizenship," to use the analysis of the Ministry of Education in 1909. That is, the informal, particularistic ties that had characterized a highly commercialized but basically agrarian state were starting to give way to the impersonal regulation of the industrialized West and Japan. The modern school system was a hallmark of the transition. One of its more perceptive observers, Shu Xincheng, wrote, "[in 1908] I left the sishu produced by agricultural society and embarked on the school life that was a product of modern industrialized society"—a life characterized by impersonality, division of labor, mechanical routine, and the isolation of the school from the rest of society.[105]

Under duress, China attempted to weave patches of new cloth into the fabric of national life in the hope of protecting the whole against further rents. In the process, homespun was discarded—the indigenous sishu, academies, and examination system, which had served the empire for hundreds, even thousands, of years were thrown into the rag-bag because they gave China no advantage in the struggle for survival. The prestige of the victorious West and Japan overrode all other considerations.

It would be fallacious to say that "advanced" institutions that have functioned effectively in one society can never be adopted in another more "backward" society. Japan, which had a premodern level of education similar to China's, adapted Western education very successfully to its own purposes. China's attempt to remodel education along Western lines was by no means a ludicrous failure: although only 1.5 million students—a little under 4 percent of the estimated school-age population, or 8 percent of school-age boys—had transferred to the new schools by 1909, this nonetheless represented rapid progress compared with 1,274 students only five years earlier. By the dynasty's end, tens of thousands of the new schools were in existence, tens of thousands of teachers had been trained, and the original rigidity of the system had been modified to allow for sishu-like establishments teaching approved patriotic texts. Many of the innovations of the new system proved durable. The division of schooling vertically into primary, secondary, and tertiary study and horizontally into academic, normal, and technical training; the Ministry of Education; the triad of mental, physical, and moral development; and some of modern China's most famous educational institutions, including Beijing, Qinghua, and Nankai universities, all date from the last years of the Qing.

Other sensible adjustments, however, fell victim to political maneuvering, lack of funds, or changes in personnel. It took mass education decades to return to the principle of the simple reading school. The use of romanized Chinese in education suffered a similar setback.

Modest though it was in absolute terms, educational progress was already out of kilter with the hopes and needs of the multitude of villagers in areas little affected by Western contact. The discrepancy widened in succeeding decades, as top city schools copied the Western model more and more successfully while peasant communities lived and died unlettered. One cannot blame the framers of the new school system for not having seen that internal warfare and external trade cycles would retard China's progress into the industrialized world, although they should have foreseen the burden that an enormous population and land area and limited agricultural surplus would place on its forward movement.

The unfounded optimism of reformers left the next generation with a sense of frustration and indignation. Personal and national expectations had been raised but not fulfilled. The new school system did not give everybody an education, but it inculcated the belief that everyone should have one; it did not provide the schooled with jobs, but left them feeling cheated and dissatisfied at being unable to find positions for which they had been trained. The shortfall between expectation and performance led to the radicalization of a substantial minority of students, teachers, and educationalists.

Nor did the central government achieve its goals of increased strength and central control. On the contrary, schools at the upper levels proved something of a Trojan horse, introducing Western ideas of patriotism that overtook the Confucian ideal of loyalty and accustomed the young to trials of strength with their superiors. With the abolition of the state examinations and the rise of overseas training and private colleges, the court in effect lost its monopoly on the granting of gentry status and dissolved the link between scholarship and office holding that had fortified Chinese dynasties for over a thousand years. Furthermore, gentry involvement in educational funding and administration fueled demands for local and provincial self-government, issues that, mishandled by the Qing, contributed as much as radical ideology to the Revolution of 1911.

For education to play its part in producing the citizens of a modern society whose "every action is like the rhythm of a machine, every move is like soldiers marching in step,"[106] much had to change besides the schools themselves. Despite the vicissitudes of political change, China has gone a long way since 1949 toward realizing the reformers' goals of a strong army, modern industry, and universal schooling; but universal education has not meant universal equality, or practical subjects full employment. The aspirations raised by education and increased knowledge continue to outpace the gains brought by education itself, and the debate over the place of foreign models and local needs in the "training of talent" and the "transformation of the people" continues.

Notes

Introduction

1. Marianne Bastid, *Aspects de la réforme de l'enseignement en Chine au début du 20ᵉ siècle: D'après des écrits de Zhang Jian* (Paris: Mouton & Cie, 1971), p. 5.

2. Guo Moruo, *Wo de younian* (Shanghai: Guanghua shuju, 1930), pp. 166–68.

Chapter One

1. The country *xuegong* ("palace" or "hall" of learning) began in the Song as government schools. To become a shengyuan was known as "entering school" (*jinxue*). By the late Qing, they had no resident students and gave no teaching. For a discussion of their ritual functions, see Stephen Feuchtwang, "School Temple and City God," in G. William Skinner, ed., *The City in Late Imperial China* (Stanford: Stanford University Press, 1977), pp. 581–608.

2. Figures derived from Chang Chung-li, *The Chinese Gentry: Studies on Their Role in Nineteenth-Century China* (Seattle: University of Washington Press, 1955), pp. 122, 125, 152, 159; and Miyazaki Ichisada, *China's Examination Hell*, trans. Conrad Schirokauer (New York and Tokyo: Weatherhill, 1976), p. 38.

3. Tang Caichang, family letter (31 May 1895), quoted in Su Yunfeng, *Zhang Zhidong yu Hubei jiaoyu gaige* (Taibei: Zhongyang yanjiuyuan, Jindaishi yanjiusuo, 1976), p. 56.

4. *Qinding da-Qing huidian shili* (hereafter *Shili*) (Taibei: Guoli zhongyang tushuguan, 1963), 389: 1a–b. The injunctions were engraved on a tablet laid to the left of the Minglun Tang, the main shrine within the school-temple (see Shang Yanliu, *Qingdai keju kaoshi shulu* [Beijing: Sanlian shudian, 1958], p. 45).

5. See Hsiao Kung-chuan, *Rural China: Imperial Control in the Nineteenth Century* (Seattle: University of Washington Press, 1960), pp. 246–49, for examples of "bad scholars."

6. Memorial of censor Wenti impeaching Kang Youwei, in Su Yu, ed., *Yijiao congbian* (Taibei: Guofeng chubanshe, 1970), 2: 9a.

7. *Huangchao wenxian tongkao*, 21, Zhiyi.

8. *Shili*, 398: 6a.

9. The rural compact began as an association for mutual assistance and surveillance during the Song. The original Four Pledges of the Lu Family were replaced during the sixteenth century by the Six Maxims of the Hongwu emperor; the maxims were in turn succeeded by the teachings of the Qing emperors. The institution has had an abiding interest for Chinese thinkers: Zhu Xi and Wang Yangming both wrote on it, and in the twentieth century it provided inspiration for Liang Shuming.

10. *Shili*, 398: 11b.

11. Wu Jingzi, *Rulin waishi*, chapter 42, contains a description of the invocation of spirits by officials presiding over the examinations (Chen Dongyuan, *Zhongguo jiaoyushi* [Shanghai: Shangwu yinshuguan, 1937], pp. 388–89). Chen comments that Wu's account accords with the memory of elderly scholars; thus the ceremony was evidently still practiced late in the dynasty. *Rulin waishi* has been translated into English under the title *The Scholars* by Yang Hsien-yi and Gladys Yang (Beijing: Foreign Languages Press, 1957).

12. Zhan Ruoshui (Ming), quoted in Liu Boji, *Guangdong shuyuan zhidu yange* (Shanghai: Shangwu yinshuguan, 1939), pp. 413–14.

13. For a discussion of the attitudes of some noted Qing thinkers toward examination requirements, see Charles P. Ridley, "Educational Theory and Practice in Late Imperial China: The Teaching of Writing as a Specific Case" (Ph.D. diss., Stanford University, 1973), pp. 73, 465–66.

14. *Shili*, 395: 1b.

15. Ibid., 395: 6a.

16. Ibid., 395: 3b.

17. Expenditures appear to have been lower in the eighteenth century (see Liu Boji, *Guangdong shuyuan zhidu yange*, pp. 209–11).

18. For Guangdong, see Tilemann Grimm, "Academies and Urban Systems in Kwangtung," in Skinner, *The City in Late Imperial China*, pp. 482–83. For further details on merchant support of academies, see Ōkubo Hideko, *Min Shin jidai shoin no kenkyū* (Tokyo: Kokusho kankō kai, 1976), pp. 221–361.

19. For the relationship between the urban and the academic hierarchy, see Grimm, "Academies and Urban Systems," pp. 487–90.

20. Ibid., p. 478.

21. Liu Boji, *Guangdong shuyuan zhidu yange*, p. 293.

22. *Shili*, 395: 5a.

23. Ibid., 395: 2b–3a.

24. Liu Jincao, comp., *Huangchao xu wenxian tongkao* (Taibei: Xinxing shuju, 1963), Xuexiao: 7. The passage is written from the point of view of an advocate of reform and gives a one-sided picture.

25. See Chen Dongyuan, *Zhongguo jiaoyushi*, pp. 285–86.

26. *Shili*, 395: 3a.

27. Yuan dynasty study rules, quoted in Liu Boji, *Guangdong shuyuan zhidu yange*, pp. 420–23.

28. Ibid., pp. 424–25.

29. For government involvement in public education, see Evelyn Rawski, *Education and Popular Literacy in Ch'ing China* (Ann Arbor: University of Michigan Press, 1979), pp. 33–35; and Ogawa Yoshiko, "A Study of the Foundation of the Premodern Educational System in the Ching Era," (M.A. thesis, Stanford University, 1958). Rawski holds that *shexue* and *yixue* are variant names for publicly funded schools rather than terms denoting different institutions.

30. The early Ming promoted community schools on a large scale. The court ordered the establishment of one community school for every 50 families in 1375 and again in 1383. The main text taught was the Great Proclamation of the Hongwu emperor. Both in its attempt at nationwide coverage and in the use of education for propaganda, the Ming plan for community schools recalls the development of modern education in Europe and Japan; it was, however, never fully realized by its founding dynasty, and by the nineteenth century the few community schools still functioning may have been merely "staging points for admonishing the population to behave" (Grimm, "Academies and Urban Systems," p. 480).

31. Rawski, *Education and Popular Literacy*, p. 184.

32. Chiang Yee, *A Chinese Childhood* (London: Methuen, 1940), p. 52.

33. Y. K. Leong and L. K. Tao, *Village and Town Life in China* (London: Allen & Unwin, 1915), p. 19.

34. To use an American sociologist's distinction, the Chinese system resembles the "sponsored mobility" of English education, "in which the elite or their agents choose recruits early and carefully induct them into elite status" rather than the "contest mobility" supposed to characterize American education, in which "elite status is the prize in an open contest." Although in China competition for elite status was theoretically open to all males except those of mean origin, the rules of the game ensured that entry depended on the early internalization of elite values. (See Ralph Turner, "Sponsored and Contest Mobility and the School System," *American Sociological Review* 25, no. 6 [1960], 855–67.)

35. Rawski, *Education and Popular Literacy*, pp. 38–39, 79; and Ogawa, "Premodern Educational System," pp. 9–10.

36. Rawski, *Education and Popular Literacy*, p. 186.

37. See ibid., pp. 84–88, for evaluation of data on lineage schools.

38. Liu Zizhou, "Yixuezheng Wu Gong zhuan," in Li Shizhao, ed., *Wu Xun xiansheng de zhuanji* (Shanghai: Jiaoyu shudian, 1948), p. 6.

39. Chen Daiqing, "Wu Qi xiao zhuan," in Li Shizhao, *Wu Xun xiansheng de zhuanji*, p. 11.

40. Chairman Mao's 1951 criticism of the cult of Wu Xun started a campaign to tear every shred of credit from Wu's name. For a typical product of the campaign, see Wu Xun Lishi Diaocha Tuan, *Wu Xun lishi diaocha ji* (Beijing: Renmin chubanshe, 1951).

Chapter Two

1. For the latter, see E. P. Thompson, "Time, Work-Discipline, and Industrial Capitalism," in M. W. Flinn and T. C. Smout, eds., *Essays in Social History* (London: Oxford University Press, 1974), pp. 39–77.

2. Basil Bernstein's "On the Classification and Framing of Educational Knowledge," in Michael F. D. Young, ed., *Knowledge and Control* (London: Collier-Macmillan, 1971), pp. 47–69, afforded some starting points for this analysis, although I did not find his typologies directly applicable.

3. Wang Chong, a philosopher of the second century A.D., attended a school that taught reading and writing to village children from classical texts. A millennium later, children in Song sishu were taught in similar fashion; many of the same primers continued in use into the twentieth century. (See Chen Dongyuan, *Zhongguo jiaoyushi* [Shanghai: Shangwu yinshuguan, 1937], pp. 62, 311.)

4. I have encountered only one example of a three-teacher sishu. It was run by members of three generations of one family, two of whom held the first degree, indicating an exceptional concurrence of talent and longevity. (Zhang Moseng, *Li Zongwu zhuan* [Taibei: Landeng chubanshe, 1970], p. 59.)

5. Li Zonghuang, *Li Zhonghuang huiyilu* (Taibei: Zhongguo difang zizhi xuehui, 1972), p. 42. Li was a Yunnanese writer whose father was school manager, or chief sponsor, for sishu of this size. William Liu remembers classes in his village near Guangzhou of the same size (interview).

6. The only figures I have seen that predate the new school system are for two Zhili counties in the 1880s. Average class sizes are 5 for one county and 11 for the other. The figures were for combined yixue and sishu attendance, excluding attendance at jiashu or single-family schools. Given this omission, the number of boys per school in the first county is surprisingly low (Evelyn Rawski, "Appendix 2: The System of Elementary Education in South Chihli," *Education and Popular Literacy in Ch'ing China* [Ann Arbor: University of Michigan Press, 1979], p. 188). For the period after the introduction of the new school system in 1903, sishu in Shangyuan county, Jiangsu, for example, averaged 15 pupils in 1910 (*Jiaoyu zazhi* 2, no. 3 [1910]: Jishi, 20) as did those in Beijing in the same year (*Xue Bu guanbao* 92 [1909]: Jingwai xuewu baogao, 17a). Smaller schools

were less likely to attract the notice of investigators and had more reason to hide from them since size was a partial qualification for approval by educational authorities. Incomplete statistics from 1935 showed a national average of 17. Shandong had the smallest classes, averaging 11 pupils; Anhui followed with 13. Classes in Beiping, Tianjin, and Nanjing averaged between 22 and 24. (*Jiaoyu zazhi* 26, no. 12 [1936]: 136.) The same caveats that apply to Qing statistics apply to these. If reliable, the figures for these urban sishu may indicate a demand for education rising with increased population and/or the influence of the larger size of the new schools.

7. Zhou Shizhao, *Women de shibiao* (Beijing: Beijing chubanshe, 1958), p. 9.

8. For the last case, see Liao T'ai-ch'u, "Rural Education in Transition," *Yenching Journal of Social Studies* 4, no. 2 (1949): 34. For Liao, the charity school (yixue) is a type of sishu. Another author, who lists the village school as a type of family school, defines it as managed solely by the teacher (Yu Shulin, *Zhongguo jiaoyushi* [Taibei: Taiwan shengli shifan daxue, 1961], p. 852). Yet another distinguishes the jiashu from the sishu (Zhou Zuoren, *Zhitang huixianglu* [Hong Kong: Sanyou tushu wenju gongsi, 1970], p. 21). Usage sanctions sishu as a generic term for traditional private tutorial schools, as distinct from all forms of "modern" or "foreign" schools.

9. Among them, Luo Dunwei (*Wushi nian huiyilu* [Taibei: Zhongguo wenhua gongyingshe, 1952], p. 5), Ling Hongxun (*Qishi zishu* [Taibei: Sanmin shuju, 1968], p. 6), Hu Shi (*Sishu zishu* [Shanghai: Yadong tushuguan, 1941], p. 23), and William Liu (interview) were taught by relatives, Gu Jiegang by a friend of his grandfather's (*Gushi bian*, vol. 1 [Beijing: Pu she, 1926], Zi xu, p. 7), and Ma Xulun by a former student of his father's (*Wo zai liushi sui yiqian* [Shanghai: Shenghuo shudian, 1947], p. 4).

10. Bao Tianxiao, *Chuanyinglou huiyilu* (Hong Kong: Dahua chubanshe, 1971), p. 4.

11. See Chen Tianxi, *Chizhuang huiyilu* (Taibei: Shengjing yinshuguan, 1970), p. 34.

12. Guo Moruo's tutor had been in the family since before Guo was born (*Wo de younian* [Shanghai: Guanghua shuju, 1930], p. 47). Chiang Yee's "had been my brother's teacher; his father had been my father's teacher; his son was going to be my nephew's teacher" (*A Chinese Childhood* [London: Methuen, 1940], p. 85).

13. Hsiao Kung-chuan in Sichuan was taught successively by two fellow provincials from Jiangxi (*Wenxue jianwang lu* [Taibei: Zhuanji wenxue chubanshe, 1972], pp. 17–18). Chiang Yee's teacher was not a native of the place where he taught (*A Chinese Childhood*, p. 85).

14. Evelyn Rawski estimates that in the mid-nineteenth century a pool of some 2.9 million men who had taken the lowest-level examination was available to teach 40.3 million school-age boys (*Education and Popular Literacy*, p. 96).

15. Arthur H. Smith, *Village Life in China* (New York: Fleming H. Revell Co., 1899), pp. 67–68.

16. Weng Yanzhen, "Gudai ertong duwu gaiguan," *Tushuguanxue jikan* 10, no. 1 (1936): 138.

17. Miyazaki Ichisada, *China's Examination Hell*, trans. Conrad Schirokauer (New York and Tokyo: Weatherhill, 1976), p. 57. Recognition of a teacher's role in his pupil's success was more readily claimed than acknowledged. For a fictional account of a teacher's hopes for his pupils in the lower examinations, see Li Liuru, *Liushi nian de bianqian* (Beijing: Zuojia chubanshe, 1957), pp. 66–70.

18. The appearance of "teacher" (*shī*) in the family shrine as an object of reverence in the same context as heaven, earth, emperor, and parents is often adduced as evidence of the high esteem in which teachers were held in traditional China (see Ma Xulun, *Wo zai liushi sui yiqian*, p. 15; and Chiang, *A Chinese Childhood*, p. 79). Such reverence appears to have belonged purely to the conceptual realm, in which "teacher" had honored associations with Confucius.

19. Exceptions to this generalization can be found in cases where the teacher offered advanced training and the relationship was reinforced by other ties. Chen Tianxi records three marriages within two generations between his own family and that of his father's teacher (*Chizhuang huiyilu*, p. 32).

20. Rawski, *Education and Popular Literacy*, p. 23. See also pp. 6–8 for discussion of elite and popular female literacy. A figure quoted by Rawski of a literacy rate of 25 percent among female immigrants to Hawaii in 1896 bears out Guangdong's preeminence in this sphere.

21. Liao T'ai-ch'u, "Rural Education in Transition," pp. 19–67.

22. Arthur Smith states rather confusingly that it is "uncommon" for a scholar to teach in his own village, but that it "does often happen." The preference for outside teachers apparently rested on the expectation that they would not be in a position to make troublesome demands on their pupils in later life. (*Village Life in China*, p. 74.) Liao's survey of Wenshang in the 1930s found that "83% . . . were natives of Wenshang and again 65% were members of the same village or township in which they taught" ("Rural Education in Transition," p. 35).

23. Liao T'ai-ch'u, "Rural Education in Transition," p. 34.

24. Ibid., pp. 24, 45.

25. Shu Xincheng, *Wo he jiaoyu* (Shanghai: Zhonghua shuju, 1945), p. 17, notes the operation of the canvasser, or *yaodong*, for Hunan in the 1890s.

26. Smith, *Village Life in China*, p. 67. Another foreign observer quotes a Cantonese proverb, "If I'm poor I'll teach, if I'm hungry I'll scrape the rice pot." (T. K. Dealy, "Mr E. H. Parker's China," *China Review* 25, no. 4 [1900–1901]: 201). Since, in principle, "a Confucianist does not become a farmer, craftsman, merchant or shopkeeper, the only [careers open to him] are to be an official or to teach the young" (Weng Yanzhen, "Gudai ertong duwu gaiguan," p. 138). As few could obtain the former position, many sought the latter. For further evidence on teachers' salaries and pupils' fees at the lower end of the scale, see Rawski, *Education and Popular Literacy*, pp. 104–6.

27. Shu Xincheng, *Wo he jiaoyu*, p. 17. For other mentions of the "discus-

sions of schooling," see Li Zonghuang, *Li Zonghuang huiyilu*, p. 42, for Yunnan in the late 1890s–early 1900s; and Liao T'ai-ch'u, "Rural Education in Transition," p. 56, for Sichuan in the mid-1940s.

28. Smith, *Village Life in China*, p. 74.

29. Weng Yanzhen, "Gudai ertong duwu gaiguan," p. 139.

30. Shan Weifan, "Beiping sishu de yanjiu," *Xin beizhen* 2, no. 10 (1936): 1067.

31. Shu Xincheng, *Wo he jiaoyu*, p. 17. It took Shu's mother only three half-days of work picking wild cotton to earn the cash part of his fees.

32. Hu Shi, *Sishi zishu*, p. 25.

33. Tian Lusheng, "Xuejiu jiaoyu tan," in *Yueyue xiaoshuo*, no. 12 (1907): 33–38.

34. Y. K. Leong and L. K. Tao, *Village and Town Life in China* (London: Allen & Unwin, 1915), p. 96.

35. Shan Weifan, "Beiping sishu de yanjiu," p. 1067.

36. Shu Xincheng, *Wo he jiaoyu*, pp. 38–39, 52.

37. Chen Heqin, *Wo de bansheng* (Shanghai: Shijie shuju, 1941), p. 60.

38. Chang Chung-li, *The Chinese Gentry* (Seattle: University of Washington Press, 1955), p. 183.

39. The best summary of evidence for Qing literacy is to be found in Rawski, *Education and Popular Literacy*, pp. 1–23. Rawski estimates that 30 to 45 percent of males possessed at least basic functional literacy. Appendix 2 of the same study (pp. 187–93) gives the only figures predating the new school system that I have seen for sishu: village records for three areas in southern Zhili in the 1870s and 1880s indicate the existence of 818 sishu (excluding family schools) spread over 878 villages and towns with an estimated school-age (7–14) male population of over 44,000. Vague and conflicting estimates for literacy rates at the end of the nineteenth century are given by Liang Qichao, who suggests a rate of "less than 30 percent" ("Lun xuexiao: Youxue," *Shiwu bao*, no. 16 [1897]), and his fellow reformer Xu Qin, who gives a hyperbolically low estimate of 5 percent ("Zhongguo chu hai yi," in Shu Xincheng, ed., *Jindai Zhongguo jiaoyushi ziliao* [hereafter *Ziliao*] [Beijing: Renmin jiaoyu chubanshe, 1962], 3: 963). No attempt to survey the rate of literacy was made during the Qing, nor were national statistics collected on the number of sishu. (Their very existence goes unmentioned in the statistical compilations of the Ministry of Education.) Apart from the village records mentioned above, the researcher is thrown back on local figures of uncertain validity compiled after the introduction of the new system and on extrapolation from surveys of the 1920s and 1930s, made when the new system was on the way to ousting the old. Beijing was said to have over 7,000 sishu pupils in 1909 (*Xue Bu guanbao*, no. 92 [1909]: Jingwai xuewu baogao, 17), and Shangyuan county to have 3,500 for the same year (*Jiaoyu zazhi* 2, no. 3 [1910]: Jishi, 21). It is unlikely that these or subsequent statistics include private family schools, which by their nature did not advertise their presence. The Beijing figures certainly and the Shangyuan ones possibly were collected in the course of a

drive to reduce the number of sishu. Any schoolmasters aware of this intention would have tried to avoid notice; this makes underreporting highly likely. Apart from defects in the figures as collected, it is possible that the proportion of children in "modern" schools in comparison with the number in sishu was deliberately exaggerated by educational officials interested in establishing a reputation for promoting schools and discouraging sishu. These caveats apply equally to official statistics of the Republican period. The first national survey, made in 1935, showed 101,027 sishu, with 1,757,014 pupils, still existing. Another source of figures is independent surveys: Buck's shows that 30 percent of the male population in the mid–1930s had been educated in sishu (John Lossing Buck, *Land Utilization in China* [New York: Paragon, 1968], pp. 373–74). Rawski's study gives several further examples of survey data.

40. See Leong and Tao, *Village and Town Life in China*, p. 97.

41. Liao T'ai-ch'u, "Rural Education in Transition," p. 48.

42. Shu Xincheng, *Wo he jiaoyu*, p. 10.

43. Smith, *Village Life in China*, p. 73. See Rawski, *Education and Popular Literacy*, p. 17, for further testimony on the number of rural schools.

44. A Shanxi magistrate established over 120 charity schools in his district in the 1860s (Rawski, *Education and Popular Literacy*, p. 92).

45. Ma Xulun, *Wo zai liushi sui yiqian*, p. 4. See also Chen Qitian, *Jiyuan huiyilu* (Taibei: Shangwu yinshuguan, 1965), p. 10.

46. Shu Xincheng, *Wo he jiaoyu*, p. 5. Shu's maternal grandfather had at one time been a teacher; his daughter had married into a family of well-to-do tenant farmers. Her hopes for her son may have reflected the standards of her own family rather than those of her husband's. Parallel examples of upward social mobility fueled by maternal ambition for education can be found in eighteenth-century England, where the optional, private character of schooling was similar to that given by sishu (see Victor E. Neuberg, *Popular Education in Eighteenth Century England* [London: Woburn Books, 1971], pp. 54–55).

47. Luo's mother berated him for "shaming his ancestors and his parents" when he was rude to his teacher (Luo Dunwei, *Wushi nian huiyilu*, p. 5). Hu's "placed all her hopes on my insubstantial, unforeseeable future" (Hu Shi, *Sishi zishu*, p. 19). The note of doubt is Hu's; his mother's wish to see him a graduate was unequivocal and tenacious.

48. Luo Dunwei, *Wushi nian huiyilu*, p. 5. Liang Chi recalls similar images from his childhood (quoted in Lin Yu-sheng, "The Suicide of Liang Chi," in Charlotte Furth, ed., *The Limits of Change* [Cambridge, Mass.: Harvard University Press, 1976], p. 159). For more homely recollections of maternal supervision, see Chen Bulei, *Chen Bulei huiyilu* (Hong Kong: Tianxing chubanshe, 1962), p. 3.

49. Shu Xincheng, *Wo he jiaoyu*, p. 4.

50. Cao Juren, *Jiangfan liushi nian* (Hong Kong: Chuangken chubanshe, 1957), p. 19. For further examples see Rawski, *Education and Popular Literacy*, pp. 21–22.

51. Liao T'ai-ch'u, "Rural Education in Transition," p. 32.

52. Edgar Snow, *Red Star over China*, rev. ed. (Harmondsworth, Eng.: Pelican Books, 1972), p. 156.

53. Personal communication from Ramon Myers, December 1978.

54. Cao Xueqin, *Honglou meng* (Beijing: Renmin wenxue chubanshe, 1973), pp. 112–13. English translations include *A Dream of Red Mansions* by Yang Hsien-yi and Gladys Yang (Beijing: Foreign Languages Press, 1978) and *The Story of the Stone* by David Hawkes (Harmondsworth, Eng.: Penguin, 1976).

55. Chen Tianxi, *Chizhuang huiyilu*, p. 21.

56. See Weng Yanzhen, "Gudai ertong duwu gaiguan," pp. 103–7, for the prescribed etiquette.

57. See Chen Tianxi, *Chizhuang huiyilu*, p. 12, for an example of this practice.

58. Lu Xun's Xiang Lin Sao, an uneducated maidservant, desires as much as any gentlewoman to observe the prohibition on remarriage. See Lu Xun, "Zhufu," in *Lu Xun quanji* (Shanghai: *Lu Xun quanji* chubanshe, 1946), 2: 139–62.

59. The account below is based on Ma Xulun's recollections of his experience in Zhejiang in 1889 (*Wo zui liushi sui yiqian*, pp. 1–3); Bao Tianxiao's of Suzhou in 1880 (*Chuanyinglou huiyilu*, pp. 5–6), and Chen Heqin's of Baiguan, Zhejiang, in 1899 (*Wo de bansheng*, pp. 48–50).

60. For orthodox Confucian opposition to the cult of these intruders in the Ming, see Liu Ts'un-yan, *Selected Papers from the Hall of Harmonious Wind* (Leiden: E. J. Brill, 1976), p. 130.

61. Chen Dongyuan, *Zhongguo jiaoyu shi*, p. 419. These sentiments, in particular the line exalting study above other occupations, were the subject of attack during the anti-Confucius campaign in China in 1974.

62. The requirement, abolished only recently, of classical languages for entry into Oxford and Cambridge can be seen as a survival of an archaic system rather than as a characteristic of a modern one. The same can be said of the Oxbridge tutorial system, where one-to-one contact forms an exception to the relatively impersonal teacher-student relations of other tertiary institutions.

63. Yu Jiaju, *Huiyilu* (Shanghai: Zhonghua shuju, 1948), p. 8.

64. See Shu Xincheng, *Wo he jiaoyu*, p. 29; and Smith, *Village Life in China*, pp. 104–5.

65. See Chen Tianxi, *Chizhuang huiyilu*, pp. 34–35; and Tang Ching-ping, "Mu-fu System in China Under the Ch'ing" (M.A. thesis, Australian National University, 1976), pp. 85–86.

66. Some writers (Hu Shi, *Sishi zishu*, pp. 21–22; and Xiao Gongquan [Hsiao Kung-chuan], *Wenxue jianwang lu*, p. 15) recall using materials written by a parent or ancestor. These, too, were in classical Chinese and were no more readily comprehensible than the models on which they were based.

67. Zheng Guanying, *Shengshi weiyan houbian* (Taibei: Datong shuju, 1968),

Xuewu, 2: 51a. In an article attacking the old education written in 1897, Xu Qin declared that 90 percent of those who studied the classics did not understand what they read ("Zhongguo chuhai yi," in Shu Xincheng, ed., *Ziliao*, 3: 964).

68. Gu Jiegang, *Gushi bian*, p. 7.

69. Ma Xulun, *Wo zai liushi sui yiqian*, pp. 3–4. Hu Shi received a better education only by dint of his mother's exertions; a fellow classmate of his could not even understand the salutation in a family letter (*Sishi zishu*, p. 26).

70. Ma Xulun, *Wo zai liushi sui yiqian*, p. 6.

71. Gu Jiegang, *Gushi bian*, p. 7.

72. For an analysis of the function of these primers in the teaching of reading, see Zhang Zhigong, *Chuantong yuwen jiaoyu chutan* (Shanghai: Jiaoyu chubanshe, 1962), pp. 3–26.

73. Liu Langsheng, *Nanchuan xianzhi* (Taibei: Chengwen chubanshe, 1976), 6: 8b–9a.

74. Liao T'ai-ch'u, "Rural Education in Transition," p. 45.

75. Shu Xincheng, *Wo he jiaoyu*, p. 12.

76. Guo Moruo, *Wo de younian*, pp. 54–55. William Liu recalls a similar ruse. He put a stone wrapped in rags under his cap to forfend against his teacher's blows; unfortunately the teacher's ruler knocked it off (interview).

77. See Smith, *Village Life in China*, p. 75; and for examples, Shu Xincheng, *Wo he jiaoyu*, p. 10; and Zhou Zuoren, *Zhitang huixianglu*, p. 21.

78. Chen Heqin, *Wo de bansheng*, p. 51.

79. See Liao T'ai-ch'u, "Rural Education in Transition," pp. 48–50; and for examples, Shu Xincheng, *Wo he jiaoyu*, p. 20; Ma Xulun, *Wo zai liushi sui yiqian*, p. 5; Cao Juren, *Wo yu wo de shijie* (Hong Kong: Sanyou tushu wenju gongsi, 1972), p. 22; Smith, *Village Life in China*, p. 107; and personal conversation with William Liu.

80. Liao T'ai-ch'u, "Rural Education in Transition," p. 43.

81. For irregular attendance, see ibid., pp. 42–43; Shen Congwen, *Congwen zizhuan* (Shanghai: Kaiming shudian, 1946), p. 10; and Hu Shi, *Sishi zishu*, p. 24.

82. Thomas W. Laqueur, "Working-Class Demand and the Growth of English Elementary Education, 1750–1850," in Lawrence Stone, ed., *Schooling and Society* (Baltimore: Johns Hopkins University Press, 1976), p. 201.

Chapter 3

1. Shu Xincheng, *Jindai Zhongguo jiaoyu sixiangshi* (Shanghai: Zhonghua shuju, 1932), pp. 6–7. Chinese influence may indeed have been behind Britain's adoption of civil service examinations in the mid-nineteenth century, as the first-hand accounts of British diplomats and missionaries swelled the trickle of information that had been flowing westward since the Jesuits (see Teng Ssu-yu, "Chi-

nese Influence on the Western Examination System," *Harvard Journal of Asian Studies* 7 [1942–43]: 267–312).

2. "Xiaoxue yishu qi," *Jiaohui xinbao* (1870), in Shu Xincheng, *Ziliao*, 1: 87–91. The quotation reappears in the writings of Zheng Guanying in 1893, Sun Yat-sen in 1894, and Chen Zhi and Liang Qichao in 1896. The identification made by the reformers may well have been erroneous since one of the institutions referred to by Mencius appears to mean literally "a place for nourishing the aged," while another was connected with archery. (See Howard S. Galt, *A History of Chinese Educational Institutions* [London: Probsthain and Sons, 1951], 1: 54–55.)

3. Alice H. Gregg, *China and Educational Autonomy: The Changing Role of the Protestant Educational Missionary in China, 1807–1937* (Syracuse, N.Y.: Syracuse University Press, 1946), p. 23; and *The China Mission Hand-book: First Issue* (Shanghai: American Presbyterian Mission Press, 1896), p. 285.

4. For a discussion of the early years of Allen's paper, see Adrian A. Bennett and Kwang-Ching Liu, "Christianity in the Chinese Idiom: Young J. Allen and the Early *Chiao-hui hsin-pao*, 1868–1870," in John K. Fairbank, ed., *The Missionary Enterprise in China and America* (Cambridge, Mass.: Harvard University Press, 1974), pp. 159–96. A system of traveling teachers was proposed as a means to universal education in "Xiaoxue yishu qi," *Jiaohui xinbao* (1870), in Shu Xincheng, *Ziliao*, 1: 87–91.

5. Feng Guifen, "Cai xixue yi," in *Jiaopinlu kangyi* (Taibei: Xuehai chubanshe, 1967), p. 149. Feng Guifen (1809–1894) was a scholar and reformer in the Self-Strengthening movement.

6. For some particulars of Zheng's influence see Key Ray Chong, "Cheng Kuan-ying (1841–1920): A Source of Sun Yat-sen's Nationalist Ideology?" *Journal of Asian Studies* 28, no. 2 (1969): 248.

7. For a discussion of *Yiyan*, see Kwang-Ching Liu, "Cheng Kuan-ying's *I-yen*: Reform Proposals of the Early Kwang-hsü Period (Part I)/Zheng Guanying *Yiyan*: Guangxu chunian zhi bianfa sixiang (shang)," *Tsing Hua Journal of Chinese Studies*, n.s., 8 (1970): 373–425.

8. Zheng Guanying, "Kaoshi" (1884), in Shu Xincheng, *Ziliao*, 3: 897–902.

9. Wang opened a newspaper in Hong Kong in 1874, was one of the editors of the Shanghai *Shen bao* in the 1880s, and contributed to Allen's *Wan'guo gongbao* in the early 1890s.

10. See Wang Tao, *Taoyuan wenlu waibian* (Hong Kong, 1883), 2: 4b, 8b–9a.

11. Ibid., 8: 7b–9a.

12. J. D. Frodsham, *The First Chinese Embassy to the West: The Journals of Kuo Sung-t'ao, Liu Hsi-hung and Chang Te-yi* (Oxford: Clarendon Press, 1974), p. 6.

13. Ibid., pp. lx, lxi. Guo's recall was the result of personal enmities as well as ideological outrage, but it is significant that the latter was available as an excuse for the former.

14. Huang Zunxian, *Riben guozhi* (Guangzhou: Fuwenzhai, 1898), 33:

7a–13a. Huang sent *Riben guozhi* to Fuwenzhai in Guangzhou in 1890 for publication, but it was delayed and eventually came out in 1895.

15. Zheng's readers included the leaders of three generations of Chinese: the Guangxu emperor (see Timothy Richard, *Forty-five Years in China* [London: T. Fisher Unwin, 1916], p. 257); Sun Yat-sen (see Key Ray Chong, "Zheng Guanying"), and the young Mao Zedong (see Edgar Snow, *Red Star over China*, rev. ed. [Harmondsworth, Eng.: Pelican Books, 1972], p. 156).

16. Zheng Guanying, *Shengshi weiyan zengding xinbian* (Taibei: Datong shuju, 1968), Zixu, 3a.

17. Ibid., 2: 15a.

18. Ibid., 2: 3a–b.

19. Ibid., 2: 21a–23a. The new school system did not adopt Zheng's suggestion that beginning language training be in the pupil's own dialect. Instead, an attempt was made to use the new schools to propagate Mandarin.

20. The term "jiaoyu" dates back to Mencius. When "education" in the modern sense first came east, its nomenclature was uncertain. The Japanese Ministry of Education (*Mombushō*) is literally the "civil" ministry. When the section on education in Chambers's Encyclopaedia was translated into Japanese, the word *gakumon* ("learning") was used; Fukuzawa Yukichi, the great popularizer of Western thought and institutions, used the same word. By the late 1870s, *kyōiku* (the Japanese pronounciation of jiaoyu) was becoming the standard equivalent in Japan of the English word "education." The magazine of the Ministry of Education, *Mombushō zasshi*, was renamed *Kyōiku zasshi*. "Kyōiku" was used in the title of translated works in 1875, 1876, and 1877. By 1879, it had become naturalized, being used both in the title of the American-influenced Educational Ordinance of that year and in the works of its conservative opponents. (See Nishihira Isao, "Western Influence on the Modernization of Japanese Education, 1868–1912" [Ph.D. diss., Ohio State University, 1972], pp. 267, 274, 278, 295, 375–77.)

21. See Key Ray Chong, "Cheng Kuan-ying," for the relationship between Sun and Zheng.

22. Sun Yat-sen, Letter to Li Hongzhang, in Shu Xincheng, *Ziliao*, 3: 1014–15.

23. See Paul A. Cohen, "Littoral and Hinterland in Nineteenth Century China: The 'Christian' Reformers," in Fairbank, *The Missionary Enterprise in China and America*, pp. 216–17.

24. Liang Qichao, "Lun xuexiao: Keju," *Shiwu bao*, no. 8 (1896). See also Chen Chi-yun, "Liang Ch'i-ch'ao's 'Missionary Education': A Case Study of Missionary Influence on the Reformers," *Papers on China* (Harvard University Press) 16 (1962): 112.

25. Kang Youwei, "Gongju shang shu," in Shu Xincheng, *Ziliao*, 3: 917–19.

26. *Shiwu bao*, no. 6 (1896); nos. 18, 25, 26, 30, 32–34, 50 (1897).

27. According to Liang, the *Shiwu bao*'s circulation passed 10,000 (Zhang

Jinglu, ed., *Zhongguo jindai chuban shiliao: Chubian* [Shanghai: Qunlian chuban-she, 1953], p. 92). Extrapolation from figures for sales revenues indicates for the last half of 1897 an average sale of about one thousand in Shanghai and between six and seven thousand outside it (*Shiwu bao*, no. 52 [1898]).

28. Lü Shaoyu, "Zhongguo jiaoyu shumu huibian," in *Wenhua tushuguan-xue zhuankexuexiao jikan* 4, nos. 3–4 (1932): 301–68.

29. *Shiwu bao*, no. 18 (1897).

30. Quoted in Chen Chi-yun, "Liang Ch'i-ch'ao's 'Missionary Education,'" p. 74.

31. Ibid., pp. 67, 75.

32. Gregg, *China and Educational Autonomy*, p. 23.

33. Zheng Guanying, *Shengshi weiyan zengding xinbian*, 2: 18b.

34. Paul Cohen's researches show that "before publishing his works, Wang deliberately edited out any phrasing that might identify him as a Christian" ("Littoral and Hinterland," p. 223).

35. Chen Chi-yun, "Liang Ch'i-ch'ao's 'Missionary Education,'" pp. 102–3, 112–13; and Chang Hao, *Liang Ch'i-ch'ao and Intellectual Transition in China, 1890–1907* (Cambridge, Mass.: Harvard University Press, 1971), pp. 71–72, 117.

36. Liang Qichao, "Lun xuexiao: Zonglun," *Shiwu bao*, no. 6 (1896).

37. Su Yu, ed., *Yijiao congbian* (Taibei: Guofeng chubanshe, 1970), Xu.

38. Li Duanfen, memorial requesting extension of schools, in Shu Xin-cheng, ed., *Jindai Zhongguo jiaoyu shiliao* (hereafter, *Shiliao*) (Shanghai: Zhonghua shuju, 1928), 1: 1–5.

39. Ibid., 5–7.

40. William Ayers, *Chang Chih-tung and Educational Reform in China* (Cambridge, Mass.: Harvard University Press, 1971), p. 150.

41. Zhang Zhidong, *Quanxue pian*, in *Zhang Wenxiang gong quanji* (Taibei: Wenhai chubanshe, 1963), 203: 9a–b.

42. Ibid., 13a.

43. Ibid., 3a–b.

44. Ibid., Xu, 2a. For Zhang's long-standing distrust of the capacity of the local gentry (the group that would have been enfranchised by "people's rights") to act in the public interest, see Daniel H. Bays, *China Enters the Twentieth Century: Chang Chih-tung and the Issues of a New Age, 1895–1909* (Ann Arbor: University of Michigan Press, 1978), pp. 16–17, 29–32.

45. Liang Qichao, "Lun xuexiao: Zonglun," *Shiwu bao*, no. 5 (1896).

46. See Philip C. Huang, *Liang Ch'i-ch'ao and Modern Chinese Liberalism* (Seattle: University of Washington Press, 1972), p. 33.

47. See Chen Chi-yun, "Liang Ch'i-ch'ao's 'Missionary Education,'" p. 112.

48. See Shu Xincheng, *Shiliao*, 1: 52.

49. Ye Dehui, "Fei youxue tongyi," in Su Yu, *Yijiao congbian*, 4: 72a.

50. See *Shiwu bao*, no. 24 (1897).

51. Wen Ti, memorial impeaching Kang Youwei, in Su Yu, *Yijiao congbian* (Taibei: Guofeng chubanshe, 1970), 2: 8b.

52. Knight Biggerstaff, *The Earliest Modern Government Schools in China* (Ithaca, N.Y.: Cornell University Press, 1961), p. 31.

53. Liao T'ai-ch'u found sishu, only slightly modified, operating in Sichuan in the immediate postwar period ("Rural Education in Transition"). The author's conversations with elderly Chinese in the People's Republic suggest that some sishu lingered on even after 1949.

54. The protean nature of this concept was first evident in Japan, where Fukuzawa Yukichi detached *jitsugaku* (the Japanese pronounciation of *shixue*) from its association with Confucianism and applied it to "the forty-seven letters of the (Japanese) alphabet, the composition of letters, bookkeeping, the abacus, and the use of scales," as well as geography, history, natural philosophy, economics, and ethics, all of which were to be studied from translations of Western works (see Fukuzawa Yukichi, *Gakumon no susume* [Encouragement of Learning], 1872, translated in Herbert Passin, *Society and Education in Japan* [New York: Columbia University, Teachers College, 1965], pp. 206–7).

55. The phrase forms part of the Charter Oath of the Meiji emperor, made public in April 1868 (Passin, *Society and Education in Japan*, p. 63).

56. Ayers, *Chang Chi-tung*, p. 59.

57. Chen Qingzhi, *Zhongguo jiaoyushi* (Shanghai: Shangwu yinshuguan, 1936), pp. 238–39.

58. See Xie Guozhen, "Jindai shuyuan xuexiao zhidu bianqian kao," in Cai Yuanpei et al., eds., *Zhang Jusheng xiansheng qishi shengri jinian lunwen ji* (Shanghai: Shangwu yinshuguan, 1937), p. 289.

59. A. P. Parker, "The Government Colleges of Suchow," *Chinese Recorder and Missionary Journal* 24, no. 11 (1893): 538.

60. Shu Xincheng, *Wo he jiaoyu* (Shanghai: Zhonghua shuju, 1945), pp. 44–46.

61. Ibid., p. 49.

62. Li Zonghuang, *Li Zonghuang huiyilu* (Taibei: Zhongguo difang zizhi xuehui, 1972), pp. 50–52.

63. See Hsiao Kung-chuan, *A Modern China and a New World* (Seattle: University of Washington Press, 1975), pp. 377–78.

64. For further discussion of these reforms, see Wolfgang Franke, *The Reform and Abolition of the Chinese Examination System* (Cambridge, Mass.: Harvard University Press, 1963), pp. 43–53.

65. Song Xishang, *Li Yizhi zhuan* (Taibei: Zhongyang wenwu gongyingshe, 1954), p. 6.

66. For a fictional example of the extemporaneous ramblings undertaken by such students, see Li Liuru, *Liushi nian de bianqian* (Beijing: Zuojia chubanshe, 1957), p. 68.

67. Huang Yanpei, "Qingji gesheng xingxue shi," *Renwen yuekan* 1, no. 7 (1930): 1.

68. Zongli Yamen, "Huiyi suanxue qushi," in Shu Xincheng, *Shiliao*, 4: 79–81.

69. The word *xuetang* has a long history in China. Its first use for one of the specialist schools was in 1866, when the Foochow Navy School (Chuanzheng Xuetang) was founded. The term was not used by missionaries, who adopted the more common appellations of indigenous schools (*guan* or *shuyuan*), or by the Japanese, who called their new schools *gakko* (the Japanese pronounciation of *xuexiao*).

70. Missionary schools teaching English had the same problem of losing students to foreign firms (see Jessie Gregory Lutz, *China and the Christian Colleges, 1850–1950* [Ithaca, N.Y.: Cornell University Press, 1971], p. 69).

71. Zhang Zhidong, "Zhao kao Ziqiang Xuetang xuesheng shi," in Shu Xincheng, *Shiliao*, 1: 13–16.

72. For example, Tang Caichang's stay at Lianghu Academy was broken by an appointment elsewhere and was for some time concurrent with a position as family tutor (Su Yunfeng, *Zhang Zhidong yu Hubei jiaoyu gaige* [Taibei: Zhongyang yanjiuyuan, Jindaishi yanjiusuo, 1976], p. 56).

73. "Jiangnan Chucai Xuetang zhangcheng," *Shiwu bao*, no. 42 (1897).

74. Lu Xun, *Zhaohua xishi* (Beijing: Renmin chubanshe, 1973), pp. 56–60.

75. Zhou Zuoren attended the Jiangnan Naval School from 1902 to 1906. For a description of his schooldays, see Zhou Zuoren, *Zhitang huixianglu* (Hong Kong: Sanyou tushu wenju gongsi, 1970), pp. 89–115, 148–50.

76. Ibid., pp. 96–98; and Lu Xun, *Zhaohua xishi*, p. 56.

77. Zhou Zuoren, *Zhitang huixianglu*, p. 92; and Lu Xun, *Zhaohua xishi*, p. 57. Stipends were in part a legacy from the academies, in part a practical necessity to attract students when foreign studies were still unfashionable.

78. Kuo Ping-wen, *The Chinese System of Public Education* (New York: AMS Press, 1972), p. 64.

79. See *The China Mission Hand-book: First Issue*, passim.

80. For the early colleges, see Kwang-Ching Liu, "Early Christian Colleges in China," *Journal of Asian Studies* 22, no. 1 (1960): 71–78.

81. Chen Qingzhi, *Zhongguo jiaoyushi*, p. 573.

82. "Xiangxiang Dongshan Jingshe zhangcheng," *Shiwu bao*, no. 2 (1896).

83. I have commented earlier on the bridging function of the word *shi* ("solid" or "substantial"). It forms part of the title of the academy Yan Xiu set up in Guizhou and of one in Shaanxi. Another popular name was "qiushi," part of the famous motto of the head of Nanjing Academy, *shishi qiushi*—to seek the truth from the facts. This work style is still recommended in the same words in China today.

84. Song Xishang, *Li Yizhi zhuan*, pp. 6–7. It is hard to know whether to give more or less credence to such memories than to official histories. One

history states that both Weijing and Chongshi taught "solid learning" (*shixue*) (Huang Yanpei, "Qingji gesheng xingxue shi," *Renwen yuekan* 1, no. 7 [1930]: 2).

85. Shu Xincheng, prefatory remarks to Liang Qichao, "Hunan Shiwu Xuetang gongqi," in Shu, *Shiliao*, 1: 40.

86. Ibid., pp. 40–61; and "Miluoxiangren xueyue jiuwu," in Su Yu, *Yijiao congbian*, 4: 80a–83a.

87. See Xie Guozhen, "Jindai shuyuan xuexiao zhidu bianqian kao," pp. 291–92.

88. Ibid., pp. 303–4.

89. See Gao Zhengfang, "Qingmo de Anhui xinjiaoyu" (shang), *Xuefeng* 2, no. 8 (1932): 32–33.

90. Qu Lihe, "Jin bai nian woguo de zhongdeng jiaoyu," *Shida xuebao* 22, shang (1977): 212.

91. Sheng Xuanhuai, "Zouchen kaiban Nanyang Gongxue qingxing shu, fu zhangcheng," and Nanyang Gongxue, "Mengxue keben liang ke," in Shu Xincheng, *Shiliao*, 1: 35–40; 2: 251–52.

92. Gao Zhengfang, "Qingmo de Anhui xinjiaoyu," pp. 35–36.

93. Ding Zhipin, *Zhongguo jin qishi nian lai jiaoyu jishi* (Shanghai: Guoli bianyiguan, 1935), p. 3; and Chen Dongyuan, *Zhongguo jiaoyushi* (Shanghai: Shangwu yinshuguan, 1937), p. 475.

94. For a discussion of the views of Qing educators on this subject, see Charles P. Ridley, "Theories of Education in the Ch'ing Period," *Ch'ing-shih Wen-t'i* 3, no. 8 (1977): 34–49.

95. Wang Yun, "Jiao tongzi fa," in Shu Xincheng, *Ziliao*, 1: 94.

96. Ibid., pp. 94, 99–100.

97. For an example of this attitude, see Li Ji, *Gan jiu lu* (Taibei: Zhuanji wenxue chubanshe, 1967), p. 4.

98. Wu Rulun, *Tongcheng Wu xiansheng riji* (Taibei: Guangwen shuju, 1963), Jiaoyu, 10b.

99. See "Wulei shi," "Zhongshi lidai shilei ge," and "Yudi qimeng," *Mengxue bao*, no. 10 (1898).

100. Wu Xiangxiang, *Chen Guofu de yisheng (fu: Chen Guofu huiyilu)* (Taibei: Zhuanji wenxue chubanshe, 1971), p. 40.

101. Xiao Gongquan (Hsiao Kung-chuan), *Wenxue jianwang lu* (Taibei: Zhuanji wenxue chubanshe, 1972), pp. 15–16.

102. Ba Jin, *Zizhuan* (Hong Kong: Zili shudian, 1956), p. 42.

103. See Chen Bulei, *Chen Bulei huiyilu* (Hong Kong: Tianxing chubanshe, 1962), p. 4.

104. See Li Shuhua, "Cong sishu dao xuetang," *Zhuanji wenxue* 17, no. 2 (1970): 61.

105. Wu Xiangxiang, *Chen Guofu de yisheng*, p. 41. See also Li Gufan, *Tan wang lu*, in his *Yunlu wushu* (Hong Kong: The author, 1963).

106. Wang Wentian, *Zhang Boling yu Nankai* (Taibei: Zhuanji wenxue chubanshe, 1968), p. 5. Yan Xiu's name appears in connection with almost every educational reform—of academies, of the examination system, in the extension of mass education, and the improvement (through Nankai, the school he founded in conjunction with Zhang Boling) of elite education—but no detailed study has yet been made of his life and career.

107. Li Gufan, *Tan wang lu*, pp. 22–23.

108. See "Jiangnan Chucai Xuetang zhangcheng," *Shiwu bao*, no. 42 (1897), for a warning against the characteristic faults of each group.

109. Qi Rushan, *Qi Rushan huiyilu* (Taibei: Zhongyang wenwu gongyingshe, 1956), p. 27.

110. Ibid., p. 36.

111. Huang Yanpei, "Qingji gesheng xingxue shi" (xu), *Renwen yuekan* 1, no. 8 (1930): 10.

112. Ma Xulun, *Wo zai liushi sui yiqian* (Shanghai: Shenghuo shudian, 1947), p. 8.

113. *Shuntian shibao*, 1 October 1902.

114. *Xue Bu guanbao*, no. 39 (1907): Jingwai xuewu baogao, 395a–b.

Chapter Four

1. Wang Tao, *Pu-Fa zhanji* (Hong Kong, 1886), 1: 11a–b.

2. Nishihira Isao, "Western Influences on the Modernization of Japanese Education, 1868–1912" (Ph.D. diss., Ohio State University, 1972), p. 9.

3. Herbert Passin, *Society and Education in Japan* (New York: Columbia University, Teachers College, 1965), p. 9.

4. Marius B. Jansen and Lawrence Stone, "Education and Modernization in Japan and England," *Comparative Studies in Society and History* 9 (1966–67): 225.

5. Zhang Zhidong, *Quanxue pian*, in *Zhang Wenxiang gong quanji* (Taibei: Wenhai chubanshe, 1963), 203: 7a.

6. The 1890s saw what Nishihira terms "the culmination of conservatism in Japanese education" ("Western Influences on the Modernization of Japanese Education," p. 423).

7. Justifiably, in some cases; Timothy Richard, for example, urged that China should hand over management of its affairs to British and American advisers. Zhang greeted his proposal coldly. (See Chen Chi-yun, "Liang Ch'i-ch'ao's 'Missionary Education,'" *Papers on China* [Harvard University Press] 16 [1962]: 106–7, 109.)

8. This wish was expressed by A. P. Parker at the third triennial meeting of the missionary Educational Association of China in 1899. (See Alice H. Gregg, *China and Educational Autonomy* [Syracuse, N.Y.: Syracuse University Press, 1946], p. 24.)

9. See ibid., pp. 45–50; and Wang Feng-Gang, "Japanese Influence on Educational Reform in China, from 1895 to 1911" (Ph.D. diss., Stanford University, 1931), pp. 77–78.

10. Wu Rulun, *Tongcheng Wu xiansheng riji* (Taibei: Guangwen shuju, 1963), Jiaoyu, 10a, 12b. Wu noted particularly Ito's warning that China should not concentrate on intellectual education at the expense of moral and physical education. (This trilogy, originating in Herbert Spencer's *Education, Intellectual, Moral, and Physical* [1860], had become an axiom in Japan. Transferred to China, it was to be a staple of educational discussion for decades.) Wu's reply, that knowledge of virtue presupposed intellectual comprehension of its dictates, reveals a Confucian conviction that intellectual and moral knowledge were inseparable. See also ibid., 9a, for Wu's notes on information supplied by the Japanese embassy on the Japanese education system.

11. For a description of Wu's trip and his findings, see Wu Rulun, *Dongyou conglu* (n.p., 1902).

12. William Ayers, *Chang Chih-tung and Educational Reform in China* (Cambridge, Mass.: Harvard University Press, 1971), p. 219.

13. Though numerous, these delegations were not necessarily useful; a report in a Chinese student paper in Japan criticized prefects and circuit intendants who spent their time drinking and sightseeing instead of visiting schools (*Jiangsu*, no. 2 [1903], Jishi).

14. Kanō had a long-standing interest in Chinese education. He had tutored the first Chinese students to go to Japan in 1896 and in 1899 had set up a school for them. This developed into the Kobun Shoin, the largest of the Japanese schools catering to the Chinese student market. (See Sanetō Keishū, *Chūgokujin Nihon ryūgaku shi* [Tokyo: Kuroshio shuppan, 1960], pp. 524, 526–27.

15. A Chinese bibliography lists 5 works on education published between 1893 and 1898, 2 in 1900, 1 in 1901, 7 in 1902, and 29 in 1903. Of the 29, 19 were translations from Japanese. (Lü Shaoyu, "Zhongguo jiaoyu shumu huibian," *Wenhua tushuguanxue zhuankexuexiao jikan*, 4, nos. 3–4 [1932], 301–68.) This represented only a fraction of the total. Of the 680 volumes in Chinese on modern education by 1905, 97 were from a single Japanese publishing firm. (Cyrus P. Peake, *Nationalism and Education in Modern China* [New York: Columbia University, Teachers College, 1932], p. 52.)

16. For Luo's translations, see Peake, *Nationalism and Education in Modern China*, p. 53; and Zhang Jinglu, *Zhongguo jindai chuban shiliao: Chubian* (Shanghai: Qunlian chubanshe, 1953), 1: 81. For Luo's visit to Japan, see Luo Zhenyu, *Xuetang zizhuan*, in *Luo Xuetang xiansheng quanji* (Taibei: Datong shuju, 1976), 1: 15.

17. Taga Akigorō, ed., *Kindai Chūgoku kyōikushi shiryō: Shimmatsuhen* (hereafter *Shiryō*) (Tokyo: Nihon gakujutsu shinkōkai, 1972), pp. 303–4.

18. Naka Arata, *Meiji no kyōiku* (Tokyo: Shibundō, 1967), p. 257.

19. Taga, *Shiryō*, p. 297.

20. See P. J. Maclagan, "Notes on Some Chinese Chap-books," *China Review* 23, no. 3 (1898–99): 164.

21. See Zongli Yamen's reply to Li Duanfen's memorial on extending schools, in Shu Xincheng, *Shiliao*, 1: 6.

22. *Dongfang zazhi* 4, no. 3 (1907), inside front cover.

23. My summary of the reforms leading to the 1904 regulations is based on Chen Baoquan, *Zhongguo jindai xuezhi bianqian shi* (Beijing: Beijing wenhua xueshe, 1927), pp. 13–48; Wolfgang Franke, *The Reform and Abolition of the Traditional Chinese Examination System* (Cambridge, Mass.: Harvard University Press, 1963), pp. 48–67; and *Qing shi gao* (Taibei: Guofang yanjiuyuan, 1961), p. 1298.

24. Taga, *Shiryō*, p. 121.

25. See Gong Shi, "Beijing Daxue zhi chengli ji yange," in Shu Xincheng, *Shiliao*, 3: 2.

26. Taga, *Shiryō*, p. 214.

27. Ibid., p. 209.

28. From entry to primary school to graduation from pre-university took seventeen years under Zhang's scheme, compared with only fourteen in Japan. Japanese primary schools did not give lessons in the classics, which were subsumed under classes in ethics and Japanese. Even before the Meiji reforms, however, the Confucian classics had not dominated Japanese education as they had Chinese.

29. See Taga, *Shiryō*, pp. 309–12. This again contrasts with the Japanese case, where educational authorities made strenuous efforts to achieve universal education for girls through coeducational elementary schools.

30. Presumably, as in the case of the Shang Bu (Ministry of Commerce), bureaucratic infighting was also involved, with the Board of Rites unwilling to give up areas under its jurisdiction (see Ramon H. Myers, *The Chinese Economy: Past and Present* [Belmont, Calif.: Wadsworth, 1980], p. 137).

31. Taga, *Shiryō*, pp. 224–25.

32. Duan Fang and Dai Hongci, report on education, in Shu Xincheng, *Shiliao*, 4: 11.

33. Twelve of the eighteen provincial directors of studies were replaced in September 1903, leaving only those in Zhili, Gansu, Fujian, Guangdong, Guangxi, and Yunnan unchanged (Franke, *Reform and Abolition of the Traditional Chinese Examination System*, p. 58).

34. Taga, *Shiryō*, p. 418.

35. Luo Zhenyu, *Xuetang zizhuan*, p. 21.

36. Ibid., p. 22.

37. "Zhang Wenxiang gong yu jiaoyu zhi guanxi," *Jiaoyu zazhi* 1, no. 10 (1909): Pinglun, 21–22. See also Daniel H. Bays, *China Enters the Twentieth Century* (Ann Arbor: University of Michigan Press, 1978), p. 198.

38. See Taga, *Shiryō*, pp. 634–35.

39. See Jiang Mengmei, "Qian-Qing Xue Bu bianshu zhi zhuangkuang," in Shu Xincheng, *Shiliao*, 2: 260.

40. *Xue Bu guanbao*, no. 91 (1909): Shending shumu, 2a.

41. Japan, Department of Education, *Education in Japan* (Tokyo, 1914), pp. 5–6.

42. Passin, *Society and Education in Japan*, pp. 75–80. Early public schooling fared little better in England, where the problem of introducing a foreign culture did not exist (see G. A. N. Lowndes, *The Silent Social Revolution: An Account of the Expansion of Public Education in England and Wales, 1895–1935* [London: Oxford University Press, 1947], pp. 21–44).

43. Albert Feuerwerker, *The Chinese Economy, ca. 1870–1911* (Ann Arbor: University of Michigan Press, 1969), p. 67.

44. Myers, *The Chinese Economy*, pp. 160–61.

45. Taga, *Shiryō*, pp. 439–40.

46. *Xue Bu guanbao*, no. 76 (1908): Benbu zhangzou, 1a–3b.

47. *Jiaoyu zazhi* 2, no. 7 (1910): Jishi, 55.

48. Franke, *Reform and Abolition of the Traditional Chinese Examination System*, p. 53.

49. Ibid., pp. 56, 59–60.

50. J. Stafford Ransome, *Japan in Transition* (London: Harper & Brothers, 1899), pp. 87–89. Stephen MacKinnon's study of Zhili under Yuan Shikai finds the same to be true at the county level. MacKinnon finds police reform to be another case in which "size did not seem to relate to population or geopolitical importance," with some small, remote counties having bigger forces than large, important ones. (*Power and Politics in Late Imperial China* [Berkeley and Los Angeles: University of California Press, 1980], pp. 146, 159.)

51. See China [Qing], Xue Bu, *Xuantong yuannian: Disanci jiaoyu tongji tubiao* (Beijing, 1911), Shanxi, pp. 2–9, and Yunnan, pp. 5–10.

52. Ho Ping-ti, *The Ladder of Success in Imperial China* (New York: John Wiley & Sons, 1962), p. 210.

53. China [Qing], Xue Bu, *Xuantong yuannian . . . tongji tubiao*, Xu.

54. *Xue Bu guanbao*, no. 21 (1907): Wendu, 117.

55. For example, Chen Qitian writes, "In this period, the old education was completely overthrown" (*Zuijin sanshinian Zhongguo jiaoyushi* [Taibei: Wenxing shudian, 1962], p. 29).

56. For 1909, the last year of the dynasty for which statistics are available, 44,774 lower primary schools are recorded. Nearly half of these were in Zhili and Sichuan; Anhui is listed as having 421, Fujian as having 275. (Taga, *Shiryō*, p. 103.)

57. Yu Jiaju, *Huiyilu* (Shanghai: Zhonghua shuju, 1948), p. 21.

58. Personal communications from Liu Ts'un-yan, Lo Hui-min, and May Wong of the Australian National University.

59. Zhuang Yu, "Lun xiaoxue jiaoyu," *Jiaoyu zazhi* 1, no. 2 (1909): Sheshuo, 23. Liao T'ai-ch'u noted the same phenomenon in Shandong nearly thirty years later: ". . . 18 sishu teachers out of the total of 198 . . . had at one point in their career been government school teachers and even principals" ("Rural Education in Transition," *Yenching Journal of Social Studies* 4, no. 2 [1949]: 36). The figures for the national survey made in 1935 show that out of 101,813 sishu teachers, over 8 percent had had teacher training in a normal school or course, and another 22 percent had attended a modern school at the primary or middle school level (*Jiaoyu zazhi* 26, no. 12 [1936]: 137).

60. See Zhuang Yu, "Lun xiaoxue jiaoyu," p. 23.

61. See Liao T'ai-ch'u, "Rural Education in Transition," pp. 46–47; and Tang Lei, "Xiangcun xiaoxuexiao zhi kunnan ji qi bujiufa," *Jiaoyu yanjiu*, no. 5 (1913): 4. Although written in the Republican period, the points these articles make appear applicable to the late Qing.

62. Liang Qichao, "Lun xuexiao: Youxue," in *Shiwu bao*, no. 16 (1896).

63. Tang Lei, "Xiangcun xiaoxuexiao zhi kunnan ji qi bujiufa," p. 6.

64. *Jiaoyu zazhi* 1, no. 2 (1909): Jishi, 10.

65. "Sishu Gailiang Hui zhangcheng," in Shu Xincheng, *Shiliao*, 2: 149–56.

66. Ibid., p. 150.

67. Taga, *Shiryō*, p. 424.

68. *Xue Bu guan bao*, no. 92 (1909): Jingwai xuewu baogao, 17.

69. Taga, *Shiryō*, p. 663.

70. *Dongfang zazhi* 1, no. 7 (1904): Jiaoyu, 169.

71. Ibid., 1, no. 2 (1904): Jiaoyu, 43.

72. Taga, *Shiryō*, p. 663. See also *Xue Bu guanbao*, no. 1 (1906): Wendu, 14a, prohibiting illegal taxes on sishu.

73. "Quanxue jishi: Jingshi zhengli sishu shimo," *Jingshi jiaoyu yanjiu*, no. 1 (1914): 1–12.

74. Liao T'ai-ch'u, "Rural Education in Transition," p. 22.

75. Harold Frederick Smith, *Elementary Education in Shantung, China* (Nashville, Tenn.: AMESSU, 1931), p. 33.

76. For an examination of returned students from Japan and the degrees awarded to them, see Huang Fuqing, *Qingmo liu-Ri xuesheng* (Taibei: Zhongyang yanjiuyuan, Jindaishi yanjiusuo, 1975), pp. 65–82.

77. Figures from early 1907 show that 60 percent of Chinese students in Japan were doing short-term courses. Ten percent were at Waseda and another 10 percent at other private universities and colleges, 15 percent were preparing for entry into tertiary education at one of the special schools for Chinese students, and only 5 percent were enrolled in government institutions for higher education. (*Zhili jiaoyu zazhi*, dingwei nian, no. 1 [1907]: Shiwen, 108.)

78. Wang Feng-Gang, "Japanese Influence on Educational Reform in China," p. 125.

79. Roger F. Hackett, "Chinese Students in Japan, 1900–1910," *Papers on China* (Harvard University Press) 3 (1949): 144.

80. Sanetō Keishū, *Chūgokujin Nihon ryūgaku shi*, p. 68. By the time it closed in 1909, the Kobun Shoin had taken in 7,192 students (ibid., p. 532).

81. Hackett, "Chinese Students in Japan," pp. 144–45.

82. Ibid., p. 153.

83. Wang Feng-Gang, "Japanese Influence on Educational Reform in China," pp. 123–24.

84. Ibid., p. 129.

85. Ibid.

86. Sanetō Keishū, *Chūgokujin Nihon ryūgaku shi*, p. 104; and Hackett, "Chinese Students in Japan," p. 143.

87. Hackett, "Chinese Students in Japan," p. 141.

88. Taga, *Shiryō*, pp. 399–408.

89. *Jiaoyu zazhi* 1, no. 6 (1909): Jishi, 39, and 2, no. 5 (1910): Pinglun, 13.

90. The quotas had ensured, if not equal opportunity for all, at least a fairly equitable sharing of places as far down as the county level. Some areas had a low ratio of candidates to places, while in others competition was fierce; moreover, the practice during the Taiping Rebellion of increasing the quota of counties that made substantial monetary contributions for the suppression of the rebels had disturbed the original ratios.

91. Cao Juren, *Jiangfan liushi nian* (Hong Kong: Chuangken chubanshe, 1957), p. 19.

Chapter Five

1. William Ayers, *Chang Chih-tung and Educational Reform in China* (Cambridge, Mass.: Harvard University Press, 1971), pp. 219–23.

2. Su Yunfeng, *Zhang Zhidong yu Hubei jiaoyu gaige* (Taibei: Zhongyang yanjiuyuan, Jindaishi yanjiusuo, 1976), p. 192.

3. G. A. N. Lowndes, *The Silent Social Revolution* (London: Oxford University Press, 1947), pp. 46–47.

4. Su Yunfeng, *Zhang Zhidong yu Hubei jiaoyu gaige*, p. 191; and Ayers, *Chang Chih-tung and Educational Reform*, p. 217.

5. *Xue Bu guanbao*, no. 34 (1907): Jingwai xuewu baogao, 280–95.

6. See *Zhili jiaoyu zazhi* 3, no. 1 (1907): Baogao, 45–60, for the Education Office's budget for 1906.

7. Another advocate of Wang's alphabet was the scholar Wu Rulun, who commended it to Zhang Boxi. The 1904 Outline of Education stated that Mandarin, specifically the Beijing dialect, should be included in Chinese lessons as a means of unifying the people. The phonetic alphabet, though not mentioned

specifically, was almost indispensable to spreading a knowledge of Beijing pronunciation. Unfortunately Wang was later jailed as a supporter of Kang Youwei and Liang Qichao, and his alphabet was taken out of circulation. (Fang Shiduo, *Wushinianlai Zhongguo guoyu yundong shi* [Taibei: Guoyu ribao she, 1965], pp. 10–13.)

8. *Zhili jiaoyu zazhi* 2, no. 7 (1906): advertisement for Education Office publications.

9. Cyrus P. Peake, *Nationalism and Education in Modern China* (New York: Columbia University, Teachers College, 1932), p. 58.

10. Stephen R. MacKinnon, *Power and Politics in Late Imperial China* (Berkeley and Los Angeles: University of California Press, 1980), p. 146.

11. Report on the primary schools of Laishui county, *Zhili jiaoyu zazhi* 1, no. 1 (1905): 40b–41a.

12. *Dongfang zazhi* 1, no. 10 (1904): Jiaoyu, 233.

13. Shu Xincheng, *Shiliao*, 3: 146.

14. Su Yunfeng, *Zhang Zhidong yu Hubei jiaoyu gaige*, p. 194.

15. Ibid., p. 195.

16. Ayers, *Chang Chih-tung and Educational Reform*, p. 234.

17. Taga, *Shiryō*, p. 288.

18. Yan Xiu developed the bureau during his period of office in the Zhili educational administration. Its members should be distinguished from the canvasser of the communal sishu; the bureau's personnel came from a higher social stratum and operated at a higher administrative level, from the county seat rather than the village. For Yan's connection with the bureau, see *Qing shi gao* (Taibei: Guofang yanjiuyuan, 1961), p. 1305.

19. "Jiaoyu ganyan," *Dongfang zazhi* 4, no. 11 (1907): Jiaoyu, 237.

20. Zhuang Yu, "Lun difang xuewu gongkuan," *Jiaoyu zazhi* 1, no. 7 (1909): Sheshuo, 85.

21. *Shuntian shibao*, 17 August 1902.

22. Ibid., 2 August 1903.

23. "Lun Zhongguo xuetang chengdu huanjin zhi yuanyin," *Dongfang zazhi* 1, no. 6 (1904): Jiaoyu, 126.

24. Taga, *Shiryō*, p. 288.

25. MacKinnon, *Power and Politics in Late Imperial China*, p. 149.

26. "Lun Zhongguo xuetang chengdu huanjin zhi yuanyin," pp. 126–27.

27. Wang Guowei, "Jiaoyu xiaoyan shi'er ze," Shu Xincheng, *Ziliao*, 3: 1012.

28. "Lun xuetang zhi fubai," *Dongfang zazhi* 1, no. 9 (1904): Jiaoyu, 201.

29. Li Renren, "Tongmenghui zai Guilin, Pingle de huodong he Guangxi xuanbu duli de huiyi," in Zhongguo Renmin Zhengzhi Xieshang Huiyi Quanguo Weiyuanhui, Wenshi Ziliao Yanjiu Weiyuanhui, ed., *Xinhai geming huiyilu* (Beijing: Zhonghua shuju, 1961), 2: 454–55.

30. Zhang Zhidong, *Quanxue pian*, in *Zhang Wenxiang gong quanji* (Taibei: Wenhai chubanshe, 1963), 203: 9a.

31. Herbert Passin, *Society and Education in Japan* (New York: Columbia University, Teachers College, 1965), p. 74.

32. Lowndes, *The Silent Social Revolution*, p. 7.

33. Guo Moruo, *Wo de younian* (Shanghai: Guanghua shuju, 1930), pp. 114–15.

34. Abe Hiroshi, "Shimmatsu no kigaku bōdō," in Taga Akigorō, ed., *Kindai Ajia kyōikushi kenkyū* (Tokyo: Iwasaki gakujutsu shuppansha, 1975), p. 78. For a study of temple expropriation and popular resentment in Jiangsu in the last years of the dynasty, see Wang Shuhuai, "Qingmo Jiangsu difang zizhi fengchao," *Zhongyang yanjiuyuan, Jindaishi yanjiusuo jikan* 6 (1977): 313–27.

35. Luo Dunwei, *Wushi nian huiyilu* (Taibei: Zhongguo wenhua gongyingshe, 1952), p. 16.

36. *Shuntian shibao*, 30 January 1904.

37. See *Dongfang zazhi* 1, no. 2 (1904): Jiaoyu, 72; 1, no. 9 (1904): Jiaoyu, 214; and 2, no. 2 (1905): Jiaoyu, 29.

38. Tian Zhi, "Lun xuetang jingfei yi xian zheng ming," *Jiaoyu zazhi* 2, no. 2 (1910): Sheshuo, 17–18.

39. The 1904 regulations had stated that public money spent on processions and operas and "all expenditures that bring no benefits" could be diverted to the foundation of higher primary schools (Taga, *Shiryō*, p. 288).

40. Abe Hiroshi, "Shimmatsu no kigaku bōdō," p. 78.

41. Wang Fen, *Hangzhou fuzhi* (Taibei: Chengwen chubanshe, 1974), pp. 15b–20b.

42. "Lun xuetang zhi fubai," *Dongfang zazhi* 1, no. 9 (1904): Jiaoyu, 201.

43. Taga, *Shiryō*, p. 472.

44. "Lun shifu wuchi wei jiruo zhi yuanyin," *Dongfang zazhi* 4, no. 2 (1907): Sheshuo, 33.

45. "Lun xuetang xianxiang ji xuesheng jianglai zhi weizhi," *Zhili jiaoyu zazhi* 2, no. 8 (1906): Lunshuo, 9a–b.

46. *Zhejiang chao*, no. 8 (1903): Diaochahui gao, 1–10.

47. *Zhili jiaoyu zazhi* 1, no. 1 (1905): 33b.

48. Shu Xincheng, *Wo he jiaoyu* (Shanghai: Zhonghua shuju, 1945), p. 51.

49. Zhuang Yu, "Lun difang xuewu gongkuan," p. 83.

50. Meng Sen, "Difang zizhi yu jiaoyu," *Jiaoyu zazhi* 1, no. 3 (1909): Sheshuo, 33.

51. David D. Buck, "Educational Modernization in Tsinan, 1899–1937," in Mark Elvin and G. William Skinner, eds., *The Chinese City Between Two Worlds* (Stanford: Stanford University Press, 1974), pp. 185–86.

52. Ichiko Chūzō, "The Role of the Gentry: An Hypothesis," in Mary

Clabaugh Wright, ed., *China in Revolution: The First Phase, 1900–1913* (New Haven, Conn.: Yale University Press, 1968), p. 300.

53. Wang Shuhuai, "Qingmo Jiangsu difang zizhi fengchao," p. 322.

54. Taga, *Shiryō*, pp. 638, 674.

55. Quoted in Joseph W. Esherick, *Reform and Revolution in China: The 1911 Revolution in Hunan and Hubei* (Berkeley and Los Angeles: University of California Press, 1976), p. 116. Esherick points out that "tax revenues were in fact diverted from projects which benefited the poor in order to finance the schemes of the reformist elite."

56. Abe Hiroshi, "Shimmatsu no kigaku bōdō," p. 78.

57. Wang Shuhuai, "Qingmo Jiangsu difang zizhi fengchao," pp. 319–20.

58. Ibid., pp. 325–26.

59. Ichiko Chūzō, "The Role of the Gentry," p. 302.

60. Daniel Bays sees a similar process at work in increased gentry assertiveness at the provincial level over the recovery of railway rights. Here, too, the mobilization of the gentry over one issue created conditions for a change in the balance of power between gentry and officialdom (*China Enters the Twentieth Century* [Ann Arbor: University of Michigan Press, 1978], pp. 5–6 and 163–84.)

61. Stephen MacKinnon shows that in Zhili gentry involvement in educational reform was not necessarily inimical to provincial government control; rather, "it had the effect of cementing ties between provincial government and local elites . . . Through educational reform, Yuan [Shikai] was also selecting and giving experience to his team of administrators, at both the provincial and *xian* (county) level . . . In the process, Yuan was extending his influence and that of the provincial government below the *xian* level." Zhili, however (as MacKinnon himself allows), was not a representative case; Yuan was not only an extremely active governor-general, but also exceptionally careful about the men appointed to serve under him in the key position of county magistrate. (*Power and Politics in Late Imperial China*, pp. 150–51.)

Chapter Six

1. See Liang Qichao, "Jiaoyu zhengce siyi," in Shu Xincheng, *Ziliao*, 3: 953; Taga, *Shiryō*, pp. 178–79; and Luo Zhenyu, "Jiaoyu jihua caoan," *Xue Bu guanbao*, nos. 23–26 (1907): Fulu.

2. For the former view, see Richard A. Orb, "Chihli Academies and Other Schools in the Late Ch'ing," in Paul A. Cohen and John E. Schrecker, eds., *Reform in Nineteenth-Century China* (Cambridge, Mass.: Harvard University Press, 1976), p. 238; for the latter, see Y. C. Wang, "Western Impact and Social Mobility in China," *American Sociological Review* 25, no. 6 (1960): 843–55.

3. Small accretions were made to the numbers of the educated by the establishment of schools for women (dealt with later in this chapter) and by permit-

ting "mean people" (yamen runners, South China's boat people, actors, barbers, brothel keepers) to ascend the educational ladder. In Guangdong in 1904, the prohibition on the boat people's taking the examinations was removed in toto, but the Ministry of Education ruled more cautiously in 1906 that "mean people" could enter government schools only if they had forsaken their previous calling. In practice, many schools required that their pupils come of a "pure family background," and reports to the ministry on middle school students had to give their ancestry to the fourth generation. Even without this limitation, it seems doubtful that many from such humble origins had the money or the motivation for schooling. (*Dongfang zazhi* 1, no. 10 [1904]: Jiaoyu, 240; and *Xue Bu guanbao*, no. 1 [1906]: Wendu, 7a–9a.)

4. See Shu Xincheng, *Wo he jiaoyu* (Shanghai: Zhonghua shuju, 1945), p. 37, for an example. See also P'an Kuang-tan and Fei Hsiao-tung's study on the examination system and social mobility, "City and Village: The Inequality of Opportunity," in Johanna Menzel, ed., *The Chinese Civil Service: Career Open to Talent?* (Boston: D. C. Heath & Co., 1963), especially pp. 15–16.

5. Liu Zijing et al., comps., *Wanyuan xianzhi* (Taibei: Chengwen chubanshe, 1976), 5: 42b (p. 640). In Zhihli in 1905, a county claiming 207 lower primary schools had two higher primary schools and a normal school in its county seat but only one higher primary outside it (Orb, "Chihli Academies," p. 233).

6. Taga, *Shiryō*, p. 167.

7. *Zhili jiaoyu zazhi* 1, no. 1 (1905): 42.

8. Bao Tianxiao, *Chuanyinglou huiyilu* (Hong Kong: Dahua chubanshe, 1971), pp. 285–86, 294.

9. Huang Yanpei, "Qingji gesheng xingxue shi," *Renwen yuekan* 1, no. 9 (1930): 26.

10. Li Liejun, *Li Liejun jiangjun zizhuan* (Chongqing: Sanhu tushushe, 1944), p. 3.

11. *Zhejiang chao*, no. 8 (1903): Diaochahui gao, 1–10.

12. Taga, *Shiryō*, p. 458.

13. Shu Xincheng, *Wo he jiaoyu*, pp. 42–43.

14. Zhuang Yu, "Lun xiaoxue jiaoyu," *Jiaoyu zazhi* 1, no. 2 (1909): Sheshuo, 21.

15. See Orb, "Chihli Academies."

16. Li Zongtong, "Cong jiashu dao Nankai Zhongxue," *Zhuanji wenxue* 4, no. 6 (1964): 44. Nine yuan could support a middle-class family for a month.

17. *Shuntian shibao*, 7 July 1903.

18. See *Mission Educational Directory for China* (Shanghai: Educational Association of China, 1910), *passim*.

19. Wang Mingdao, *Wushi nian lai* (Kowloon: Xingzhen shuju, 1950), p. 210.

20. See *Mission Educational Directory*, p. 59.

21. St. John's and McTyeire's were in Shanghai. Other mission schools

charging over $100 a year were Canton Christian College, Tianjin's Anglo-Chinese College and Pu-tung Middle School, Hankou's Griffith John School, and Shanghai's Anglo-Chinese College. The majority of the students in the "colleges" and "universities" on this list were actually taking secondary courses. See ibid., pp. 16–17, 38, 55–58, 70.

22. David D. Buck, "Educational Modernization in Tsinan, 1899–1937," in Mark Elvin and G. William Skinner, eds., *The Chinese City Between Two Worlds* (Stanford: Stanford University Press, 1974), p. 176.

23. China [Qing], Xue Bu, *Xuantong yuannian, disanci jiaoyu tongji tubiao* (Beijing, 1911), Gesheng, 9. These figures do not include pupils attending combined lower and higher primary schools, for which no breakdown is given.

24. G. A. N. Lowndes, *The Silent Social Revolution* (London: Oxford University Press, 1947), pp. 15, 19.

25. China [Qing], Xue Bu, *Xuantong yuannian . . . tongji tubiao*, Gesheng, p. 9.

26. Duan Fang, "Esheng puji xueshu zhangcheng bing shi," in Shu Xincheng, *Ziliao*, 1: 100–2.

27. For the Welfare Bureau and other attempts "to deal constructively with Tientsin's lumpenproletariat," see Stephen R. MacKinnon, "Police Reform in Late Ch'ing Chihli," *Ch'ing-shih Wen-t'i* 3, no. 4 (1974): 82–99. For the Craft Bureau, see *Dongfang zazhi* 3, no. 8 (1906): Shiye, 173.

28. *Shuntian shibao*, 25 February 1904.

29. Ibid., 5 March 1904 and 14 December 1902.

30. China [Qing], Xue Bu, *Xuantong yuannian . . . tongji tubiao*, Gesheng, p. 6.

31. *Xue Bu guanbao*, no. 30 (1907): Jingwai xuewu baogao, 234b.

32. *Jiaoyu zazhi* 3, no. 4 (1911): Jishi, 30.

33. See John Caiger, "Tejima Seiichi (1849–1918) and Schooling for Industry in Japan" (unpublished paper, Australian National University, 1976), p. 15.

34. Li Gufan, *Tan wang lu*, in *Yunlu wushu* (Hong Kong, 1963), p. 26.

35. *Dongfang zazhi* 2, no. 2 (1905): Jiaoyu, 27.

36. *Shuntian shibao*, 2 August 1903 and 13 September 1903.

37. *Xue Bu guanbao*, no. 19 (1907): Jingwai xuewu baogao, 129a.

38. *Dongfang zazhi* 1, no. 10 (1904): Jiaoyu, 236.

39. "Cishan jiaoyu shuo," *Dongfang zazhi* 1, no. 9 (1904): Jiaoyu, 197.

40. Taga, *Shiryō*, p. 409.

41. China [Qing], Xue Bu, *Xuantong yuannian . . . tongji tubiao*, Gesheng, p. 9. Xinjiang claimed a quarter of them. This may reflect Xinjiang's enthusiasm for part-time education, or simply be another example of the rule that the number of schools claimed increases with distance from the center and consequent difficulty of verification.

42. *Xue Bu guanbao*, no. 22 (1907): Jingwai xuewu baogao, 154a.

43. There is some confusion in the sources about whom the half-day schools attracted. One report says that in Tianjin their pupils came mainly from "well-off families" (*Shuntian shibao*, 23 January 1904); another that the poor attended (*Xue Bu guanbao*, no. 21 [1907]: Jingwai xuewu baogao, 129a). Both agree that the schools did not attract those who worked during the day. Discrepancies can be resolved if one allows that the words "poor"—not rich—and "well off"— not destitute—are relative and may be applied to the same group of people.

44. Zhou Jiachun, "Shuo yexuexiao," *Jiaoyu zazhi* 1, no. 11 (1909): She-shuo, 139–41.

45. Cyrus P. Peake, *Nationalism and Education in Modern China* (New York: Columbia University, Teachers College, 1932), p. 58.

46. Taga, *Shiryō*, p. 627.

47. *Jiaoyu zazhi* 3, no. 6 (1911): Jishi, 46.

48. Taga, *Shiryō*, p. 627.

49. *Jiaoyu zazhi* 3, no. 10 (1912): Jishi, 71–72. A warning against letting simple reading schools and reformed sishu interfere with the progress of lower primary schools was given by the Jiangsu Provincial Assembly at the end of 1910. (see ibid., 2, no. 11 [1910]: Jishi, 52).

50. The Qing novel *Jinghua yuan* depicted the Tang empress Wu Zetian as holding examinations for women at which the most erudite obtained the same titles as their male counterparts. This point was used as propaganda for women's education in the late Qing feminist novel, Yi-suo's *Huang Xiuqiu*, reprinted in [Qian Xingcun] Ah Ying, comp., *Wan-Qing wenxue congchao: Xiaoshuo*, vol. 1, parts 1 and 2 (Beijing: Zhonghua shuju, 1960), pp. 167–389.

51. See Bao Tianxiao, *Chuanyinglou huiyilu*, p. 123.

52. Mary Raleigh Anderson, *Protestant Mission Schools for Girls in South China* (Mobile, Ala.: Heiter-Starke Printing Co., 1943), pp. 26–27, 52–53.

53. For Liang's school, see *Shiwu bao*, no. 47 (1896).

54. *The China Mission Hand-book: First Issue* (Shanghai: American Presbyterian Mission Press, 1896), p. 232.

55. For the former, see *Shuntian shibao*, 26 December 1902; for the latter, ibid., 6 April 1902.

56. See Taga, *Shiryō*, pp. 309–12. The thought of female pupils having to walk through the streets to get to class horrified Zhang.

57. *Dongfang zazhi* 1, no. 7 (1904): Jiaoyu, 161.

58. Ibid., 1, no. 2 (1904): Jiaoyu, 42.

59. Ibid., pp. 41–42.

60. Arnold Foster, "The Educational Outlook in Wuchang," *Chinese Recorder and Missionary Journal* 37, no. 4 (1906): 208.

61. *Shuntian shibao*, 11 June 1903.

62. *Dongfang zazhi* 1, no. 2 (1904): Jiaoyu, 41.

63. Shu Xincheng, *Wo he jiaoyu* (Shanghai: Zhonghua shuju, 1945), pp. 420–37.

Notes to pages 116–120

64. See Guo Moruo, *Wo de younian* (Shanghai: Yadong tushuguan, 1941), pp. 120–21.

65. See Bao Tianxiao, *Chuanyinglou huiyilu*, p. 338.

66. Taga, *Shiryō*, p. 468.

67. Bao Tianxiao, *Chuanyinglou huiyilu*, pp. 335–38.

68. *Xue Bu guanbao*, no. 39 (1907): Jingwai xuewu baogao, 390a.

69. Taga, *Shiryō*, p. 460.

70. *Xue Bu guanbao*, no. 47 (1908): Wendu, 211a–b.

71. Luo Dunwei, *Wushi nian huiyilu* (Taibei: Zhongguo wenhua gongying-she, 1952), p. 14.

72. *Xingqi huabao*, no. 23 (1907).

73. *Liangri huabao*, no. 58 (1908).

74. *Xue Bu guanbao*, no. 35 (1907): Jingwai xuewu baogao, 304b.

75. Buwei Yang Chao, *Autobiography of a Chinese Woman*, trans. Chao Yuen-ren (Westport, Conn.: Greenwood Press, 1970), p. 73.

76. Shu Xincheng, *Ziliao*, 1: 382.

77. Cao Juren, *Wo yu wo de shijie* (Hong Kong: Sanyu tushu wenju gongsi, 1972), p. 34.

78. China [Qing], Xue Bu, *Xuantong yuannian . . . tongji tubiao*, Gesheng, p. 9.

79. Yang Buwei's modern education helped her to break off an arranged marriage (Chao, *Autobiography of a Chinese Woman*, pp. 79–81). The mother of Dr. Wang Ling ran away from home to attend school in the 1900s (personal communication, Dr. Wang Ling, Australian National University).

80. For Qiu Jin's career, see Mary Backus Rankin, *Early Chinese Revolutionaries: Radical Intellectuals in Shanghai and Chekiang, 1902–1911* (Cambridge, Mass.: Harvard University Press, 1971), pp. 40–46, 172, 176–78, 185.

81. There were between five and six hundred Japanese teachers in China in 1906. See Saneto Keishū, *Chūgokujin Nihon ryūgaku shi* (Tokyo: Kuroshio shuppan, 1960), pp. 94–97.

82. See Wang Wentian, *Zhang Boling yu Nankai* (Taibei: Zhuanji wenxue chubanshe, 1968), p. 8.

83. For the Herbartian movement in Japan, see Nishihira Isao, "Western Influences on the Modernization of Japanese Education, 1868–1912" (Ph.D. diss., Ohio State University, 1972), pp. 440–45. For its use in sishu, see *Xue Bu guanbao*, no. 93 (1909): Jingwai xuewu baogao, 19b.

84. See Taga, *Shiryō*, p. 335.

85. *Shuntian shibao*, 5 May 1902.

86. Bao Tianxiao, *Chuanyinglou huiyilu*, p. 250.

87. Guo Moruo, *Wo de younian*, p. 194.

88. Liao T'ai-ch'u, "Rural Education in Transition," *Yenching Journal of Social Studies* 4, no. 2 (1949): 36–38.

89. William Liu, interview.

90. *Xue Bu guanbao*, no. 38 (1907): Jingwai xuewu baogao, 356a–57a.

91. Ibid., no. 28 (1907): Jingwai xuewu baogao, 202a–3b.

92. Taga, *Shiryō*, p. 681. *Kexue*, now translated as "science," was originally used for all learning divided into separate units along Western lines. Humane studies were later reassimilated into the Chinese world of knowledge, leaving only the natural sciences as discrete intruders.

93. According to the Ministry of Education's figures for 1909, 68,000 Chinese had graduated at the post-elementary level in the eight years from 1902 to 1909, including nearly 40,000 who had studied at either normal schools or short-term teacher-training centers. The majority appear to have gone into teaching, as figures for teacher qualifications show that more than 80 percent of the 19,067 teachers at the post-elementary level had graduated from modern schools in China. At the elementary level, 33,348 teachers had had modern teacher training and 30,978 had not; some of the latter had probably attended modern schools, although no breakdown is given. (China [Qing], Xue Bu, *Xuantong yuannian . . . tongji tubiao*, Gesheng, pp. 14–15, 31–36.) Internal inconsistencies make it unlikely that these figures are completely reliable, but they perhaps indicate a trend.

94. Chen Qitian, for example, started his modern school career at an agricultural school but changed to regular higher primary after only one year (*Jiyuan huiyilu* [Taibei: Shangwu yinshuguan, 1965], p. 12).

95. Missionaries had set up a few medical schools, but not many were founded by Chinese. The Jiangxi Medical School, which taught both Chinese and Western medicine, deserves note as an early example of the principle of walking on two legs: unfortunately, its course in Western medicine was of a low standard. (See Huang Yanpei, "Qingji gesheng xingxue shi," *Renwen yuekan* 1, no. 9 [1930]: 25–26.)

96. For a scathing satire of *lunhuan jiaoyu*, see Lao She's novel *Maocheng ji*.

97. Arthur H. Smith, *Village Life in China* (New York: Fleming H. Revell Co., 1899), pp. 107–9.

98. Shu Xincheng, *Shiliao*, 2: 254–57.

99. Jiang Mengmei, "Qian-Qing Xue Bu bianshu zhi zhuangkuang," in ibid., p. 260.

100. For the history of the Commercial Press, see Wang Yunwu, *Shangwu yinshuguan yu xin jiaoyu nianpu* (Taibei: Shangwu yinshuguan, 1973). For the contribution made by missionary publishers, see Wang Shuhuai, "Jidujiao Jiaoyuhui ji qi chuban shiye/The Educational Association of China and Its Publications, (1890–1912)," *Zhongyang yanjiuyuan, Jindaishi yanjiusuo jikan* 2 (1971): 365–96. For further details on textbook publishing in the late Qing, see "Jiaokeshu zhi fakan gaikuang," in Zhang Jinglu, *Zhongguo jindai chuban shiliao: Chubian* (Shanghai: Qunlian chubanshe, 1953), pp. 225–44.

101. Peake, *Nationalism and Education in Modern China*, p. 180.

102. Wang Shuhuai, "Jidujiao Jiaoyuhui ji qi chuban shiye," p. 388. Not all these works were textbooks.

103. See Peake, *Nationalism and Education in Modern China*, p. 58.

104. *Xue Bu guanbao*, no. 4 (1906): Shending shumu, 5b–7b. These and other texts were supposed to inculcate bravery, love of country, and self-reliance.

105. The edition I have used, the *Dingzheng nüzi guowen jiaokeshu*, is actually a revision made early in 1912 of the Qing edition. The changes appear to consist mainly of extra material on domestic science and hygiene.

106. Liang Ruochen, "Yige shancunli de geming fengbao," in Zhongguo Renmin Zhengzhi Xieshang Huiyi Quanguo Weiyuanhui, Wenshi Ziliao Yanjiu Weiyuanhui, ed., *Xinhai geming huiyilu* (Beijing: Zhonghua shuju, 1961), 2: 366.

107. The *Nüzi guowen jiaokeshu*, for example, came in four volumes: the first two cost 20¢ each and the second two 25¢ each.

108. Pupils at a Guangdong village sishu, for example, were still chanting "wash your face, then plait your pigtail" from a Qing ethics textbook even after the Republic had done away with the queue (see Liang Ruochen, "Yige shancunli de geming fengbao," p. 367).

109. William Liu, interview. A similar danger was associated with the color white; one pupil used to change out of the white hat and shoes of his summer uniform at school rather than alarm his grandmother by wearing them home (see Yang Yinpu, "Sishiba zishu," in Zhuo Li and Wu Fan, eds., *Dangdai zuojia zizhuan ji* [Chongqing: Chubanjie yuekanshe, 1945], p. 34).

110. Quoted in Y. C. Wang, *Chinese Intellectuals and the West, 1872–1949* (Chapel Hill: University of North Carolina Press, 1968), p. 182.

111. Lao Xiang, "Guanyu kang-Ri *Sanzi jing*," *Kangzhan wenyi* 1, no. 7 (1938): 19. I am indebted to Dr. Mary Farquhar of Griffith University for this reference.

112. Chen Deyun, *Chen Zibao xiansheng jiaoyu yiyi* (Hong Kong: n.p., 1952?).

113. New buildings could cause alarm on other than aesthetic grounds if erected without regard for geomancy. A Chinese school in Zhejiang was destroyed by local people in 1907 because it went against geomantic principles. (Abe Hiroshi, "Shimmatsu no kigaku bōdō," in Taga Akigorō, *Kindai Ajia kyōikushi kenkyū* [Tokyo: Iwasaki gakujutsu shuppansha, 1975], p. 73). Similar superstitious objections to the conversion of a graveyard into school property are chronicled in Ye Shengtao's novel, *Ni Huanzhi* (Hong Kong: n.p., 1930), pp. 81–86.

114. A similar discrepancy between the expectations of rulers and ruled appears to have existed in Ghana, where "the close relationship existing between differential rewards of the occupational structure and the educational systems of colonial areas" meant that an "academic" education in English was vocational training for clerical work, while apparently practical technical education was little use in the absence of job openings for those with modern technical training (Philip J. Foster, *Education and Social Change in Ghana* [London: Routledge and Kegan Paul, 1965], p. 65 and *passim*).

115. In 1896, Shanghai's Anglo-Chinese College (a mission establishment) was one of the few schools teaching English. It boasted that former pupils were "scattered throughout China in the telegraph offices, the Custom Houses, Yamêns, etc." (*China Mission Hand-book*, p. 232.)

116. See *Mengxue bao*, nos. 9–11 (1896).

117. See Ma Xulun, *Wo zai liushi sui yiqian* (Shanghai: Shenghuo shudian, 1947), pp. 10–11; and Bao Tianxiao, *Chuanyinglou huiyilu*, pp. 158–59. Neither Bao nor Ma took their study of "the devils' language" seriously: it was not yet the stepping-stone to study abroad and consequent high rank that it became during the Republican period.

118. Taga, *Shiryō*, pp. 214–15.

119. Yan Fu, their most famous graduate, headed the Anhui Higher School for a year in 1906–7. Under him were eight English-language teachers and three English-teaching administrators (out of a total staff of 23). Their combined salaries cost the school over 1,500 taels a year. (See *Xue Bu guanbao*, no. 38 [1907]: Jingwai xuewu baogao, 363b–64a.)

120. On Japanese teachers in China, see Sanetō Keishū, *Chūgokujin Nihon ryūgaku shi*, pp. 94–97.

121. Among the former must be classed Wang Guowei, whose interest in Kant and Schopenhauer was fired by his Japanese teachers of European languages in 1899 (see Zhao Wanli, *Wang Jing'an xiansheng nianpu* [Taibei: Guangwen shuju, 1971], p. 4).

122. *Zhili jiaoyu zazhi* 1, no. 1 (1905): 39a.

123. *Xue Bu guanbao*, no. 20 (1907): 134a.

124. See comments in Bao Tianxiao, *Chuanyinglou huiyilu*, p. 336. At Qinghua, too, all other subjects were subordinated to the study of English (see Li Ji, *Gan jiu lu* [Taibei: Zhuanji wenxue chubanshe, 1967], p. 13).

125. "Lun shifu wuchi wei jiruo zhi yuanyin," *Dongfang zazhi* 4, no. 2 (1907): Sheshuo, 32.

126. Yu Ziyi, "Ershi nian qian xiangcun xuexiao shenghuoli de wo," *Jiaoyu zazhi* 19, no. 12 (1927): 3.

127. Guo Moruo, *Wo de younian*, pp. 187–88.

128. *Su bao* (Taibei, 1968), no. 2,454.

129. *Xue Bu guanbao*, no. 30 (1907): Jingwai xuewu baogao, 227a–31b.

Chapter Seven

1. Liang Qichao, "Xinmin shuo: Qi," *Xinmin congbao*, no. 7 (1902): 7–8.

2. "Zhongguo dang zhong guomin jiaoyu," and "Guomin jiaoyu," *Hubei xueshengjie*, nos. 1 and 2 (1903): 23–32, 197–208, 331–339.

3. *Jiangsu*, no. 2 (1903): Jishi, 372–73.

4. Shu Xincheng, *Jindai Zhongguo jiaoyu sixiangshi* (Shanghai: Zhonghua shuju, 1932), pp. 114–15.

5. See Nishihira Isao, "Western Influence on the Modernization of Japanese Education" (Ph.D. diss., Ohio State University, 1972), pp. 416–19.

6. Taga, *Shiryō*, pp. 634–35.

7. *Zhili jiaoyu zazhi* 1, no. 1 (1905): 40a.

8. *Shuntian shibao*, 19 August 1902.

9. Wen Tian, "Shu neidi banxue qingxing," *Jiaoyu zazhi* 1, no. 7 (1909): Zazuan, 43–44.

10. *Xue Bu guanbao*, no. 39 (1907): Jingwai xuewu baogao, 389b.

11. *Jiaoyu zazhi* 3, no. 6 (1911): Jishi, 46–47.

12. See *Zhili jiaoyu zazhi* 1, no. 1 (1905): 45b; and *Xue Bu guanbao*, no. 83 (1909): Jingwai xuewu baogao, 19b–23a.

13. Shu Xincheng, *Wo he jiaoyu* (Shanghai: Zhonghua shuju, 1945), p. 55.

14. Tian Lusheng, "Xuejiu jiaoyu tan," *Yueyue xiaoshuo*, no. 12 (1907): 33–38. "Palmer" was an English reader put out for Indian schools: the Commercial Press produced a version with notes in Chinese in 1897 (see Wang Yunwu, *Shangwu yinshuguan yu xin jiaoyu nianpu* [Taibei: Shangwu yinshuguan, 1973], p. 2; and Bao Tianxiao, *Chuanyinglou huiyilu* [Hong Kong: Dahua chubanshe, 1971], p. 159).

15. China [Qing], Xue Bu, *Xuantong yuannian, disanci jiaoyu tongji tubiao* (Beijing, 1911), Zhili, pp. 1–2; Gesheng, pp. 1–2.

16. *Xue Bu guanbao*, no. 8 (1906): 45a.

17. *Shili*, 395: 3a.

18. Chen Guofu, for example, graduated from higher primary school three times. A year of study at Hunan's famous Mingde at middle-school level was insufficient preparation for entry to the first year of middle school in Huzhou and Nanjing. (See Wu Xiangxiang, *Chen Guofu de yisheng* [Taibei: Zhuanji wenxue chubanshe, 1971], pp. 42–46.) More fortunate students were able to leap a grade (see Li Shuhua, "Cong sishu dao xuetang," *Zhuanji wenxue* 17, no. 2 [1970]: 62–63, and Zhou Fohai, *Kuxue ji*, in Zhou Fohai and Chen Gongbo, *Huiyili hebian* [Hong Kong: Chunqiu chubanshe, 1967], p. 93).

19. In 1868 a fief school set up in Numazu introduced the week to Japan. All primary schools later adopted the seven-day system. (See Nishihira, "Western Influence on the Modernization of Japanese Education," p. 52.)

20. *Xue Bu guanbao*, no. 34 (1907): 284a.

21. Shu Xincheng, *Wo he jiaoyu*, pp. 49, 51.

22. "Lun jinri zhi jiaoyu," *Dongfang zazhi* 3, no. 12 (1907): Jiaoyu, 344.

23. See *Jiaoyu zazhi* 1, no. 10 (1909): Sheshuo, 124, for the economic background to this practice.

24. Bao Tianxiao, *Chuanyinglou huiyilu*, pp. 276–79. For informal appointment of friends in Shanghai, see ibid., pp. 331–39.

25. Cao Juren, *Jiangfan liushi nian* (Hong Kong: Chuangken chubanshe, 1957), p. 29.

26. Guo Moruo, *Wo de younian* (Shanghai: Guanghua shuju, 1930), p. 153.

27. Li Zongtong, "Wu da chen chuyang yu Beijing diyike zhadan," *Zhuanji wenxue* 4, no. 4 (1964): 36.

28. Li Zongtong, "Cong jiashu dao Nankai Zhongxue," *Zhuanji wenxue* 4, no. 6 (1964): 44.

29. Yu Jiaju, *Huiyilu* (Shanghai: Zhonghua shuju, 1948), p. 21.

30. Wen Tian, "Shu neidi banxue qingxing," pp. 43–44.

31. See *Shuntian shibao*, 5 April 1902. The practice is still universal among U.S. state universities and colleges.

32. Guo Moruo, *Wo de younian*, p. 167.

33. Ibid., p. 178.

34. Liu Zhi, *Wo de huiyi* (Taibei: Rongtai yinshuguan, 1966), p. 2.

35. *Shuntian shibao*, 1 January 1904.

36. *Dongfang zazhi* 2, no. 2 (1905): Jiaoyu, 27.

37. *Shuntian shibao*, 15 May 1904.

38. *Dongfang zazhi* 1, no. 7 (1904): Jiaoyu, 168.

39. See Taga, *Shiryō*, p. 382.

40. See Shu Xincheng, *Wo he jiaoyu*, pp. 57–58.

41. Bao Tianxiao, *Chuanyinglou huiyilu*, pp. 296–97.

42. *Jiaoyu zazhi* 1, no. 7 (1909): Pinglun, 9–11.

43. *Xingqi huabao*, no. 45 (1907).

44. Ibid., no. 39 (1907).

45. Taga, *Shiryō*, p. 472.

46. See *Shuntian shibao*, 21 September 1903, 22 November 1903, and 10 January 1904.

47. See Bao Tianxiao, *Chuanyinglou huiyilu*, p. 343.

48. "Nanyang Gongxue de yijiulinger nian bake fengchao he Aiguo Xue-she," in Zhongguo Renmin Zhengzhi Xieshang Huiyi Quanguo Weiyuanhui, Wenshi Ziliao Yanjiu Weiyuanhui, ed., *Xinhai geming huiyilu* (Beijing: Zhonghua shuju, 1963), 4: 72.

49. *Xingqi huabao*, no. 53 (1907). See Illustration 7.

50. *Chinese Recorder* 37, no. 9 (1906): 509.

51. See Shu Xincheng, *Wo he jiaoyu*, p. 116.

52. Liu Bannong, "Xiepuluchen ji," *Xiaoshuo huabao*, no. 1 (1917): 5.

53. Taga, *Shiryō*, pp. 383–84.

54. Ibid., p. 214.

55. Ibid., pp. 384–85.

56. Chang Chung-li, *The Chinese Gentry* (Seattle: University of Washington Press, 1955), p. 125.

57. Chong You, "Xuetang jiangli zhangcheng yiwen," *Jiaoyu zazhi* 2, no. 1 (1910): Pinglun, 1–5. This does not indicate an increase in social mobility; the number studying to become juren was probably larger under the old system than

under the new, but with the examinations almost no one passed while with the new schools almost everyone did. The abolition of quotas led to the dilution of standards and consequently to the relative lowering of the juren's status.

58. Bao Tianxiao, *Chuanyinglou huiyilu*, p. 290.

59. *Shuntian shibao*, 2 May 1903.

60. Guo Moruo, *Wo de younian*, pp. 153–54.

61. See especially the debate on the student walkout from Zhejiang University, "Xuejie fengchao," *Su bao*, 11 May, 13 May, 18 May, and 19 May 1903.

62. *Zhili jiaoyu zazhi* 1, no. 1 (1905): 356.

63. Shu Xincheng, *Wo he jiaoyu*, p. 56.

64. *Shuntian shibao*, 20 September 1903.

65. Ibid., 15 November 1903.

66. Ibid., 10 May 1903.

67. Ibid., 10 July 1903.

68. See Bao Tianxiao, *Chuanyinglou huiyilu*, p. 302; Guo Moruo, *Wo de younian*, p. 168; and *Shuntian shibao*, 17 July 1903 and 26 July 1904.

69. Chen Duxiu, *Shi'an zizhuan* (Taibei: Zhuanji wenxue chubanshe, 1967), p. 39.

70. *Xue Bu guanbao*, no. 38 (1907): Jingwai xuewu baogao, 384a–b; and Mary Backus Rankin, *Early Chinese Revolutionaries* (Cambridge, Mass.: Harvard University Press, 1971), p. 180.

71. *Jiaoyu zazhi* 2, no. 5 (1910): Jishi, 39.

72. Ibid., 2, no. 4 (1910): Jishi, 32.

73. "Lun jinri zhi jiaoyu," p. 344.

74. See Guo Moruo, *Wo de younian*, p. 76.

75. Ibid., p. 140.

76. Ma Xulun, *Wo zai liushi sui yiqian* (Shanghai: Shenghuo shudian, 1947), pp. 12, 18, 19. Even outside the new schools, the historical temper was a threat to the Manchus: Xiong Kewu recalls that the teacher in the Sichuan sishu he attended in the early 1900s, a historian whose special interest was the fall of the Song and the Ming, had his pupils read *Yangzhou shiri ji* (Ten Days at Yangzhou) and other anti-Manchu works ("Xinhai qian wo canjia de Sichuan jici wuzhuang qiyi," in *Xinhai geming huiyilu*, 3: 1).

77. Roger F. Hackett, "Chinese Students in Japan, 1900–1910," *Papers on China* (Harvard University Press) 3 (1949): 147.

78. "Lun youxue buke tailan," *Dongfang zazhi* 1, no. 9 (1904): 199–200.

79. Harold Z. Schiffrin, *Sun Yat-sen and the Origins of the Chinese Revolution* (Berkeley and Los Angeles: University of California Press, 1968), p. 261.

80. "Nanyang Gongxue . . . bake fengchao," pp. 72–73.

81. See biographies of Huang Xing, Wu Zhihui, and Zhang Ji in Howard L. Boorman, ed., *Biographical Dictionary of Republican China* (New York: Columbia University Press, 1967–1970).

82. "Nanyang Gongxue . . . bake fengchao," p. 67.

83. Zou Taofen, *Jingli* (Shanghai: Taofen chubanshe, 1947), p. 9.

84. Sa Mengwu, *Xuesheng shidai* (Taibei: Sanmin shuju, 1959), p. 51.

85. Li Renren, "Tongmeng Hui zai Guilin, Pingle de huodong he Guangxi xuanbu duli de huiyi," in *Xinhai geming huiyilu*, 2: 449.

86. William Liu, interview. Geography lessons continued to be a useful stimulus to patriotism under the Republic. Martin Yang, at primary school from 1914 to 1918, vividly remembers that "it was taught that the map of China ought to be the shape of a crab-apple leaf. This leaf has recently been damaged by many kinds of diseases and insects." It was up to the younger generation to repair the damage. (*Chinese Social Structure* [Taibei: Eurasia Book Co., 1969], p. 361.)

87. Cao Juren, *Wo yu wo de shijie* (Hong Kong: Sanyu tushu wenju gongsi, 1972), p. 34.

88. William Liu, interview.

89. Quoted in Zhou Shizhao, *Women de shibiao* (Beijing: Beijing chubanshe, 1958), p. 10.

90. *Jiaoyu zazhi* 1, no. 13 (1910): Jishi, 98–99.

91. Ma Xulun, *Wo zai liushi sui yiqian*, pp. 25–26.

92. Huang Zhong, *Hu Yuantan xiansheng zhuan* (Taibei: Zhonghua shuju, 1971), pp. 20–21.

93. Quoted in Joseph W. Esherick, *Reform and Revolution in China* (Berkeley and Los Angeles: University of California Press, 1976), p. 162.

94. See Bao Tianxiao, "Cha gongke," *Yueyue xiaoshuo* 1, no. 8 (1907): 170–71; and Li Jianhou, "Wuchang shouyi qianhou yishi baze," in *Xinhai geming huiyilu*, 2: 81.

95. For example, Li Jianhou: "From 1906 to 1910, I attended the provincial Central Area Primary School. Among my 240 schoolmates were . . . three who received special treatment from the rest of us and from the teachers, the supervisor, and . . . the head teacher. Their schoolwork was poor, but they liked reading forbidden books and progressive periodicals and had resolved to take part in revolutionary activities . . . because of this, everyone thought of them as future heroes of our race." ("Wuchang shouyi qianhou yishi baze," p. 79.)

96. The figures for civil schools (including higher and middle schools and upper and lower normal and industrial schools) come from China [Qing], Xue Bu, *Xuantong yuannian . . . tongji tubiao*, pp. 2–9. Plans for a hierarchy of military schools were drawn up in 1904, but only the lower levels—basic or primary schools (equivalent to the civil system's higher primary schools) and intermediate or middle schools—were set up. In 1906 China had 35 military schools and training establishments, in 1911 about 70. (Ralph L. Powell, *The Rise of Chinese Military Power, 1895–1912* [Princeton, N.J.: Princeton University Press, 1955], pp. 180–82, 236, 299.)

97. For figures on the number of "foreign-trained" (mainly in Japan)

teachers in specialist, technical, and normal schools, see China [Qing], Xue Bu, *Xuantong yuannian . . . tongji tubiao*, Gesheng, pp. 31–34.

98. See ibid., Sichuan, pp. 3–7; and Zhang Chonglei, "Qingmo Minchu Sichuan de junshi xuetang ji Chuanjun paixi," in *Xinhai geming huiyilu*, 3: 345–51.

99. Shi Tiyuan, "Yi Chengdu baolu yundong," in *Xinhai geming huiyilu*, 3: 49.

100. Chen Rigang, "Dazu Tongzhijun," in *Xinhai geming huiyilu*, 3: 258–59.

101. Wang Yinglou, "Huizhoufu zhongxuesheng zai Xinhai geming shiqi de huodong," in *Xinhai geming huiyilu*, 2: 348.

102. Li Jianhou, "Wuchang shouyi qianhou yishi baze," p. 81; quoted in Esherick, *Reform and Revolution in China*, p. 162.

103. See China [Qing], Xue Bu, *Xuantong yuannian . . . tongji tubiao*, Gesheng, pp. 2–9; and Powell, *Rise of Chinese Military Power*, p. 299.

104. Lao Xiang, "Guanyu kang-Ri *Sanzi jing*," *Kangzhan wenyi* 1, no. 7 (1938): 79; quoted in M. A. Farquhar, "Children's Literature in China" (Ph.D. diss., Griffith University, 1981), pp. 118–19.

105. Shu Xincheng, *Wo he jiaoyu*, pp. 49, 51.

106. Liang Qichao, "Xin min shuo," 16a.

Glossary

chongtu

冲突

cuanju

爨局

cunxue

村学

daguan

大馆

daibiao

代表

daxue

大学

dongcao

冬漕

dushu ren

读书人

fansi

藩司

gangchang

纲常

geming

革命

gongren

公认

gongli

公立

gongyi ju

工艺局

guan

馆

guanxue dachen

管学大臣

guohun

国魂

guomin jiaoyu

国民教育

Guomin bidu

国民必读

huiguan

会馆

jianyi shizi xueshu

简易识字学塾

jiao

教

jiaohua

教化

jiaoyang

教养

jiaoyang ju

教养局

jiaoyu

教育

jiashu

家塾

jiazu zhuyi

家族主义

jingyi

经义

jinshi

进士

jinxue

进学

junguomin zhuyi

军国民主义

juren

举人

keju

科举

kexue

科学

lejuan

乐捐

liedeng

躐等

lunhuan jiaoyu

轮换教育

mengguan

蒙馆

Ming

明

mou

亩

Napolun

拿破仑

niesi

臬司

paijuan

派捐

po meng

破蒙

qi meng

启蒙

Qing

清

quanxuesuo

劝学所

rencai

人才

shang gong

尚公

shang shi

尚实

shang wu

尚武

shangyuan

上院

shanzhang

山长

shengyuan

生员

shexue

社学

shī

师

shí

实

shifan yuan

师范院

shishi qiushi

实事求是

shixue

实学

shiye

实业

shuyuan

书院

sishu

私塾

Song

宋

sulun

俗论

tianlong jingxiang

天龙景象

tianran jingxiang

天然景象

tixueshi

提学史

Tongmeng Hui

同盟会

tu

土

tuanti

团体

waiyuan

外院

wenming

文明

xi ru

西儒

xi xue

西学

xian ru wei zhu

先入为主

xiang

乡

xiangyue

乡约

xiaoxue

小学

xing xue

兴学

Xing Zhong Hui

兴中会

xingqi

星期

xisheng

牺牲

xue

学

Xue Bu

学部

xuegong

学宫

xueshu

学术

xuetang

学堂

xuewu

学务

Xuewu chu

学务处

xuewu juan

学务捐

xuexiao

学校

xuewu dachen

学务大臣

Xuewu gangyao

学务纲要

xuezheng

学政

yang

洋

yang jinshi

洋进士

yang juren

洋举人

yaodong

邀东

yeman

野蛮

yixue

义学

yi xue

议学

yuanzhang

院长

yucai

育才

yulun

舆论

yundong

运动

zhishi

治事

zhiyuan

职员

zhong jun

忠君

zhongxue

中学

zhongyuan

中院

zong jiaoxi

总教习

zongli xuewu dachen

总理学务大臣

Zongli yamen

总理衙门

zuxue

族学

zuzhi

组织

zun Kong

遵孔

Bibliography

Works in Chinese and Japanese

Primary Sources

Official Sources and Collections of Documents

China [Qing]. Xue Bu. *Guangxu sanshisannian, diyici jiaoyu tongji tubiao.* Beijing, 1909.

———. *Xuantong yuannian, disanci jiaoyu tongji tubiao.* Beijing, 1911.

Liu Jincao, comp. *Huangchao xu wenxian tongkao.* Taibei: Xinxing shuju, 1963 [1915].*

Qinding da-Qing huidian shili. Taibei: Guoli zhongyang tushuguan, 1963 [1899].

Qing shi gao. Taibei: Guofang yanjiuyuan, 1961 [1927].

Shu Xincheng, ed. *Jindai Zhongguo jiaoyu shiliao.* 4 vols. Shanghai: Zhonghua shuju, 1933 [1928].

———. *Jindai Zhongguo jiaoyushi ziliao.* 3 vols. Beijing: Renmin jiaoyu chubanshe, 1962.

Taga Akigorō, ed. *Kindai Chūgoku kyōikushi shiryō: Shimmatsuhen.* Tokyo: Nihon gakujutsu shinkōkai, 1972.

---

*Dates in brackets are those of first publication.

Zhang Jinglu, ed. *Zhongguo jindai chuban shiliao: Chubian.* Shanghai: Qunlian chubanshe, 1953.

Other Contemporary Works

Books

Cao Xueqin. *Honglou meng.* Beijing: Renmin wenxue chubanshe, 1973.

Chen Deyun. *Chen Zibao xiansheng jiaoyu yiyi.* Hong Kong: n.p., 1952?

Dingzheng nüzi guowen jiaokeshu. Nos. 4–8. Shanghai: Shangwu yinshuguan, 1912.

Feng Guifen. *Jiaopinlu kangyi.* Taibei: Xuehai chubanshe, 1967.

Huang Zunxian. *Riben guozhi.* Guangzhou: Fuwenzhai, 1898.

Liu Langsheng. *Nanchuan xianzhi.* Taibei: Chengwen chubanshe, 1976 [1926].

Liu Zijing et al. comps. *Wanyuan xianzhi.* Taibei: Chengwen chubanshe, 1976, [1932].

Su Yu, ed. *Yijiao congbian.* Taibei: Guofeng chubanshe, 1970 [1899].

Wang Fen. *Hangzhou fuzhi.* Taibei: Chengwen chubanshe, 1974 [1922].

Wang Tao. *Pu-Fa zhanji.* Hong Kong, 1886.

———. *Taoyuan wenlu waibian.* Hong Kong, 1883.

Wu Rulun. *Dongyou conglu.* N.p., 1902.

———. *Tongcheng Wu xiansheng riji.* Taibei: Guangwen shuju, 1963.

Xinmin congbao huibian. Taibei: Datong shuju, 1969 [1903].

Yi-suo. *Huang Xiuqiu.* Reprinted in [Qian Xingcun] Ah Ying, ed., *Wan-Qing wenxue congchao: Xiaoshuo.* Vol. 1, parts 1 and 2. Beijing: Zhonghua shuju, 1960, pp. 167–389.

Zhang Zhidong. *Zhang Wenxiang gong quanji.* Taibei: Wenhai chubanshe, 1963.

Zheng Guanying. *Shengshi weiyan houbian.* Taibei: Datong shuju, 1968 [1909].

———. *Shengshi weiyan zengding xinbian.* Taibei: Datong shuju, 1968 [1895].

Articles

(Note: Page numbers in brackets are those of the reprint edition of the journal cited.)

Bao Tianxiao. "Cha gongke." *Yueyue xiaoshuo* 1, no. 8 (1907): 170–71.

Chong You. "Xuetang jiangli zhangcheng yiwen." *Jiaoyu zazhi* 2, no. 1 (1910): Pinglun, 1–8 [01329–336].

"Cishan jiaoyu shuo." *Dongfang zazhi* 1, no. 9 (1904): Jiaoyu, 197–200 [2123–126].

"Guomin jiaoyu." *Hubei xueshengjie,* no. 2 (1903): [331–39].

"Jiangnan Chucai Xuetang zhangcheng." *Shiwu bao,* no. 42 (1897).

Lao Xiang. "Guanyu kang-Ri *Sanzi jing*." *Kangzhan wenyi* 1, no. 7 (1938).

Liang Qichao. "Bianfa tongyi: Lun xuexiao." *Shiwu bao,* nos. 5–33 (1896–1897).

————. "Xinmin shuo: Qi." *Xinmin congbao*, no. 7 (1902): 1–8.

Liu Bannong. "Xiepuluchen ji." *Xiaoshuo huabao*, no. 1 (1917): 1–14.

Lu Xun. "Zhufu." *Panghuang*. Reprinted in *Lu Xun quanji*. Shanghai: *Lu Xun quanji* chubanshe, 1946, 2: 139–62.

"Lun jinri zhi jiaoyu." *Dongfang zazhi* 3, no. 12 (1907): Jiaoyu, 341–50 [8169–178].

"Lun shifu wuchi wei jiruo zhi yuanyin." *Dongfang zazhi* 4, no. 2 (1907): Sheshuo, 29–33 [8749–753].

"Lun xuetang xianxiang ji xuesheng jianglai zhi weizhi." *Zhili jiaoyu zazhi* 2, no. 8 (1906): Lunshuo, 8b–12a.

"Lun xuetang zhi fubai." *Dongfang zazhi* 1, no. 9 (1904): Jiaoyu, 200–202 [2126–128].

"Lun Zhongguo xuetang chengdu huanjin zhi yuanyin." *Dongfang zazhi* 1, no. 6 (1904): Jiaoyu, 126–27 [1382–383].

Luo Zhenyu. "Jiaoyu jihua caoan." *Xue Bu guanbao*, nos. 23–26 (1906): Fulu.

Meng Sen. "Difang zizhi yu jiaoyu." *Jiaoyu zazhi* 1, no. 3 (1909): Sheshuo, 31–37 [00191–197].

"Miluoxiangren xueyue jiuwu." In Su Yu, ed., *Yijiao congbian*, 4: 72a–79b.

Shan Weifan. "Beiping sishu de yanjiu." *Xin beizhen* 2, no. 10 (1936): 1061–70; 2, no. 12 (1936): 1261–274.

Tang Lei. "Xiangcun xiaoxuexiao zhi kunnan ji qi bujiufa." *Jiaoyu yanjiu*, no. 5 (1913): 1–6.

Tian Lusheng. "Xuejiu jiaoyu tan." *Yueyue xiaoshuo*, no. 12 (1907): 33–38.

Tian Zhi. "Lun xuetang jingfei yi xian zheng ming." *Jiaoyu zazhi* 2, no. 2 (1910): Sheshuo, 17–20 [01381–384].

Wang Guowei. "Jiaoyu xiaoyan shi'er ze." In Shu Xincheng, ed., *Jindai Zhongguo jiaoyushi ziliao*, 3: 1010–13.

Wang Yun. "Jiao tongzi fa." In Shu Xincheng, ed., *Jindai Zhongguo jiaoyushi ziliao*, 1: 93–100.

Wen Tian. "Shu neidi banxue qingxing." *Jiaoyu zazhi* 1, no. 7 (1909): Zazuan, 43–44 [00619–620].

"Xiangxiang Dongshan Jingshe zhangcheng." *Shiwu bao*, no. 2 (1968).

Ye Dehui. "Fei youxue tongyi." In Su Yu, ed., *Yijiao congbian*, 4: 80a–83a.

"Zhang Wenxiang gong yu jiaoyu zhi guanxi." *Jiaoyu zazhi* 1, no. 10 (1909): Pinglun, 21–22.

"Zhongguo dang zhong guomin jiaoyu." *Hubei xueshengjie*, no. 1 (1903): [23–32, 197–208].

Zhou Jiachun. "Shuo yexuexiao." *Jiaoyu zazhi* 1, no. 11 (1909): Sheshuo, 139–41.

Zhuang Yu. "Lun difang xuewu gongkuan." *Jiaoyu zazhi* 1, no. 7 (1909): Sheshuo, 83–96 [00551–564].

————. "Lun xiaoxue jiaoyu." *Jiaoyu zazhi* 1, no. 2 (1909): Sheshuo, 19–26 [00109–116].

Biographies and Memoirs

Collections

Tao Kangde, ed., *Zizhuan zhi yizhang*. Guangzhou: Yuzhou feng she, 1938.

Zhongguo Renmin Zhengzhi Xieshang Huiyi Quanguo Weiyuanhui. Wenshi Ziliao Yanjiu Weiyuanhui, ed. *Xinhai geming huiyilu*. 5 vols. Beijing: Zhonghua shuju, 1961–1963.

Zhuo Li and Wu Fan, eds. *Dangdai zuojia zizhuan ji*. Chongqing: Chubanjie yuekanshe, 1945.

Books

Ba Jin (Li Feigan). *Zizhuan*. Hong Kong: Zili shudian, 1956.

Bao Tianxiao. *Chuanyinglou huiyilu*. Hong Kong: Dahua chubanshe, 1971.

Cao Juren. *Jiangfan liushi nian*. Hong Kong: Chuangken chubanshe, 1957.

———. *Wo yu wo de shijie*. Hong Kong: Sanyu tushu wenju gongsi, 1972.

Chen Bulei. *Chen Bulei huiyilu*. Hong Kong: Tianxing chubanshe, 1962.

Chen Duxiu. *Shi'an zizhuan*. Taibei: Zhuanji wenxue chubanshe, 1967.

Chen Heqin. *Wo de bansheng*. Shanghai: Shijie shuju, 1941.

Chen Qitian. *Jiyuan huiyilu*. Taibei: Shangwu yinshuguan, 1965.

Chen Tianxi. *Chizhuang huiyilu*. Taibei: Shengjing yinshuguan, 1970.

Gu Jiegang. *Gushi bian*. Vol. 1. Beijing: Pu she, 1926.

Guo Moruo. *Wo de younian*. Shanghai: Guanghua shuju, 1930.

Hu Shi. *Sishi zishu*. Shanghai: Yadong tushuguan, 1941.

Huang Baoshi. *Xiantan wangshi*. Taibei: Zhuanji wenxue chubanshe, 1962.

Huang Shaohong. *Huang Shaohong wushi huiyi*. Hong Kong: n.p., 1969.

Huang Zhong. *Hu Yuantan xiansheng zhuan*. Taibei: Zhonghua shuju, 1971.

Li Feigan, *see* Ba Jin.

Li Gufan. *Tan wang lu*. Reprinted in *Yunlu wushu*. Hong Kong: The author, 1963.

Li Ji. *Gan jiu lu*. Taibei: Zhuanji wenxue chubanshe, 1967.

Li Liejun. *Li Liejun jiangjun zizhuan*. Chongqing: Sanhu tushushe, 1944.

Li Xianwen. *Li Xianwen zizhuan*. Taibei: Shangwu yinshuguan, 1970.

Li Zonghuang. *Li Zonghuang huiyilu*. Taibei: Zhongguo difang zizhi xuehui, 1972.

Ling Hongxun. *Qishi zishu*. Taibei: Sanmin shuju, 1968.

Liu Zhi. *Wo de huiyi*. Taibei: Rongtai yinshuguan, 1966.

Lu Xun (Zhou Shuren). *Zhaohua xishi*. Beijing: Renmin chubanshe, 1973.

Luo Dunwei. *Wushi nian huiyilu*. Taibei: Zhongguo wenhua gongyingshe, 1952.

Luo Zhenyu. *Xuetang zizhuan*. In *Luo Xuetang xiansheng quanji*. Vol. 1. Taibei: Datong shuju, 1976.

Ma Xulun. *Wo zai liushi sui yiqian*. Shanghai: Shenghuo shudian, 1947.

Qi Rushan. *Qi Rushan huiyilu.* Taibei: Zhongyang wenwu gongyingshe, 1956.

Sa Mengwu. *Xuesheng shidai.* Taibei: Sanmin shuju, 1959.

Shen Congwen. *Congwen zizhuan.* Shanghai: Kaiming shudian, 1946.

Shu Xincheng. *Wo he jiaoyu.* Shanghai: Zhonghua shuju, 1945.

Song Xishang. *Li Yizhi zhuan.* Taibei: Zhongyang wenwu gongyingshe, 1954.

Wang Mingdao. *Wushi nian lai.* Kowloon: Xingchen shuju, 1950.

Wang Wentian. *Zhang Boling yu Nankai.* Taibei: Zhuanji wenxue chubanshe, 1968.

Wang Yunwu. *Wo de shenghuo pianduan.* N.p.: Huayu chubanshe, 1952.

Wu Xiangxiang. *Chen Guofu de yisheng (fu: Chen Guofu huiyilu).* Taibei: Zhuanji wenxue chubanshe, 1971.

Xiao Gongquan [Hsiao Kung-chuan]. *Wenxue jianwang lu.* Taibei: Zhuanji wenxue chubanshe, 1972.

Yu Jiaju. *Huiyilu.* Shanghai: Zhonghua shuju, 1948.

Zhang Moseng. *Li Zongwu zhuan.* Taibei: Landeng chubanshe, 1970.

Zhao Wanli. *Wang Jing'an xiansheng nianpu.* Nianpu congshu 61. Taibei: Guangwen shuju, 1971.

Zhou Fohai. *Kuxue ji.* Reprinted in Zhou Fohai and Chen Gongbo, *Huiyilu hebian.* Hong Kong: Chunqiu chubanshe, 1967.

Zhou Shizhao. *Women de shibiao.* Beijing: Beijing chubanshe, 1958.

Zhou Shujen, *see* Lu Xun.

Zhou Zuoren. *Zhitang huixianglu.* Hong Kong: Sanyou tushu wenju gongsi, 1970.

Zou Taofen. *Jingli.* Shanghai: Taofen chubanshe, 1947.

Articles

Chen Rigang. "Dazu Tongzhijun." In *Xinhai geming huiyilu,* 3: 258−71.

Fu Zhongtao. "Shenghuo de huiyi." In Tao Kangde, ed., *Zizhuan zhi yizhang,* pp. 129−34.

Li Jianhou. "Wuchang shouyi qianhou yishi baze." In *Xinhai geming huiyilu,* 2: 79−89.

Li Renren. "Tongmenghui zai Guilin, Pingle de huodong he Guangxi xuanbu duli de huiyi." In *Xinhai geming huiyilu,* 2: 448−66.

Li Shuhua. "Cong sishu dao xuetang." *Zhuanji wenxue* 17, no. 2 (1970): 61−64.

Li Zongtong. "Cong jiashu dao Nankai Zhongxue." *Zhuanji wenxue* 4, no. 6 (1964): 43−45.

———. "Wu da chen chuyang yu Beijing diyike zhadan." *Zhuanji wenxue* 4, no. 4 (1964): 35−37.

Liang Ruochen. "Yige shancunli de geming fengbao." In *Xinhai geming huiyilu,* 2: 363−67.

"Nanyang Gongxue de yijiulinger nian bake fengchao he Aiguo Xueshe." In *Xinhai geming huiyilu,* 4: 63−77.

Shi Tiyuan. "Yi Chengdu baolu yundong." In *Xinhai geming huiyilu,* 3: 42−67.

Wang Yinglou. "Huizhoufu zhongxuesheng zai Xinhai geming shiqi de huo-dong." In *Xinhai geming huiyilu*, 2: 348–51.

Xiong Kewu. "Xinhai qian wo canjia de Sichuan jici wuzhuang qiyi." In *Xinhai geming huiyilu*, 3: 1–25.

Yang Yinpu. "Sishiba zishu." In Zhuo Li and Wu Fan, eds., *Dangdai zuojia zizhuan ji*, pp. 33–38.

Yu Ziyi. "Ershi nian qian xiangcun xuexiao shenghuoli de wo." *Jiaoyu zazhi* 19, no. 12 (1927): 1–13.

Zhang Chonglei. "Qingmo Minchu Sichuan de junshi xuetang ji Chuanjun paixi." In *Xinhai geming huiyilu*, 3: 345–64.

Periodicals and Newspapers

The following were selectively scanned:

Dongfang zazhi	*Xinmin congbao*
Hubei xueshengjie	*Xinming huabao*
Jiangsu	*Xingqi huabao*
Jiaoyu zazhi (Shanghai)	*Xue Bu guanbao*
Liangri huabao	*Yueyue xiaoshuo*
Shiwu bao	*Zhejiang chao*
Shuntian shibao	*Zhili jiaoyu zazhi*
Su bao	*Zhixin bao*
Xiangxue bao	

Only the first issues of the following were available:

Jiangning xuewu zazhi	*Jingshi jiaoyu yanjiu*

Secondary Sources

Books

Cai Yuanpei et al. *Zuijin sanshiwu nian lai zhi Zhongguo jiaoyu*. Shanghai: Shangwu yinshuguan, 1931.

Chen Baoquan. *Zhongguo jindai xuezhi bianqian shi*. Beijing: Beijing wenhua xue-she, 1927.

Chen Dongyuan. *Zhongguo jiaoyushi*. Shanghai: Shangwu yinshuguan, 1937.

Chen Qingzhi. *Zhongguo jiaoyushi*. Shanghai: Shangwu yinshuguan, 1936.

Chen Qitian. *Zuijin sanshinian Zhongguo jiaoyushi*. Taibei: Wenxing shudian, 1962.

Ding Zhipin. *Zhongguo jin qishi nian lai jiaoyu jishi*. Shanghai: Guoli bianyiguan, 1935.

Fang Shiduo. *Wushinianlai Zhongguo guoyu yundong shi*. Taibei: Guoyu ribao she, 1965.

Huang Fuqing. *Qingmo liu-Ri xuesheng*. Taibei: Zhongyang yanjiuyuan, Jindaishi yanjiusuo, 1975.

Li Liuru. *Liushi nian di bianqian.* Beijing: Zuojia chubanshe, 1957.

Liu Boji. *Guangdong shuyuan zhidu yange.* Shanghai: Shangwu yinshuguan, 1939.

Naka Arata. *Meiji no kyōiku.* Tokyo: Shibundō, 1967.

Ōkubo Hideko. *Min Shin jidai shoin no kenkyū.* Tokyo: Kokusho kankō kai, 1976.

Sanetō Keishū. *Chūgokujin Nihon ryūgaku shi.* Tokyo: Kuroshio shuppan, 1960.

Shang Yanliu. *Qingdai keju kaoshi shulu.* Beijing: Sanlian shudian, 1958.

Sheng Langxi. *Zhongguo shuyuan zhidu.* Shanghai: Zhonghua shuju, 1934.

Shu Xincheng. *Jindai Zhongguo jiaoyu sixiangshi.* Shanghai: Zhonghua shuju, 1932 [1929].

Su Yunfeng. *Zhang Zhidong yu Hubei jiaoyu gaige.* Taibei: Zhongyang yanjiuyuan, Jindaishi yanjiusuo, 1976.

Wang Yunwu. *Shangwu yinshuguan yu xin jiaoyu nianpu.* Taibei: Shangwu yinshu-guan, 1973.

Wu Xun Lishi Diaocha Tuan. *Wu Xun lishi diaocha ji.* Beijing: Renmin chuban-she, 1951.

Yu Shulin. *Zhongguo jiaoyushi.* Taibei: Taiwan shengli shifan daxue, 1961.

Zhang Zhigong. *Chuantong yuwen jiaoyu chutan.* Shanghai: Jiaoyu chubanshe, 1962.

Articles

Abe Hiroshi. "Shimmatsu gakudō kō: Chokurei-shō o chūshin toshite." *Bunka ronshu* 1 (1966): 45–88.

———. "Shimmatsu no kigaku bōdō." In Taga Akigorō, ed., *Kindai Ajia kyōikushi kenkyū.* Tokyo: Iwasaki gakujutsu shuppansha, 1975.

———. "Shimmatsu no kindai gakkō: Kōsei-shō o chūshin ni." *Rekishi hyōron* 175 (1965): 56–66.

———. "*Tōhō zasshi* ni mirareru Shimmatsu kyōikushi shiryō ni tsuite." *Rekishi hyōron* 137 (1962): 23–33.

Chen Daiqing. "Wu Qi xiao zhuan." In Li Shizhao, ed., *Wu Xun xiansheng de zhuanji.* Shanghai: Jiaoyu shudian, 1948, pp. 11–12.

Gao Zhengfang. "Qingmo de Anhui xinjiaoyu" (shang). *Xuefeng* 2, no. 8 (1932): 30–36.

Gong Shi. "Beijing Daxue zhi chengli ji yange." In Shu Xincheng, ed., *Jindai Zhongguo jiaoyu shiliao,* 3: 1–4.

Huang Yanpei. "Qingji gesheng xingxue shi." *Renwen yuekan* 1, no. 7 (1930): 1–9; no. 8 (1930): 9–17; no. 9 (1930): 19–36; no. 10 (1930): 37–43.

Jiang Mengmei. "Qian-Qing Xue Bu bianshu zhi zhuangkuang." In Shu Xin-cheng, ed., *Jindai Zhongguo jiaoyu shiliao,* 2: 259–60.

Liu Zizhou. "Yixuezheng Wu Gong zhuan." In Li Shizhao, ed., *Wu Xun xiansheng de zhuanji.* Shanghai: Jiaoyu shudian, 1948, pp. 3–7.

Lü Shaoyu. "Zhongguo jiaoyu shumu huibian." *Wenhua tushuguanxue zhuankexue-xiao jikan* 4, nos. 3–4 (1932): 297–400.

Qu Lihe. "Jin bai nian woguo zhongdeng jiaoyu." *Shida xuebao* 22, shang (1977): 211–98.

Saitō Akio. "Chūgoku gakusei kaikaku no shisō to genjitsu." *Shinshu jimbun ronshu* 4 (1969): 1–25.

Tanaka Kenji. "Kyū Shina ni okeru jidō no gakujuku seikatsu." *Tōhō gakuho* (Kyoto) 15 (1946): 217–31.

Wang Shuhuai. "Jidujiao Jiaoyuhui ji qi chuban shiye/The Educational Association of China and Its Publications (1890–1912)." *Zhongyang yanjiuyuan, Jindaishi yanjiusuo jikan* 2 (1971): 365–96.

———. "Qingmo Jiangsu difang zizhi fengchao." *Zhongyang yanjiuyuan, Jindaishi yanjiusuo jikan* 6 (1977): 313–27.

Weng Yanzhen. "Gudai ertong duwu gaiguan." *Tushuguanxue jikan* 10, no. 1 (1936): 91–146.

Xie Guozhen. "Jindai shuyuan xuexiao zhidu bianqian kao." In Cai Yuanpei et al., eds., *Zhang Jusheng xiansheng qishi shengri jinian lunwen ji*. Shanghai: Shangwu yinshuguan, 1937, pp. 281–321.

Works in European Languages

Primary Sources

Books

The China Mission Hand-book: First Issue. Shanghai: American Presbyterian Mission Press, 1896.

King, H. E. *The Educational System of China as Recently Reconstructed*. Bulletin 15, no. 469. Washington, D.C.: U.S. Bureau of Education, 1911.

Lo Hui-min. *The Correspondence of G. E. Morrison, 1895–1912*. Cambridge, Eng.: Cambridge University Press, 1976.

Mission Educational Directory for China: Containing a Brief Description of Educational Institutions Connected with Protestant Missions. Shanghai: Educational Association of China, 1910.

Morse, Hosea Ballou. *The Trade and Administration of China*. 3rd rev. ed. London: Longmans, Green & Co., 1921.

Reinsch, Paul S. *Intellectual and Political Currents in the Far East*. Boston and New York: Houghton Mifflin Company, 1911.

Richard, Timothy. *Forty-five Years in China*. London: T. Fisher Unwin, 1916.

Smith, Arthur H. *Village Life in China: A Study in Sociology*. New York: Fleming H. Revell Co., 1899.

Articles

Foster, Arnold. "The Educational Outlook in Wuchang." *Chinese Recorder and Missionary Journal* 37, no. 4 (1906): 208–16.

Gage, Brownell. "Government Schools in Hunan." *Chinese Recorder and Missionary Journal* 38, no. 12 (1907): 667–74.

Harada, J. "Japanese Educational Influence in China." *Chinese Recorder and Missionary Journal* 36, no. 7 (1905): 356–61.

J. D. "Educational Issues from Native Presses." *Chinese Recorder and Missionary Journal* 37, no. 7 (1906): 384–91.

Liao T'ai-ch'u. "Rural Education in Transition: A Study of the Old-fashioned Chinese Schools (Szu Shu) in Shantung and Szechuan." *Yenching Journal of Social Studies* 4, no. 2 (1949): 19–67.

Maclagan, P. J. "Notes on Some Chinese Chap-books." *China Review* 23, no. 3 (1898–99): 163–67.

Parker, A. P. "The Government Colleges of Suchow." *Chinese Recorder and Missionary Journal* 24, no. 11 (1893): 534–40; 24, no. 12 (1893): 579–84.

Autobiographies

Chiang Monlin. *Tides from the West: A Chinese Autobiography*. New Haven, Conn.: Yale University Press, 1947.

Chiang Yee. *A Chinese Childhood*. London: Methuen, 1940.

Chao, Yang Buwei, *Autobiography of a Chinese Woman*. Translated by Chao Yuenren. Westport, Conn.: Greenwood Press, 1970 [1947].

Periodicals

The following were selectively scanned:

China Review   *Chinese Recorder and Missionary Journal*

Secondary Sources

Books and Theses

Anderson, Mary Raleigh. *Protestant Mission Schools for Girls in South China (1827 to the Japanese Invasion)*. Mobile, Ala.: Heiter-Starke Printing Co., 1943.

Ayers, William. *Chang Chih-tung and Educational Reform in China*. Cambridge, Mass.: Harvard University Press, 1971.

Bastid, Marianne. *Aspects de la réforme de l'enseignement en Chine au début du 20e siècle: D'après des écrits de Zhang Jian*. Paris: Mouton & Cie, 1971.

Bays, Daniel H. *China Enters the Twentieth Century: Chang Chih-tung and the Issues of a New Age, 1895–1909*. Ann Arbor: University of Michigan Press, 1978.

Biggerstaff, Knight. *The Earliest Modern Government Schools in China*. Ithaca, N.Y.: Cornell University Press, 1961.

Boorman, Howard L., ed. *Biographical Dictionary of Republican China*. 4 vols. New York: Columbia University Press, 1967–1970.

Britton, Roswell S. *The Chinese Periodical Press, 1800–1912*. Taibei: Cheng-wen Publishing Co., 1966 [1933].

Buck, John Lossing. *Land Utilization in China.* New York: Paragon, 1968.

Chang Chung-li. *The Chinese Gentry: Studies on Their Role in Nineteenth-Century China.* Seattle: University of Washington Press, 1955.

Chang Hao. *Liang Ch'i-ch'ao and Intellectual Transition in China, 1890–1907.* Cambridge, Mass.: Harvard University Press, 1971.

Chuang Chai-hsuan. *Tendencies Toward a Democratic System of Education in China.* Shanghai: Commercial Press, 1922.

Cohen, Paul. *Between Tradition and Modernity: Wang T'ao and Reform in Late Ch'ing China.* Cambridge, Mass.: Harvard University Press, 1974.

Esherick, Joseph W. *Reform and Revolution in China: The 1911 Revolution in Hunan and Hubei.* Berkeley and Los Angeles: University of California Press, 1976.

Farquhar, M. A. "Children's Literature in China." Ph.D. dissertation, Griffith University, 1981.

Feuerwerker, Albert. *The Chinese Economy, ca. 1870–1911.* Ann Arbor: University of Michigan Press, 1969.

Foster, Philip J. *Education and Social Change in Ghana.* London: Routledge and Kegan Paul, 1965.

Franke, Wolfgang. *The Reform and Abolition of the Traditional Chinese Examination System.* Cambridge, Mass.: Harvard University Press, 1963.

Frodsham, J. D. *The First Chinese Embassy to the West: The Journals of Kuo Sung-t'ao, Liu Hsi-hung and Chang Te-yi.* Oxford: Clarendon Press, 1974.

Furth, Charlotte, ed. *The Limits of Change: Essays on Conservative Alternatives in Republican China.* Cambridge, Mass.: Harvard University Press, 1976.

Galt, Howard S. *A History of Chinese Educational Institutions.* Vol. 1. London: Probsthain and Sons, 1951.

Gregg, Alice H. *China and Educational Autonomy: The Changing Role of the Protestant Educational Missionary in China, 1807–1937.* Syracuse, N.Y.: Syracuse University Press, 1946.

Ho Ping-ti. *The Ladder of Success in Imperial China.* New York: John Wiley & Sons, 1962.

Hsiao Kung-chuan. *A Modern China and a New World.* Seattle: University of Washington Press, 1975.

———. *Rural China: Imperial Control in the Nineteenth Century.* Seattle: University of Washington Press, 1960.

Huang, Philip C. *Liang Ch'i-ch'ao and Modern Chinese Liberalism.* Seattle: University of Washington Press, 1972.

Kuo Ping-wen. *The Chinese System of Public Education.* New York: AMS Press, 1972 [1915].

Japan. Department of Education. *Education in Japan.* Tokyo, 1914.

Latourette, Kenneth Scott. *A History of Christian Missions in China.* Taibei: Chengwen Publishing Co., 1966 [1929].

Leong, Y. K., and Tao, L. K. *Village and Town Life in China.* London: Allen & Unwin, 1915.

Liu Ts'un-yan. *Selected Papers from the Hall of Harmonious Wind.* Leiden: E. J. Brill, 1976.

Lowndes, G. A. N. *The Silent Social Revolution: An Account of the Expansion of Public Education in England and Wales, 1895–1935.* London: Oxford University Press, 1947.

Lutz, Jessie Gregory. *China and the Christian Colleges, 1850–1950.* Ithaca, N.Y.: Cornell University Press, 1971.

MacKinnon, Stephen R. *Power and Politics in Late Imperial China: Yuan Shi-kai in Beijing and Tianjin, 1901–1908.* Berkeley and Los Angeles: University of California Press, 1980.

Miyazaki Ichisada. *China's Examination Hell.* Translated by Conrad Schirokauer. New York and Tokyo: Weatherhill, 1976. Originally published in Japanese in 1963 by Chūō Kōron-sha under the title *Kakyo: Chūgoku no shiken jigoku.*

Myers, Ramon H. *The Chinese Economy: Past and Present.* Belmont, Calif.: Wadsworth, 1980.

Neuberg, Victor E. *Popular Education in Eighteenth Century England.* London: Woburn Books, 1971.

Nishihira Isao. "Western Influence on the Modernization of Japanese Education, 1868–1912." Ph.D. dissertation, Ohio State University, 1972.

Ogawa Yoshiko. "A Study of the Foundation of the Premodern Educational System in the Ching Era." M.A. thesis, Stanford University, 1958.

Passin, Herbert. *Society and Education in Japan.* New York: Columbia University, Teachers College, 1965.

Peake, Cyrus P. *Nationalism and Education in Modern China.* New York: Columbia University, Teachers College, 1932.

Powell, Ralph L. *The Rise of Chinese Military Power, 1895–1912.* Princeton, N.J.: Princeton University Press, 1955.

Rankin, Mary Backus. *Early Chinese Revolutionaries: Radical Intellectuals in Shanghai and Chekiang, 1902–1911.* Cambridge, Mass.: Harvard University Press, 1971.

Ransome, J. Stafford. *Japan in Transition.* London: Harper & Brothers, 1899.

Rawski, Evelyn. *Education and Popular Literacy in Ch'ing China.* Ann Arbor: University of Michigan Press, 1979.

Rhoads, Edward. *China's Republican Revolution: The Case of Kwangtung, 1895–1913.* Cambridge, Mass.: Harvard University Press, 1975.

Ridley, Charles P., "Educational Theory and Practice in Late Imperial China: The Teaching of Writing as a Specific Case." Ph.D. dissertation, Stanford University, 1973.

Schiffrin, Harold Z. *Sun Yat-sen and the Origins of the Chinese Revolution.* Berkeley and Los Angeles: University of California Press, 1968.

Shipman, M. D. *Education and Modernisation.* London: Faber & Faber, 1971.

Skinner, G. William, ed. *The City in Late Imperial China.* Stanford: Stanford University Press, 1971.

Skinner, G. William, and Elvin, Mark, eds. *The Chinese City Between Two Worlds.* Stanford: Stanford University Press, 1974.

Smedley, Agnes. *The Great Road: The Life and Times of Chu Teh.* New York and London: Monthly Review Press, 1972 [1956].

Smith, Harold Frederick. *Elementary Education in Shantung, China.* Nashville, Tenn.: AMESSU, 1931.

Snow, Edgar, *Red Star over China.* Rev. ed. Harmondsworth, Eng.: Pelican Books, 1972 [1937].

Tang Ching-ping. "Mu-fu System in China Under the Ch'ing." M.A. thesis, Australian National University, 1976.

Wang Feng-Gang, "Japanese Influence on Educational Reform in China, from 1895 to 1911." Ph.D. dissertation, Stanford University, 1931.

Wang, Y. C. *Chinese Intellectuals and the West, 1872–1949.* Chapel Hill: University of North Carolina Press, 1968.

Wilkinson, Rupert. *The Prefects: British Leadership and the Public School Tradition, a Comparative Study in the Making of Rulers.* London: Oxford University Press, 1964.

Yang, Martin. *Chinese Social Structure.* Taibei: Eurasia Book Co., 1969.

Yin Chiling. *Reconstruction of Modern Educational Organizations in China.* Shanghai: Commercial Press, 1926.

Articles

Bennett, Adrian A., and Kwang-Ching Liu. "Christianity in the Chinese Idiom: Young J. Allen and the Early *Chiao-hui hsin-pao*, 1868–1870." In John K. Fairbank, ed., *The Missionary Enterprise in China and America.* Cambridge, Mass.: Harvard University Press, 1974, pp. 159–96.

Bernstein, Basil. "On the Classification and Framing of Educational Knowledge." In Michael F. D. Young, ed., *Knowledge and Control.* London: Collier-Macmillan, 1971, pp. 47–69.

Buck, David D. "Educational Modernization in Tsinan, 1899–1937." In G. William Skinner and Mark Elvin, eds., *The Chinese City Between Two Worlds.* Stanford: Stanford University Press, 1974, pp. 171–212.

Caiger, John. "Tejima Seiichi (1849–1918) and Schooling for Industry in Japan." Unpublished paper, Australian National University, 1976.

Chen Chi-yun. "Liang Ch'i-ch'ao's 'Missionary Education': A Case Study of Missionary Influence on the Reformers." *Papers on China* (Harvard University Press) 16 (1962): 66–126.

Chong, Key Ray. "Cheng Kuan-ying (1841-1920): A Source of Sun Yat-sen's Nationalist Ideology?" *Journal of Asian Studies* 28, no. 2 (1969): 247–67.

Cohen, Paul A. "Littoral and Hinterland in Nineteenth Century China: The 'Christian' Reformers." In John K. Fairbank, ed., *The Missionary Enterprise in China and America.* Cambridge, Mass.: Harvard University Press, 1974, pp. 197–225.

Feuchtwang, Stephen. "School Temple and City God." In G. William Skinner, ed., *The City in Late Imperial China*. Stanford: Stanford University Press, 1977, pp. 581–608.

Grimm, Tilemann. "Academies and Urban Systems in Kwangtung." In G. William Skinner, ed., *The City in Late Imperial China*. Stanford: Stanford University Press, 1977, pp. 475–98.

Hackett, Roger F. "Chinese Students in Japan, 1900–1910." *Papers on China* (Harvard University Press) 3 (1949): 134–69.

Ichiko Chūzō. "The Role of the Gentry: An Hypothesis." In Mary Clabaugh Wright, ed., *China in Revolution. The First Phase, 1900 1913*. New Haven, Conn.: Yale University Press, 1968, pp. 297–317.

Jansen, Marius B., and Stone, Lawrence. "Education and Modernization in Japan and England." *Comparative Studies in Society and History* 9 (1966–67): 208–32.

Laqueur, Thomas W. "Working-Class Demand and the Growth of English Elementary Education, 1750–1850." In Lawrence Stone, ed., *Schooling and Society*. Baltimore: Johns Hopkins University Press, 1976, pp. 192–205.

Lin Yu-sheng. "The Suicide of Liang Chi." In Charlotte Furth, ed., *The Limits of Change*. Cambridge, Mass.: Harvard University Press, 1976, pp. 151–68.

Liu Kwang-Ching. "Cheng Kuan-ying's *I-yen*: Reform Proposals of the Early Kwang-hsü Period (Part I) / Zheng Guanying *Yiyan*: Guangxu chunian zhi bianfa sixiang (shang)." *Tsing Hua Journal of Chinese Studies*, n.s., 8 (1970): 373–425.

———. "Early Christian Colleges in China." *Journal of Asian Studies* 20, no. 1 (1960): 71-78.

MacKinnon, Stephen R. "Police Reform in Late Ch'ing Chihli." *Ch'ing-shih Wen-t'i* 3, no. 4 (1974): 82–99.

Mote, F. W. "China's Past in the Study of China Today." *Journal of Asian Studies* 32, no. 1 (1972): 107–20.

Orb, Richard A. "Chihli Academies and Other Schools in the Late Ch'ing: An Institutional Survey." In Paul A. Cohen and John E. Schrecker, eds., *Reform in Nineteenth-Century China*. Cambridge, Mass.: Harvard University Press, 1976.

P'an Kuang-tan and Fei Hsiao-t'ung. "City and Village: The Inequality of Opportunity." In Johanna Menzel, ed., *The Chinese Civil Service: Career Open to Talent?* Boston: D. C. Heath & Co., 1963, pp. 9–21.

Rankin, Mary Backus. "The Manchurian Crisis and Radical Student Nationalism, 1903." *Ch'ing-shih Wen-t'i* 2, no. 1 (1969): 87–106.

Rhoads, Edward J. M. "Late Ch'ing Response to Imperialism: The Case of Canton." *Ch'ing-shih Wen-t'i* 2, no. 1 (1969): 71–86.

Ridley, Charles P. "Theories of Education in the Ch'ing Period." *Ch'ing-shih Wen-t'i* 3, no. 8 (1977): 34–49.

Teng Ssu-yu. "Chinese Influence on the Western Examination System." *Harvard Journal of Asian Studies* 7 (1942–43): 267–312.

Thompson, E. P. "Time, Work-Discipline, and Industrial Capitalism." In M. W. Flinn and T. C. Smout, eds., *Essays in Social History*. London: Oxford University Press, 1974, pp. 39–77.

Turner, Ralph. "Sponsored and Contest Mobility and the School System." *American Sociological Review* 25, no. 6 (1960): 855–67.

Wang, Y. C. "Western Impact and Social Mobility in China." *American Sociological Review* 25, no. 6 (1960): 843–55.

Index